Garages & Carports

84 LUMBER

SA...

Exterior Latex Flat House & Trim Paint
7⁹⁹* gal.

10 Year Warranty!

10 Year Latex Satin . . . . . . 13⁸⁴ gal.

1000 Acrylic Flat . . . . 15⁸⁴* gal.

*Price reflects $2.00 Mfr's Mail-in Rebate

2 Gallon Exterior White Latex Paint (331-01)
9⁹⁹

More Paint Inside! See Pg. 2.

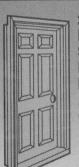

32" 6 Panel Prehung Insulated Steel Entrance Doors
$99

36" $102

Includes Brick Mould & energy saving weatherstripping. Primed and ready to paint.

More Doors Inside! See Pg. 3.

5 Gallon Asphalt Emulsion Driveway Sealer
5⁹⁹

(591-29)

Sealer/ Filler (591-36) 8⁹⁹

Rubberized Sealer (591-57) 14⁹⁹

8'x8' Wood Truss Barn Packages
with 4'x8' Inner-Seal® Siding
$384

Includes Shingles & Flooring

8'x10'. $469	10'x12'. $619	12'x12'. $849
8'x12'. $514	10'x16'. $749	12'x16'. $1049

24'x24' 2 Car Garage Packages
with Engineered Roof Trusses, Window, Service Door & 4'x8' LP Inner-Seal® Siding
$2749

with White or Almond Twin 4 Vinyl Siding $2899

16'x24' 1 1/2 Car	24'x32' 2 Car	32'x28' 3 Car
with LP Inner-Seal® $2299	with LP Inner-Seal® $3184	with LP Inner-Seal® $4484
with White Vinyl $2449	with White Vinyl $3449	with White Vinyl $4699

Self Seal Fiberglass Roofing Shingles
20 Year Warranty

18²⁷ 100 sq. ft.

Class "A" Fire Rating
6 colors in stock

Roofer's Shovel (660-84) 17⁹⁹

White Twin 4 Vinyl Siding
Armor Bond®

36⁸⁴ 100 sq. ft.

Stock Colors. 39⁸⁴

Dutchlap White 39⁸⁴

Dutchlap Stock Colors 41⁸⁴

OUTDOOR HOME IMPROVEMENT

25 Year Warranty

OWENS CORNING ™

3 Tab Self Seal Fiberglass Roofing Shingles

3 colors in stock

22⁹⁸

100 sq. ft.

SPECIAL ORDER

Premium Laminated Shingles

The Oakridge® Series, from Owens Corning™, will add a symbol of discriminating value and distinction to both new and existing homes through its rugged appearance of added dimension. Choose from several colors with 25, 30, and 40 year warranties. See store for ordering information.

4'x8' High "R" Insulating Sheathing

R-3.6

6¹⁹

(612) (752) (698-63)

The higher the R-value, the greater the insulating power. R-value fact sheets on file at store.

Fiberglass Ladders

6' Step (531-70)

59⁹⁹

8' Step (531-71) **82⁸⁴**

16' Extension (593-61) **144⁸⁴**

24' Extension (531-77) **199⁹⁹**

12" Internally Braced Galvanized
Turbine Vent
with Base (449-74)

16⁸⁴

Aluminum (451-78) **24⁹⁹**

Turbine and base packaged together for convenience • Adjustable to fit most roof slopes • Available in Aluminum or Galvanized finish

10' Low Profile Ridge Vent

11⁸⁴

White (451-50)   Brown (451-57)   Black (473-64) . . . .

40 Year Limited Warranty

Solid or Perforated
12"x12' Soffit
White or Brown

6⁹⁹

Aluminum Fascia White or Brown

6"x12'6" **4⁹⁹**

8"x12'6" **6⁹⁹**

84 LUMBER Roof and Foundation Coating

5 Gallon Fibered Foundation & Roof Coating (856) . . . .

11⁴⁹

5 Gallon Plastic Roof Cement (712-53) **11⁹⁹**

5 Gallon Aluminum Roof Coating (591-56) **25⁹⁹**

ClassiCoat® Paint

84 CLASSICOAT 10 Year Warranty Interior Latex Flat Wall Paint

Interior Latex Flat Wall Paint

10 Year Warranty

5⁸⁴*

gal.

Semi-Gloss **10 Year Warranty** . . . . **9⁸⁴*** gal.

Ceiling (591-39) **10 Year Warranty** . . . **5⁸⁴*** gal.

1000 Lo-Lustre Enamel (333-10) **Lifetime Warranty.** . . . . **11⁸⁴*** gal.

***Price reflects $2.00 Mfr's Mail-in Rebate.**

---

2 Gallon Specials!

800 square feet latex flat paint

Interior White Latex Flat Paint (332-34)

9⁹⁹

Ceiling White (330-02) **9⁹⁹**

Semi-Gloss (330-04) **16⁹⁹**

Utility Grey (330-05) **14⁹⁹**

Texture Paint
Smooth (331-50) Sand (333-00) **10⁸⁴**

Drywall Primer/ Sealer (340-46) **10⁹⁹**

2

WINDOWS & DOORS FOR YOUR HOME

Double Hung Insulated Wood Windows with stops and sash lock

Glass Size	Window Size	Wood Tilt	Clad Tilt
20"x16"	2'0"x3'2"	89⁹⁹	134⁹⁹
24"x16"	2'4"x3'2"	96⁹⁹	142⁹⁹
24"x20"	2'4"x3'10"	105⁹⁹	152⁹⁹

◣ SPECIAL ORDER

Great Prices on DOORS & WINDOWS Hundreds of styles available!

See sales associate for delivery times.

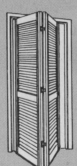

2436 Single Hung **Vinyl Tilt Windows** with Insulated Glass (840-31)

68⁸⁴

Includes Screen

3636 (840-35) 82⁸⁴
3660 (840-37) 99⁸⁴

32" Flush Prehung **Insulated Steel Entrance Doors**

$102

36" $106

Flair·Fold®

Bifold Doors

Includes Track and Hardware

size	Paint Grade Louvered Pine	Lauan Flush	Stain Grade Louvered Pine
24"	22⁹⁹	27⁸⁴	37⁹⁹
30"	28⁸⁴	30⁸⁴	42⁹⁹
36"	31⁸⁴	32⁹⁹	47⁹⁹

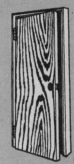

GP Georgia-Pacific

24" Interior Lauan **Prehung Doors** bored without casing

36⁹⁹

30" 38⁹⁹

32" 9 Lite 2 Panel

$145

36" $147

36" 1/2 Round Spoke

$179

Includes Brick Mould, energy saving weatherstripping. Primed and ready to paint.

6' Vinyl Sliding **Patio Door**

369⁹⁹

Screen Extra

Insulated

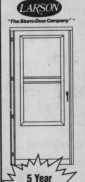

LARSON "The Storm Door Company"™

32" White Wood-Core #298 SS Self Storing **Storm Doors** (704-76)

96⁹⁹

5 Year Replacement Warranty

36" (704-77) . . . 99⁹⁹

3

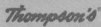

AFFORDABLE HOMES ACROSS AMERICA™

84

The Bluff City 1307 sq. ft. (Ranch) $47,900*

The Newbury 1632 sq. ft. (Split Level) $55,400*

The Cape May 1915 sq. ft. (1 1/2 Story) $68,400*

The Adrian 2016 sq. ft. (2 Story) $64,900*

• Shell and Trim Material • Kitchen Cabinets • Bath Vanities • Counter tops
Also included in this price are approximate materials and labor costs for: • Plumbing • Heating
• Electrical • Flooring • Excavating • Foundation • Grading • Construction
These basic requirements (which are not supplied by 84 Lumber) are based on national averages in
the building industry and will vary by market area.   See an 84 Associate for details.   Lot Extra*

The Wexford $47,400*
1040 sq. ft. (Bi-level)

Seasonal Closeout!

4'x8' Treated Stockade Fence Section (746-69) **22⁹⁹**

6'x8' Stockade (746-68) **28⁸⁴**

42"x8' Spaced Picket (746-82) **11⁹⁹**

6'x8' Shadow Box (751-24) **29⁹⁹**

Tools and Accessories

DeWALT High Performance Industrial Tools

12.0 Volt 3/8"
**Heavy Duty
Cordless Drill**
(711-08)

• Adjustable Clutch
• Includes 1 hour charger, Battery, and Steel Case.

164⁸⁴

12" Compound
Mitre Saw (700-07) **375⁸⁴**

3/8" Heavy Duty
Drill (700-01) **63⁸⁴**

7 1/4" Heavy Duty
Circular Saw (700-04) **154⁸⁴**

American Built For America's Builders

7 1/4 Carbide Tipped
Circular
**Saw
Blade 3³³**
(633-69)

Ideal General Purpose Saw Blade

STANLEY Contractor Grade Tools

Swivel Lock
**Retractable
Knife** **5⁴⁹**
(251-244)

Speed Square (351-873) **7⁹⁹**

Drywall Saw (351-806) **12⁸⁴**

25' Heavy Duty
Powerlock Tape (351-839) **12⁹⁹**

48" Brass Bound
Mahogany Level (351-857) **34⁹⁹**

**Step up to oil-less technology
from ATRO® and Georgia-Pacific**

1 1/2 HP
**Workhorse
Compressor**

359⁹⁹

GP Georgia-Pacific

Seasonal Closeout On All Children's Wood Playsets

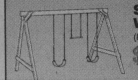

**Scout 12'
Westpoint**
(831-04-99)

$114

Pioneer 16' Trading Post
(831-01-99) $159

Mustang Renegade
Project 455 (840-05-99) $684

Eagle's Nest Clubhouse
(831-00-99) $234

Sky Fort Skyscraper
(831-09-99) $784

Sky Fort/Sky Fort
(839-34-99) $334

Covered Wagon Corral
Project 485 (831-41-99) $359

Clubhouse
Project 520 (831-48-99) $299

Star Tower Galaxy
Project 505 (831-45-99) $854

Quality Wood

Shelving Boards

1"x4" (104)	.35 ln. ft.
1"x6" (106)	.54 ln. ft.
1"x8" (108)	.75 ln. ft.
1"x10" (110)	.97 ln. ft.
1"x12" (112)	1²⁹ ln. ft.

5

BATH DEPARTMENT

19"x17" One Door Natural Ash Vanity
with Cultured Marble Top

84⁸⁴

25"x19" 1 Door/2 Drawer	154⁸⁴
31"x19" 1 Door/2 Drawer	169⁸⁴
37"x19" 2 Door/2 Drawer	219⁸⁴
49"x22" 2 Door/4 Drawer	296⁸⁴

Single Door Recessed Natural Ash Bath Cabinet (615-55)

35⁸⁴

Single Door Surface Mount (615-45)	71⁸⁴
30" Double Door (615-54)	85⁸⁴

Tri-views
30" (615-52)	89⁸⁴
36" (615-46)	116⁸⁴
48" (615-47)	145⁸⁴

Interior Products for your Kitchen & Bath

Armstrong
12"x12"
Self Stick/No Wax
Vinyl Floor Tile
.44 ea.
Vernay Series

7 Different Styles To Choose From

Armstrong
Royelle
No Wax Vinyl
Floor Covering
3⁸⁴ sq. yd.

Level Loop
Power Play
Indoor Carpet
with attached cushion back

Scotchgard Protected
Not Available at Greece Location.

3⁹⁹ sq. yd.

Cut & Loop
Ventura or Fiesta ... **6⁹⁹** sq. yd.

Georgia-Pacific
4'x8'
Prefinished
Silvery Floral Tileboard
(593-03)

16⁹⁹

White (592-78) ... **9⁹⁹**

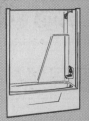

AQUA STREAM by MOEN
#84407
Two Handle Bath Faucet
w/o Pop-up
9⁹⁹ (614-02)
5 Year Limited Warranty
Not Available at Greece Location.

JAMECO
Single Handle Bath Faucet
w/ Pop-up
29⁸⁴ (630-20)
Lifetime Warranty

Two Handle w/ Pop-up (630-21) ... **17⁸⁴**
Decorative w/ Pop-up (630-22) ... **45⁸⁴**

Touch Control by MOEN
#84503
Single Handle Bath Faucet
w/ Pop-up
57⁸⁴ (611-32)
Lifetime Limited Warranty

#84417 2 Handle
w/ Pop-up (612-20) ... **42⁸⁴**

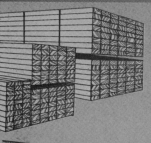

Garages & Carports
Converting, Expanding, Building

James E. Russell

CREATIVE HOMEOWNER PRESS®

A DIVISION OF FEDERAL MARKETING CORPORATION,
24 PARK WAY, UPPER SADDLE RIVER, NEW JERSEY 07458

Manufactured in United States of America

Current Printing (last digit)
10 9 8 7 6 5

Editor: Shirley M. Horowitz
Art Director: Léone Lewensohn
Designer: Paul Sochacki
Additional drawings: Norman Nuding

Cover photograph: James E. Russell

ISBN: 0–932944–32–9 (paperback)
ISBN: 0–932944–31–0 (hardcover)
LC. 81–66548

CREATIVE HOMEOWNER PRESS®
BOOK SERIES

A DIVISION OF FEDERAL
MARKETING CORPORATION
24 PARK WAY,
UPPER SADDLE RIVER, NJ 07458

FOREWORD

A garage can be an asset or an eyesore, both in its usefulness and its visual appeal. This book will enable the homeowner to build a new garage at the lowest cost possible, but also aid him or her to renovate an old garage to make it more useful and convenient — whether for use as a garage or as converted living space. A selected list of projects is presented below. For additional topics covered, refer to the Table of Contents pages.

LIST OF PROJECTS

Contents

1
Planning & Design

This attractive garage is of concrete block with a brick veneer (see Chapter 12). The curved arches require more carpentry experience and tools than do other, straight-line designs.

A breezeway connection between the main house and the garage enables entry without exposure to poor weather conditions, and provides extra living space.

Start the design of your garage addition or conversion with a listing of your needs. This listing of needs, which the design must eventually answer (when you have decided on which physical form is necessary) becomes what architects sometimes call a "design program."

If you will be converting an attached garage, start your design program by listing all the things about your current arrangement that inconvenience you and the other members of the family. Lack of storage space is one typical and justifiable complaint of many homeowners. Lack of leisure space — family and game rooms — is another. Go over the list until you reach agreement on the priorities of the problems you have listed. The design solutions should be considered in light of the total house and garage floor plan, and even of the way the house relates to the site. The priority listing is necessary because all final designs are a compromise between what you ideally want and what is physically and practically possible within your ability and budget.

You may need help from an architect with the final design you need, but you still need to go through the listing process. All the architect can do is design solutions around the needs you define for him. You can employ an architect by the hour to help you with design, working drawings (the detailed, dimensioned drawings from which construction is actually done), construction monitoring, or all the above. However, remember that planning will start from the listing of needs mentioned above, which you will — with or without an architect — carry into the actual physical planning of your project.

Whatever your needs, the design program will call for more space, or better use of existing space, or a trade-off of space when you convert a garage or carport to some other use such as a family room. Your plans and needs may call for some combination, such as a conversion of an attached garage plus a new, detached garage.

PROBLEMS AND SOLUTIONS

If all you want is weather protection and security for your car and convenient access to it, you can solve your problem by building a garage or carport. Which one you choose, and whether or not the structure is adjacent to your house (attached) or some distance away from it (detached) depends on local weather, security needs, the site plan, and your budget.

If your locality is very cold in winter, an attached garage is probably the best solution. Attached garages can be entered from the house, keeping you and the car warmer. The attached garage also offers the house itself some protection from the cold and offers energy savings. Since the attached garage shares a wall with the house, there also is some saving in con-

struction material costs. All enclosed garages offer more security for your car and tools than carports.

You may not be able to build an attached garage or carport because of the

way your house fits the site. For example, there may not be room between your house and your neighbors' house to fit on an attached garage and meet the city code. This brings up one of the very first steps:

Garages are often built oversize to allow the homeowner use of the additional space to work on activities that might be inconvenient inside the home.

Similar exterior materials offer a means of establishing continuity of design between a house and garage.

before you begin any physical planning, get all the pertinent code information from your building or planning department (this is more thoroughly discussed in the later chapter on Building Codes).

Assuming you cannot fit the garage on at the side of your house, you may not be able to fit it on the back of the house either, because of the floor plan. For example, you would not want an attached garage if you had to enter it from the bathroom. Another obstacle that can prevent your building attached garages is lack of driveway access or poor driveway access. It might be possible to work out the circulation between the floor plan and the garage but you still might not be able to work out an adequate driveway radius. If these negative considerations prevent construction of an attached garage, do not try to force the attached garage to work where physical conditions call for a detached garage.

Site Planning
A few preliminary measurements will reveal whether you can build an attached garage or carport at the side of your house. Call the building department and tell them what you are planning and ask for the minimum distance required between your new construction and your neighbors' house. Preliminary checks and measurements such as these are the most obvious elements of site planning.

Establish the legal restrictions you will be operating under, such as: building setback line from the street; distance from the building to the adjoining property lines; maximum building height; other major site considerations. Most building departments have handout sheets with all this information and more, similar to the listing given below.

Most of us in suburban areas will be doing more ''adjusting'' than actual site planning. This might involve fitting garages, carports, or additions into areas that have already been set aside by the developers or converting one space usage to another without disrupting the circulation or appearance of the house and lot. This kind of planning — making the best of few alternatives — may not seem as challenging as doing the job from scratch, but it does require understanding of the previous plan in order to follow suit with the new planning. Although this kind of restraint is difficult, it is necessary in order to harmo-

nize both freestanding and attached garages with the existing building structures.

Landscaping considerations. If you have choices as to where the construction will be, consider the building relative to the sun and prevailing winds. Remember that large expanses of glass transfer heat and cold inside the building. Try to take advantage of any existing natural landscaping elements — trees, rock outcroppings, grade changes, and so forth — by making them a part of your design. Plan the drive approach around your existing lawn; save existing trees and shrubbery where possible. Avoid steep driveways in snow country. Try to ''zig-zag'' the drive up steep slopes to keep the slopes mild. The first 20 feet from the garage or carport door should not slope (ideally) more than 2 percent. After the first 20 feet from the door, try to keep the slope at 8 percent or less (4 percent is desirable).

PLOT PLANS
If you plan to try for an FHA-approved loan to finance your improvements, you have to supply a fair amount of information in a form of which the government approves. FHA typically wants the site, or ''plot plan'' to contain at least the following information at a scale of $1'' = 20'$ or $\frac{1}{16}'' = 1'\text{-}0''$ minimum:

(1) the lot and block number;
(2) the dimensions of your lot and the north point (north arrow on drawing);
(3) the dimensions of the front, rear, and side yards (for additions, show the dimensions of the new construction relative to the above dimensions);
(4) in general, you will need only

drawings that pertain to the work to be done — but you will have to show enough of the existing property to indicate how the improvements relate;
(5) locate and dimension the garage, carport, or new construction;
(6) locate new approaches, walks, driveways;
(7) locate other site work such as steps, patios, porches, retaining walls, and fences;
(8) locate and dimension any easements and setbacks;
(9) show grade elevations of the first floor of the addition and/or garage or carport, any other storage buildings, as well as grade elevations at the curb or crown of street where the lot lines would hit, if they were extended, plus elevations at the finished grade of each main corner of the building(s);
(10) you may need additional grade elevations if the improvements require special grading, drainage, or foundations.

An architect or drafting service with experience in residential planning should be very familiar with HUD (FHA) requirements and should be able to provide plans and/or guidance that will gain you HUD approval. The above requirements, even if the government does require them, are not an unreasonable amount of information. Use of the HUD requirements as a guide should also provide you with enough information to satisfy conventional lenders, who may want to tie your plans in with their agreement to loan you money for improvements. Note the sample site plan given here. When you know the general parameters of your site — know what kind

If your home's roof uses wood shingles, use them on your new garage also.

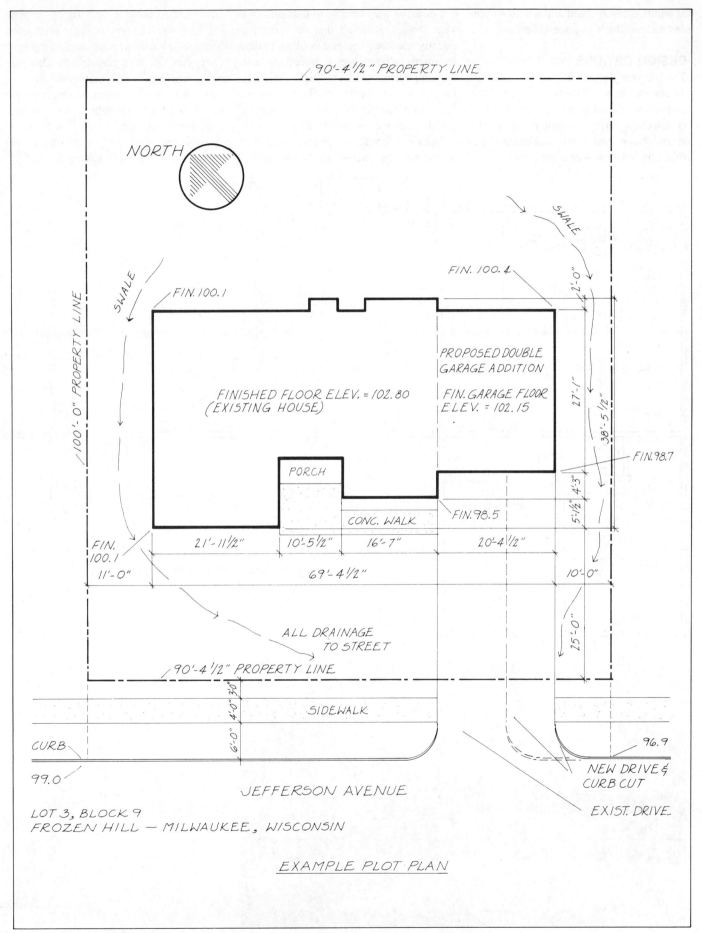

NORTH

90'-4½" PROPERTY LINE

SWALE

SWALE

FIN. 100.4

2'-0"

SWALE

FIN. 100.1

PROPOSED DOUBLE
GARAGE ADDITION

27'-1"

38'-5½"

FINISHED FLOOR ELEV. = 102.80
(EXISTING HOUSE)

FIN. GARAGE FLOOR
ELEV. = 102.15

100'-0" PROPERTY LINE

FIN. 98.7

PORCH

4'-3"

CONC. WALK

FIN. 98.5

5'-½"

FIN.
100.1

21'-11½"   10'-5½"   16'-7"   20'-4½"

11'-0"   69'-4½"   10'-0"

25'-0"

ALL DRAINAGE
TO STREET

90'-4½" PROPERTY LINE

4'-0" 3'-0"

SIDEWALK

6'-0"

CURB

96.9

99.0

NEW DRIVE &
CURB CUT

JEFFERSON AVENUE

EXIST. DRIVE

LOT 3, BLOCK 9
FROZEN HILL — MILWAUKEE, WISCONSIN

EXAMPLE PLOT PLAN

This plot plan locates the proposed double garage additions relative to the existing house and drive.

of addition can be built and where — you can decide which solution is best for you.

DESIGN OPTIONS

The following pages discuss the attached garage, the attached carport, the detached carport, the detached garage, the two-story attached garage with a room on the second floor, and a one-car detached garage converted to a two-car garage.

Since you may choose to heat and cool your project, consider that the most frequently used heating and cooling system in American residences is forced-air heating and refrigerated cooling. The same duct work is used for both systems. Forced-air furnaces typically use natural gas, heating oil, or electricity.

Gas-fired furnaces have been used most frequently, but many utility companies have pushed for electric furnaces in new installations. The type of fuel varies from location to location; your mechanical subcontractor can help you decide what furnace you need and help you buy it. Another possibility when heating attached spaces is the window unit heating/cooling unit. Especially interesting is a through-the-wall unit discussed in the chapter on "Converting for More Living Space."

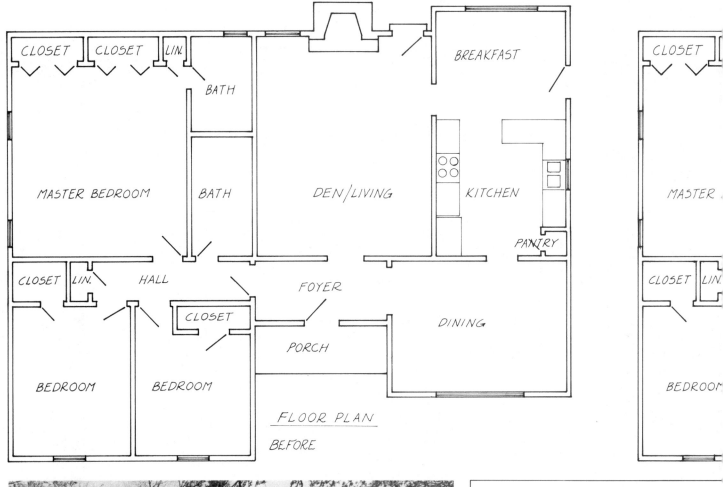

If you have space and it will not be out-of proportion with your home, build a multi-stall garage.

To aid discussion of the different projects, we will present them by example. We start with the existing floor plan of an example house. It is a rather typical builder house for a suburban lot. There is a master bedroom, two children's bedrooms, a den/living room ("great room"), a gallery-type kitchen with breakfast eating area, and a dining room. The laundry is done in the breakfast room.

This is not really desirable, but is not unusual in modest homes. Nor is it restrictive, since there is a dining room on the other side of the kitchen. But the arrangement could be considerably improved, as we will show.

The Attached Garage

The example plan below is now shown modified with a garage that has a storage-

and-laundry room. This garage is a typical solution chosen by many builders. It provides security and protection from the elements for cars, tools, and equipment. The garage can be entered from the house; it also can be entered from the outside without raising the double front door. The accompanying drawing shows the finished front elevation. The term "elevation," incidentally, has two meanings: as used

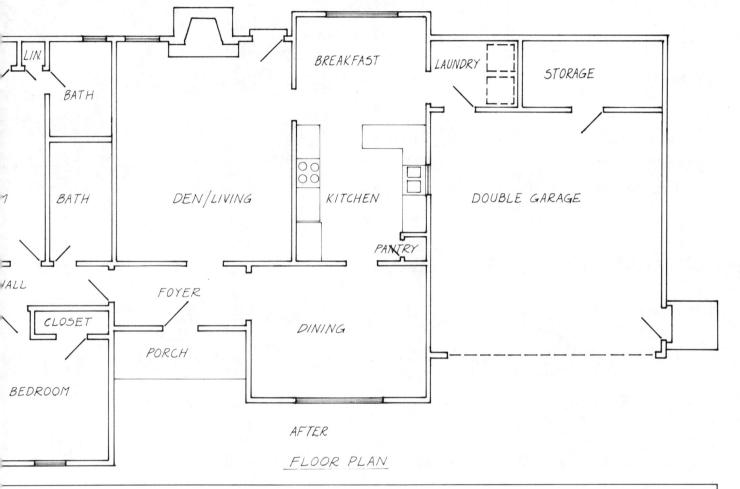

AFTER FLOOR PLAN

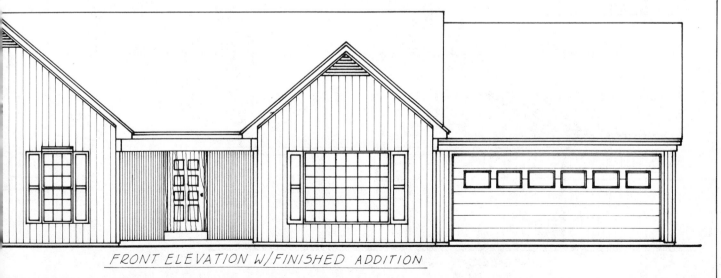

FRONT ELEVATION W/FINISHED ADDITION

below, elevation refers to a two-dimensional drawing of some vertical portion of the building — typically front, rear, and side views, although interior elevations are common; the other meaning of "elevation" refers to grade changes — typically, finished floor elevations, grades at building corners, curb and street elevations, and so forth.

The front elevation was first studied with a sketch; that is, tracing paper was laid over a scaled drawing of the front of the house (front elevation) and various shapes were tried to see which one looked best for the addition. The garage roof could have been a hip roof, a flat roof, or a number of other shapes. But the one shown in the sketch was chosen to blend in

RIGHT SIDE ELEVATION — BEFORE ADDITION

RIGHT SIDE ELEVATION W/FINISHED ADDITION

4" COLUMNS   RIGHT SIDE ELEVATION

with the existing roofline and to complement the house. Additional drawings show the right side elevation of the house before and after the addition and the rear elevation after the addition. It also indicates what the elevation would be with an open carport. Dimensions for an attached one-story garage will vary, but a one-car garage usually ranges from 20 to 23 feet long, and from 12 to 15 feet wide. A two-car garage will be the same length, but will be anywhere from 18 to 24 feet wide.

The Attached Carport

In moderate and hot climates, and when security is not an important consideration, the carport will provide cheaper weather protection than a garage. The carport is cheaper than the attached garage because

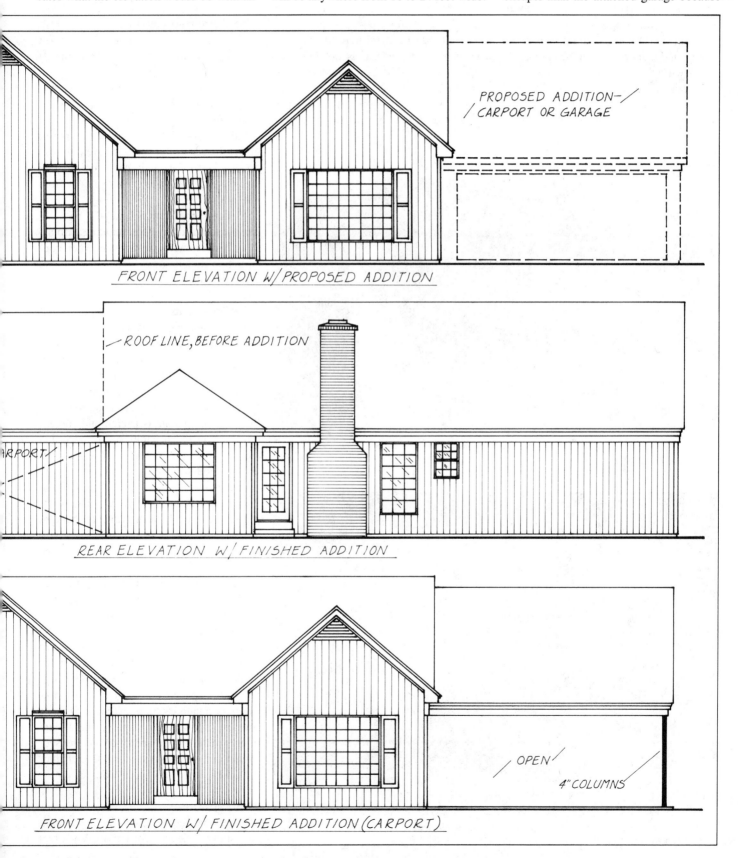

PROPOSED ADDITION—/
/ CARPORT OR GARAGE

FRONT ELEVATION W/ PROPOSED ADDITION

—ROOF LINE, BEFORE ADDITION

ARPORT/

REAR ELEVATION W/ FINISHED ADDITION

OPEN/
4" COLUMNS

FRONT ELEVATION W/ FINISHED ADDITION (CARPORT)

there is less construction material involved (fewer side walls), and there is less labor involved in building the carport (important if you are hiring some of the work done). If you really need a garage, but your budget is too tight, you may first build an open carport like the one chosen for the example in this text; you can then wall it in later. Or you could incorporate a storage and laundry area in the carport, as shown earlier for the attached garage, and then wall in the rest of the carport later. The example carport is a simplified version of the attached garage. The walls have been eliminated, but it uses the same roofline and all the remaining dimensions are the same. There are no significant differences in the physical site planning and layout of the carport versus the attached garage.

Completely open carports are seen in many areas. Their purpose is to protect the car from the weather in mild climates. However, when the car is not in it, the carport can be used as an outdoor game room or barbecue area.

Fully or partially open carports are particularly desirable in the Southwest, to provide the ventilation and relief from an otherwise stuffy, humid structure.

Instead of a slab, as for a garage, concrete piers underneath the support posts. This significantly reduces construction time and cost.

The Detached Carport

There are cases where an attached carport or garage is impossible or undesirable. If aesthetics prevent an attached carport or attached garage — for example, where the house facade is arranged symmetrically about the door with an equal number of windows on both sides — you may prefer not to disturb this appearance by adding on to one end of it. This calls for separate utility spaces, such as carports, away from the house.

Because the framing and flat roof are simple to build for a freestanding carport, it is one of the easiest homeowner construction undertakings. Packaged kits are available also.

The Detached Garage

The detached garage is more expensive to build than either the carport or the attached garage. There are more construction materials required — more lumber, more concrete to get the drive to the garage, and longer runs of electrical and plumbing lines. If the garage is heated and cooled, you will need an additional furnace and cooling unit and duct lines (this is assuming, of course, a garage large enough to warrant having a central heating and cooling unit instead of a window or through-the-wall unit). Attached garages can usually tap onto the house mechanical, plumbing, and electrical systems.

The detached garage does, however, have certain advantages over attached units. It usually can be built larger than attached carports or attached garages, because attached units are generally at the side of the house in the typical suburban fashion. This area offers less space for building than does the backyard. The larger garage space can be used for a workshop, or a laundry, or a recreation area, or storage facilities, or all these things and more (including an apartment on the second floor, as discussed in the chapter "Building the Two-Story Garage").

Conversions

Conversions require just as much planning and study as new construction. When you

In hot climates, an attached carport is often preferred to a garage. A ledger connects the carport roof to the side of the house.

This salt-box double two-car garage (it will hold four cars) also has a separate-entry storage area underneath its low shed roof. Note extended slab and support poles.

convert house space, even if it is changing the garage from one use to another, you are altering the traffic patterns and relationships of the whole house. So you must review the entire plan in light of your proposed conversion. Study the circulation that will result from the change. For example, you do not want to have to go from a newly converted bedroom through the kitchen to reach a bathroom. Examine the new usage relative to the other spaces; for example, do you really want a workshop next to the kitchen? Study every aspect of the change relative to the rest of the house.

Basic measurements. Your existing garage or carport space probably is large enough for any interior use you have in mind. Typical interior dimensions for a one-car garage are 11 feet 6 inches x 21 feet 10 inches; for a two-car garage, the basic measurements are 18 feet 4 inches x 21 feet 10 inches. For extra storage or working space, add 2 to 3 feet to the width of the garage.

Expanding a One-Car to a Two-Car Garage

Most houses built today have two-car garages or carports. But older homes were often built with one-car detached garages. If you have a one-car garage, you can convert it to a two-car garage. The conversion requires hard work, but since the existing garage provides all the reference points, it is simple to carry out.

Is it worth it? First, determine if the garage you have is worth expanding: is the slab in good condition, with few and only minor cracks? Are the rafters fairly straight, with no serious sags obvious to the eye? Will you be able to match the old siding or brick when you build the new wall sections? If you do not believe the old garage is worth expanding, do not try it. You still will be able to use much of the old materials, even if you decide to dismantle the old garage and build a new, larger one.

Double-door expansion. If the old ga-

rage is basically sound, it can be expanded. If the garage is presently wide enough for one modern car (some of the older garages are too narrow for comfort) and has an overhead or lift-up door you are satisfied with, you can double the existing garage space by building a double-door garage in order to utilize the existing door. This means you will have to build a short section of wall between the old door and the new door to separate them and to accommodate framing around the doors. This wall section is usually not less than about a foot wide, but not more than several feet wide.

Single-door expansion. If the existing garage is not wide enough, it will probably be best to discard the old door (sell it if you can) and make the expanded garage a double-car garage with one large door.

Two-Story Attached Garage

There are differing structural requirements for building a two-story garage as opposed

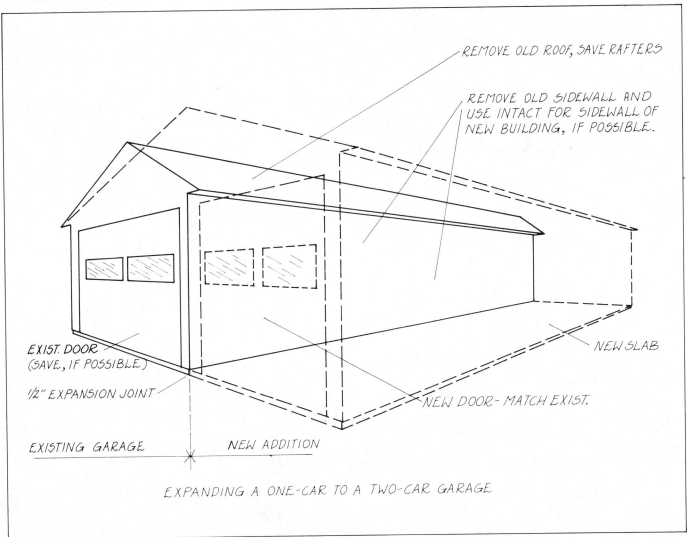

EXPANDING A ONE-CAR TO A TWO-CAR GARAGE

Expansion of a garage involves removing one side wall and then filling in the necessary framing and finishing.

to a one-story structure. However, the increased living space possible over the garage is gained at relatively little additional cost, since much of the work has to be done anyway for a one-story garage. For structural requirements, see the later chapter on ''Building a Two-Story Garage.''

With a two-story garage addition even more care must be taken to match the existing roof line and veneer. Otherwise, a ''tacked-on'' appearance will result. However, if it is impossible to match the veneer, a strong contrast is better than a close match.

DRIVEWAYS
Planning

Timing and trucks. There is some flexibility in scheduling the driveway. You can lay it when you lay the floor slab for your carport. If you use ready-mix, this combination pour is the most economical way, since the truck will then come only once. But if you rent your own power mixer, you can lay the driveway and floor slab any time and in any sequence that suits your schedule.

You may choose to lay the driveway first to accommodate the transport of ma-terials to the building area and to cut down on mud and/or dust during construction. However, keep extremely heavy trucks, such as cement trucks, off the driveway.

Routes and designs. With many suburban lots, the distance from the proposed carport or garage is a short, straight distance to the street. This means that doubling an existing driveway or building a new double driveway all the way to the street will not be an expensive project. Shown opposite page is a straight double driveway to the street, as well as other layout possibilities.

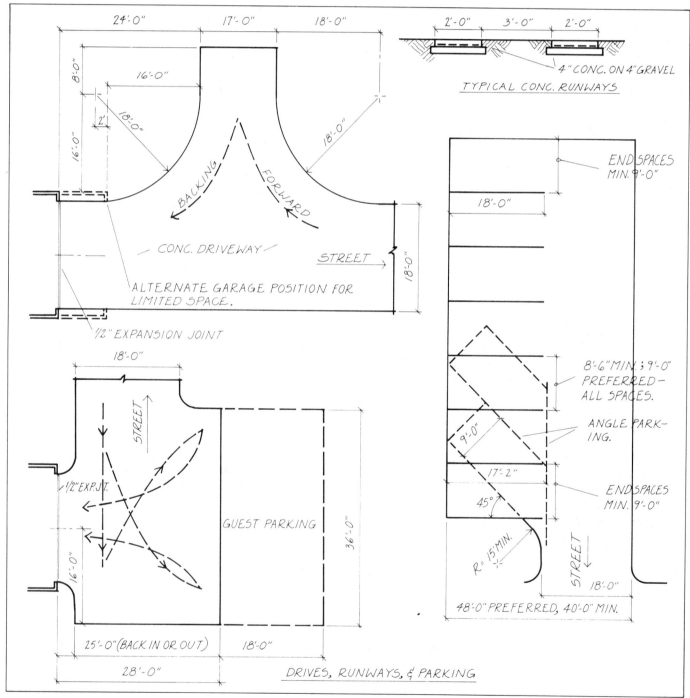

DRIVES, RUNWAYS, & PARKING

Parking may need to be expanded off an existing drive, or a drive may be enlarged for a garage expansion. Pay attention to the turning radius.

Enlarging a Driveway

To expand a concrete driveway for an extra car or for parking, use the old driveway for reference points. For example, secure a form board at a corner of the existing driveway (or butt the form board up against the driveway if your driveway addition does not come off a corner) with a 2x4 stake, so it is visually level with the top of the existing driveway. You can check for level with a straight section of 2x4 laid across the form board and the existing driveway. Then stake the form board down as you would for any other slab, checking for level with a spirit level as you go.

Expansion and control joints. Remember to use a ½-inch expansion joint between the existing drive and the addition poured next to it. It is recommended that you use ½-inch expansion joints longitudinally, 9 feet apart. Therefore, for an 18-foot driveway, you would have one longitudinal expansion joint down the center of the driveway. If the driveway were 27 feet wide, you would need two ½-inch longitudinal expansion joints, dividing the driveway into three 9-foot sections. Transverse (across) expansion joints, also ½ inch, should be used every 90 to 120 feet. Transverse control joints should be used every 15 to 25 feet. If you are in doubt about how many control joints to use, then use more, not less. Remember that control joints can be used to etch patterns in the concrete, adding interest to wide expanses of concrete.

If you have considerable acreage, then building a double driveway all the way to the street is expensive and probably unnecessary. You can instead build a double driveway from the garage or carport entry out a comfortable distance to about the same as the typical suburban double driveway — less than a hundred feet, depending on your preference and budget — and then build a single lane to the street. Or you can use runways (two strips or "ribbons" of concrete for the car wheels) out a distance from the house to the street. In snow country it is wise to fill the center section with gravel to aid drainage. Illustration 1 shows a typical runway setup: two 4-inch thick strips of concrete 3 feet apart (inside of runway to inside of runway). The concrete is laid on 4 inches of gravel and is reinforced with 6x6 #10 wire mesh.

Parking and turnaround standards. The basic standards can be used as shown or can be manipulated to fit most homeowner driveway needs. Where a two-car driveway (minimum 18 feet wide) enters the street, the radius at the corners should be at least 15 feet and preferably 20 feet. The minimum width of a one-car driveway is 9 feet and, where it meets the street, the radius at the corners should be the same as for the 18-foot two-car driveway.

Study the sections on preparing and pouring concrete and concrete slabs, and on building formwork, presented in Chapter 6, before you start building your driveway or expanding an existing one. Use the same construction techniques for laying out and pouring concrete driveways as for slabs, and refer to Chapter 15.

OUTSIDE RADIUS

Driveway Width	Minimum
9'6" (2.7 meters, 152.4 mm)	55' (16.7 meters)
10'6" (3 meters, 152.4 mm)	31' (9.4 meters)
11'6" (3.3 meters, 152.4 mm)	24'9" (7.3 meters 228.6 mm)

A concrete slab driveway can be part of the landscaping, particularly if the control joints are a design of permanent redwood strips.

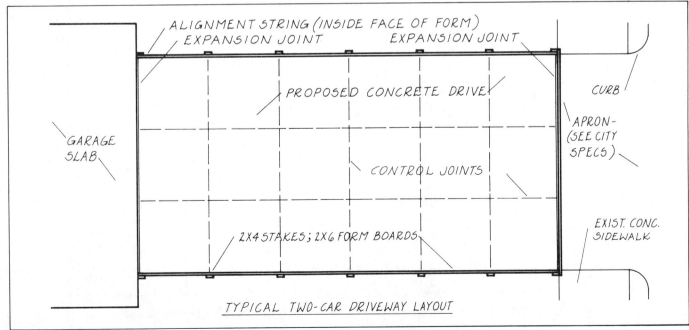

TYPICAL TWO-CAR DRIVEWAY LAYOUT

The typical two-car driveway extends from the garage to the street. Use frequent control joints. Use a ½-inch expansion joint between the drive and the garage slab and at the drive apron at the street.

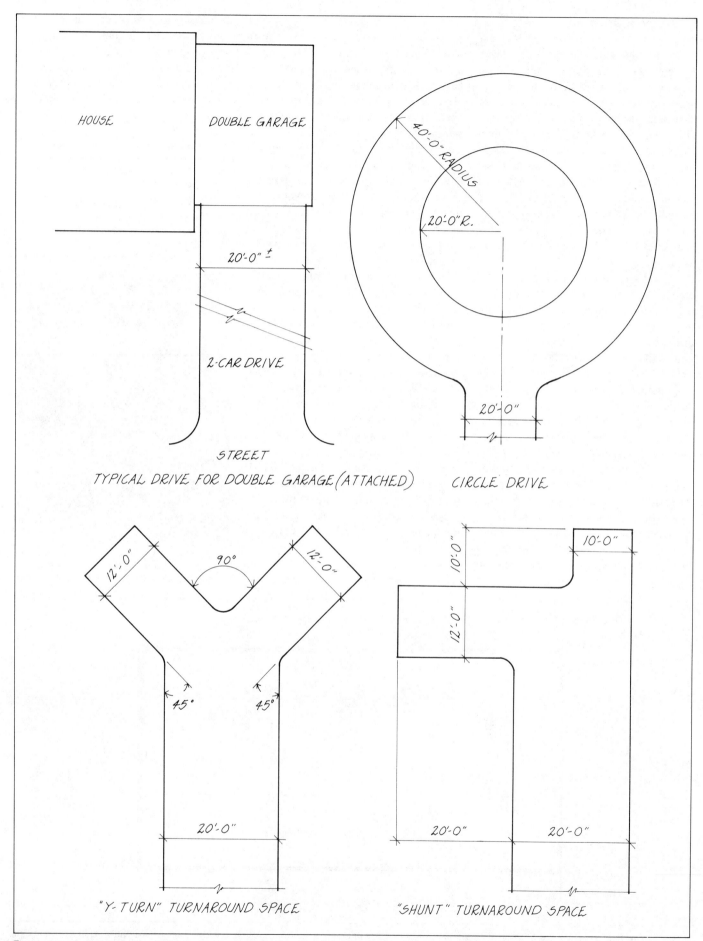

HOUSE

DOUBLE GARAGE

20'-0" ±

2-CAR DRIVE

STREET

TYPICAL DRIVE FOR DOUBLE GARAGE (ATTACHED)

40'-0" RADIUS

20'-0" R.

20'-0"

CIRCLE DRIVE

12'-0"   90°   12'-0"

45°   45°

20'-0"

"Y-TURN" TURNAROUND SPACE

10'-0"

10'-0"

12'-0"

20'-0"   20'-0"

"SHUNT" TURNAROUND SPACE

The design of your driveway will depend on your needs, the size of your lot and the siting of your house on the lot.

2
Working with Contractors

Before beginning a discussion of how you relate to contractors, it will be helpful to discuss briefly how contractors relate to each other. In textbook situations, the client (you) contracts with a "general contractor" to build a structure. It is the responsibility of the general contractor to select and administer the mechanical, plumbing, electrical, landscaping, and other contractors needed to perform the work — these contractors under the general contractor are called "subcontractors," relative to the general contractor.

If an architect is used, he acts as a kind of professional "referee" between the owner and the general contractor, assuming the owner (you again) contracts with the architect to perform job inspections, instead of just providing a set of plans. The architect, if he does job inspection, usually handles the owner's purse strings for him, approving or disapproving payments and deciding when the work has been done satisfactorily. There are two kinds of architects: building architects, normally called simply "architects", and landscape architects, who usually are called "landscape architects" to distinguish them from the building architect, who often has the wider administrative authority. Both architects and landscape architects are highly trained and licensed professionals.

The most important item you buy from any contractor is his knowledge. Much of the work he does is simple to execute — if you know what you are doing. Knowing what you are doing also means that you understand the relationship of each building element to the other. So, in working with the various subcontractors, you want the contractor to plan the technical details and the work flow, help get you started, and then let you do as much of the work as

possible. He should check back with you as your work speed requires, and keep you going. In short, you become his helper.

AGREEMENT AND CONTRACTS

Your relationship should start by signing a contract spelling out exactly what each subcontractor is to do for you.

The subcontractor should have overall responsibility for seeing each type of work through to completion. He should arrange for all permits and inspections, and meet with the inspectors when necessary. But even in these areas, you may be able to do the leg work of gaining the permits or even gaining code approvals; whether you will or not is largely a matter of time and personal relationships with individuals. If the inspectors see that competent, known professionals are guiding and supplementing the work, you may be able to handle more of the contact. Still, your subcon-

tractor should be responsible for permits, code approvals, as well as coordination with the other building trade elements. This should be spelled out in the contract.

A contract usually has a time frame for work completion. Contractors are often pushed hard to get through as quickly as possible. Therefore, the subcontractors may be hesitant to sign a contract with someone (you) who, as part of the contract understanding, insists on doing a great deal of the work. For this reason, a contract based on an hourly rate will probably be the best and fairest way for both of you. You are buying a contractor's knowledge and time and as much of his hands-on work as is necessary to get the job done when you need it. Choose those who will be satisfied to be paid by the hour, and only when he is on the job or doing work elsewhere that concerns your project. Do not enter into an agreement with anyone

It will cost more to have all or part of a new garage built by professionals, but it will save time. Uncut lumber for this job was delivered six hours before this photo was taken.

who is hesitant or not sympathetic with your efforts to build your own garage. If you do, the relationship will not last long. Once you have the subcontractors under contract, you can begin.

Materials

Small contractors often want the owner to pay for the materials on the front end. Then they install the materials. Avoid this situation if possible. The materials are a considerable investment. If they are installed improperly, and if you have hired a contractor whom you do not know — often by the hour — all he has to do is walk off the job for you to be stuck with damaged or improperly installed materials plus the cost of removing them before you can start again. Try to arrange the contract so that the subcontractor buys the materials and you make partial payments as the job goes along. This method will encourage quality work from the subcontractor and will prompt him to properly store materials and protect them against theft. He will be more careful because until the materials are in place (this should be in the contract) the materials are his, not yours.

WORKING WITH A HEATING AND COOLING SUBCONTRACTOR
Responsibilities

Heating and cooling jobs often call for too many code requirements and skill require-

ments to be attempted alone by an amateur. In fact, in selecting a subcontractor, you want to be sure that he presently works in the residential heating and cooling field. A general knowledge of the subject is not enough. Code inspections and approvals are an inherent part of the building business, and the contractor's working relationships with the inspectors is of significant value to you. Do not get involved with a subcontractor for any portion of the work who does not work well with the building officials.

Heating and cooling systems typically use natural gas, heating oil, and electric energy. But the most-used heating and cooling system in America is presently forced-air heating (gas-fired) and refrigerated cooling.

Heating and cooling, often referred to as the ''mechanical'' section of building plans, like plumbing and electrical work, is controlled by building codes and installation is inspected by some government authority (building department). For this reason, you are advised to find yourself a mechanical subcontractor early on.

Work diagrams. When you find a mechanical subcontractor, get him to sketch a heating and cooling distribution diagram on a blueline print (or sketch with dimensions, if you do not have a house plan) of your floor plan. The diagram should show the ductwork, locate the supply and return

grilles, and show duct connections to the furnace.

The work schedule. To begin, discuss the heating and cooling diagram with your subcontractor and make out a work plan. He will probably need to fabricate the duct runs (or at least some of them), perhaps in sections, and then install a run with you to help you get the hang of it. Have him itemize the duct connectors, sealing tape, hangers, fasteners, and tools. You may want him to call the supply house and let you pick up the items (remember, if you do not do the errands, you are paying skilled labor to do them). The contractor should deal with the authorities when getting any new gas line. He should also hire and instruct any excavators needed to dig trenches for the line, and be responsible for seeing that the line gets to the proper point at the house or garage.

After the contractor does a complete diagram, and you know where the equipment goes, he can install a sample portion of duct and let you install as much as you can afterwards. You can either agree with him to make scheduled inspections of your work, or you can call him when you need him. An essential part of your agreement with the contractor is that he arrange all applicable inspections with building inspectors and be present, and in charge, when the inspectors come. In other words, the official building inspections are the responsibility of the contractor. Relative to code approvals, you are strictly a laborer.

The subcontractor will arrange the schedule, decide when and how to install a furnace, if one is needed. You should be able to install the main supply duct and the branch ducts, with his guidance. He should advise on how to get the duct work through the framing without weakening it. The ducts should be run through the framing before the plumbing and electrical work are in position. After you see him install one grill and register, you should be able to do the rest. In general, try to handle all the repetitive work.

The thermostat wiring. There is considerable latitude in scheduling the installation of the thermostat. The wiring is simple to install and little space is required. But the contractor should locate the thermostat. You may choose to bring the wiring from the thermostat to the heating and cooling unit. But do not make the final thermostat hookup at this time.

If your garage addition will require extension of the existing roofline, you will find it safer and more efficient to contract out the extended roof framing work to a professional.

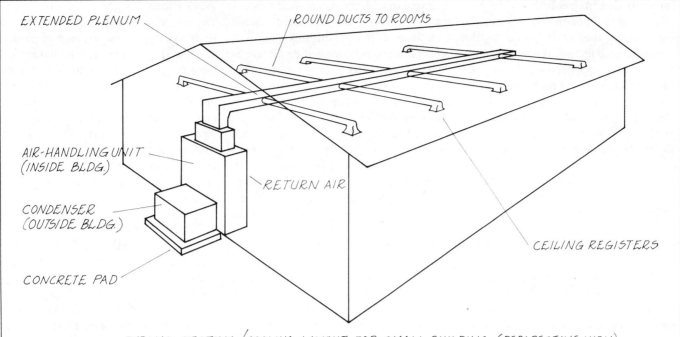

EXTENDED PLENUM

ROUND DUCTS TO ROOMS

AIR-HANDLING UNIT
(INSIDE BLDG.)

RETURN AIR

CONDENSER
(OUTSIDE BLDG.)

CONCRETE PAD

CEILING REGISTERS

TYPICAL HEATING/COOLING LAYOUT FOR SMALL BUILDING (PERSPECTIVE VIEW)

NOTE: PLENUM, DUCTS, REGISTERS, AND OTHER COMPONENTS
OF SYSTEM TO BE SIZED BY CONTRACTOR.

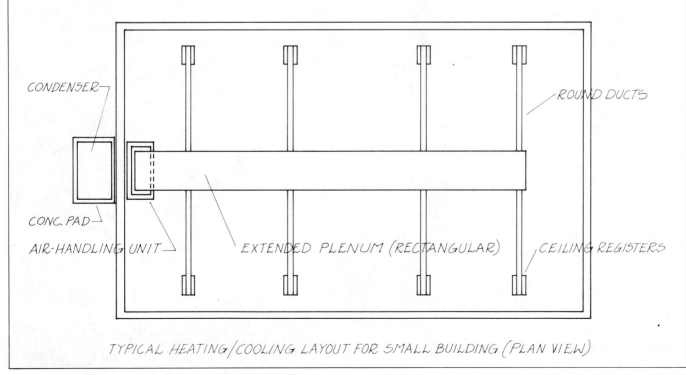

CONDENSER

ROUND DUCTS

CONC. PAD

AIR-HANDLING UNIT

EXTENDED PLENUM (RECTANGULAR)

CEILING REGISTERS

TYPICAL HEATING/COOLING LAYOUT FOR SMALL BUILDING (PLAN VIEW)

Heating for a detached garage will require a new furnace. When converting an attached garage to living space, existing ducts can be extended.

Carrying Out Inspections

Creating a "punch" list. After the complete system is in place — the ductwork, heating and cooling elements, thermostat(s), supply and return grilles — have the contractor inspect the system and make up a "punch list." A punch list is a listing of all the minor details that inevitably are overlooked in construction work: tape around the duct connections, dirt or mud in the heating and cooling unit, and so forth, are typical items that get left out. You should be able to examine the punch list items. When you think you are through with the punch list items, have the contractor inspect the system again, to be sure everything is complete.

When the power is on, the contractor should make another complete inspection of the system, then connect the thermostat, and start the system up. He should adjust the controls and balance the register system. This process may result in another punch list of minor items to do, like securing rattling supply and return grilles and other details.

The final check. The installation and final checkout of the heating and cooling system may take weeks or months. Be sure that the contractor agrees to be responsible through this period, as well as responsible for servicing the unit for one year from the time of final completion and checkout.

The above work schedule is a brief synopsis of dozens of work details that have to be done and done right. The quality of the heating and cooling system will depend on the ability of the contractor and your own ability, patience, attention to detail and — perhaps most important — on your ability to work well with the mechanical subcontractor.

WORKING WITH THE PLUMBING SUBCONTRACTOR

The planning and installation of plumbing, like the planning and installation of mechanical and electrical systems, is too much for the inexperienced to take on alone. Plumbing for a conversion, or for a second-floor bedroom over the garage, or similar projects, can be complicated work. Get a plumbing contractor under contract to help you.

Responsibilities

Your relationship with the plumbing subcontractor will be very similar to your relationship with the mechanical subcontractor. That is, he will have overall coordination responsibilities and will schedule all inspections and be present as your representative at the inspections. You are the plumbing subcontractor's helper. The subcontractor should be responsible for any necessary permits, although you may do the leg work for him just as you may pick up various supplies that he orders from suppliers. The material should be paid for by the subcontractor and you should pay him when the materials are satisfactorily installed. He should coordinate the work with excavators and other contractors, with building officials, and with you.

If you do not make it clear in the contract that the subcontractor is ultimately responsible for the progress of the work and that you are the helper, you may find yourself responsible for major mistakes and failures in coordination. This means you owe it to the plumber to in fact be the helper, and not impose your inexpertise on him. You will simply be replacing the plumber's hours (and his salary) with your own time, whenever you can. He will carry out the work you cannot do.

Work Plans

The plumbing work should start with a study of the type and location of fixtures on your floor plan: toilets, lavatories, bathtubs, sinks, and so forth. Have the plumbing subcontractor work out a plumbing diagram showing how the plumbing lines run and what size and type pipe they are, and so forth. Then have him work out a work sequence schedule. Divide the work according to what you think you can handle and have him help you get started.

WORKING WITH THE ELECTRICAL SUBCONTRACTOR

Electrical work demands careful planning beyond the capacity of the do-it-yourselfer. Electricity is very unforgiving of mistakes or sloppy work; mistakes with electrical wiring can result in fires, serious injuries, or even death. You need an electrical subcontractor under contract for expert planning and execution of your electrical system.

However, the actual hands-on-work of installing the electrical service is not difficult. You can save a lot of money by doing the labor yourself.

Construction of a two-story garage offers more living area per dollar investment.

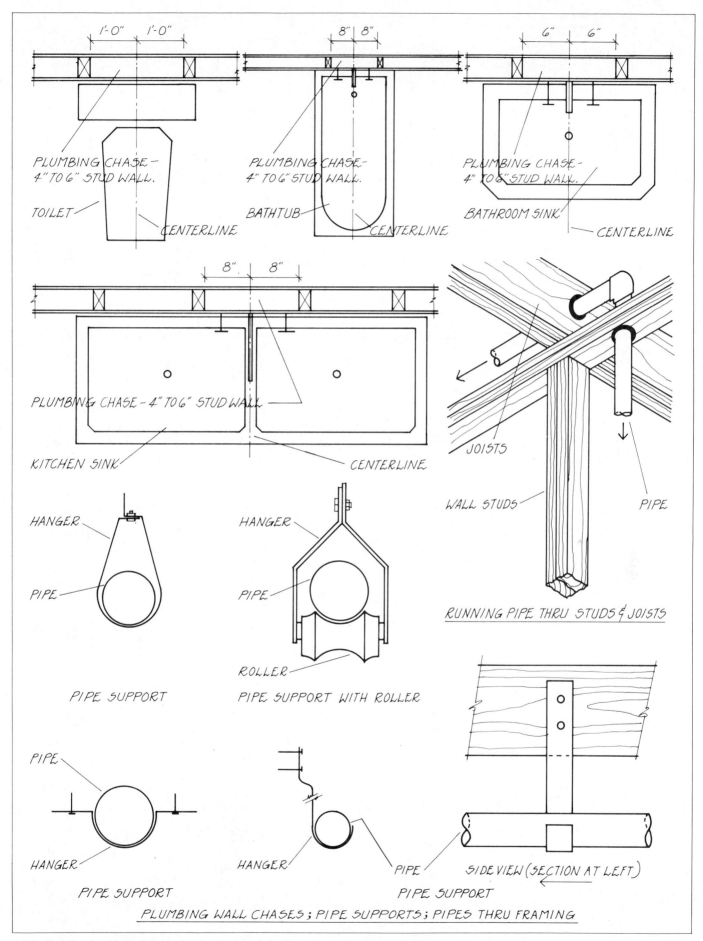

PLUMBING CHASE –
4" TO 6" STUD WALL.

TOILET

CENTERLINE

1'-0"   1'-0"

PLUMBING CHASE –
4" TO 6" STUD WALL.

BATHTUB

CENTERLINE

8"   8"

PLUMBING CHASE –
4" TO 6" STUD WALL.

BATHROOM SINK

CENTERLINE

6"   6"

8"   8"

PLUMBING CHASE – 4" TO 6" STUD WALL

KITCHEN SINK

CENTERLINE

JOISTS

WALL STUDS

PIPE

RUNNING PIPE THRU STUDS & JOISTS

HANGER

PIPE

PIPE SUPPORT

HANGER

PIPE

ROLLER

PIPE SUPPORT WITH ROLLER

PIPE

HANGER

PIPE SUPPORT

HANGER

PIPE

PIPE SUPPORT

SIDE VIEW (SECTION AT LEFT)

PLUMBING WALL CHASES; PIPE SUPPORTS; PIPES THRU FRAMING

A "plan" of the plumbing, similar to (and perhaps on) the floor plan, shows the routes of various lines and plumbing construction details.

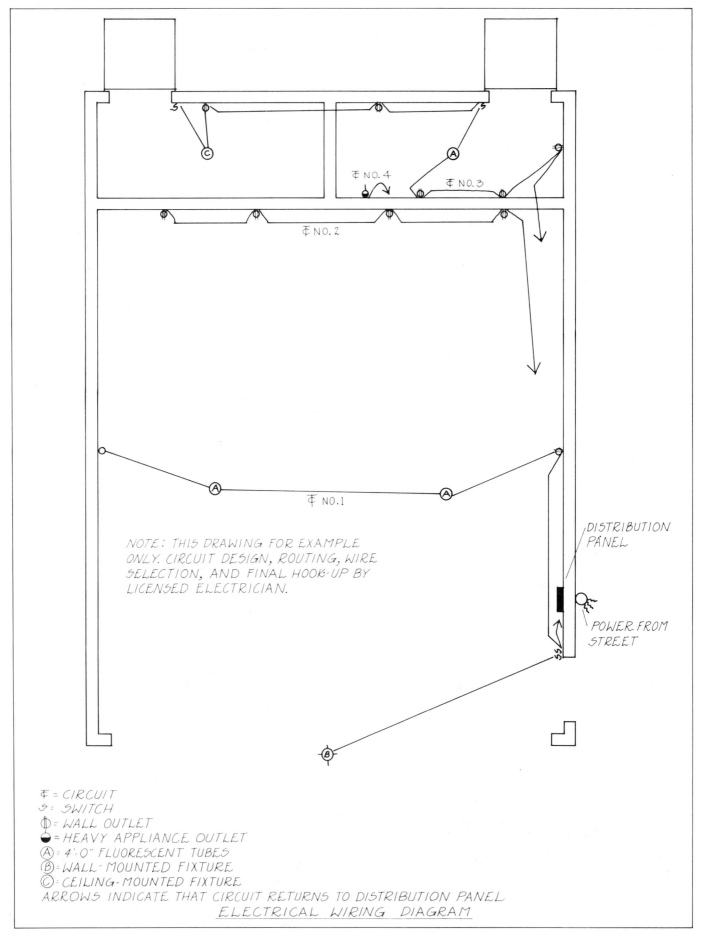

NOTE: THIS DRAWING FOR EXAMPLE ONLY. CIRCUIT DESIGN, ROUTING, WIRE SELECTION, AND FINAL HOOK-UP BY LICENSED ELECTRICIAN.

₵ = CIRCUIT
S = SWITCH
⏀ = WALL OUTLET
⬤ = HEAVY APPLIANCE OUTLET
Ⓐ = 4'-0" FLUORESCENT TUBES
Ⓑ = WALL-MOUNTED FIXTURE
Ⓒ = CEILING-MOUNTED FIXTURE
ARROWS INDICATE THAT CIRCUIT RETURNS TO DISTRIBUTION PANEL
ELECTRICAL WIRING DIAGRAM

This sample electrical plan identifies the various items and their locations.

Responsibilities

Begin with a study of the floor plan. The lighting plan is shown right on the floor plan. Builders typically turn the floor plan over to an electrical subcontractor, who figures how many circuits are needed, how many service panels are needed, and figures any other equipment needed. He may or may not draw a wiring diagram when he works for builders. You want him to draw one for you. Electrical and other residential subs are often so familiar with design and installation of their services that they can store the information in their heads. You do not want the subcontractor

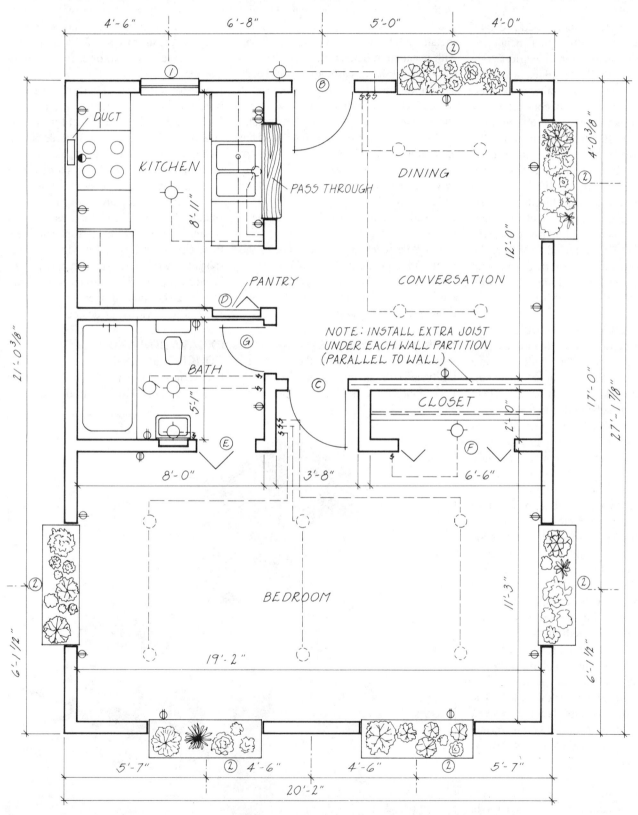

FLOOR PLAN & ELECTRICAL PLAN: 2ND. FLOOR, GARAGE APARTMENT

Here is a floor plan for a luxurious bedroom with window greenhouses, showing the electrical plan markings.

to do that. Get the electrical subcontractor to draw a wiring diagram and to divide the work to be done between you and himself. Plan a work sequence schedule, as you did with the mechanical and plumbing subcontractors.

The construction and installation details not shown on the floor plan mentioned above are standard in the electrical code and the local building code, which licensed electricians are familiar with. Contract with the electrical subcontractor such that he is responsible for overall coordination of the construction, installation of the electrical work, scheduling all inspections (he should be your representative at the inspections). Specify that he is responsible for *successful* inspection by officials — that is, he should correct any deficiencies found and call the inspector back when they are corrected. Further, he should coordinate the electrical work with excavators and other contractors, with building officials, and with you.

Setting Up a Work Schedule

After the electrical subcontractor does the wiring diagram and the work sequence plan, have him get you started on the job. Remember that when you are talking to the electrical subcontractor the clock is running, so plan your work questions carefully before he comes to the job to save valuable time. Take notes. Because he will not always be able to come exactly when you need him. He may be moonlighting from a regular job, or he may be a small but busy contractor.

You will be performing the work of the general contractor and a laborer, or helper, at the same time. It will be necessary for you to talk to the electrical subcontractor and plan several days, or a week's work at a time. Find out what materials and supplies you need and get them for him. Do the work and arrange for him to come and check what you have done and to help you overcome any snags.

Doing some of the work yourself. The circuitry work and installation of outlets, switches, and so forth, is repetitive and simple to do. You will gain work skills as you proceed.

The first step will be to bring the conduit or through-wall cable to the garage. Here is an example of how you might proceed: have the electrician come out before you start the work, advise you how to run the conduit to the garage and through

the wall. You can dig necessary trenches, cut access holes, and secure the conduits, but let the electrician make the final connections. You also will need a system ground. As you can see, this method of work will require an electrical plan and good rapport between you and your electrician. Unless you have an electrical plan with installation details, you will have to carry the instructions around in your head.

Again, the electrical subcontractor should help you plan each work stage, check what you have done, and then make the final connections. Then he will call the appropriate inspectors and be present when they come. If there are deficiencies, he will note and correct them (or have you correct them). Local code and utility company variables make this procedure a must for the inexperienced.

It will be necessary to take some of the wiring through framing members. Have the electrical subcontractor instruct you how to do this without weakening the framing members significantly.

Setting Up Electrical Service

Electric service comes from the street via a utility pole or an underground cable; it goes to the hose accordingly. Most often,

you will be able to use the same service box when you add new service. However, this is for the electrical subcontractor to decide. If you have to add a new service box and/or new line to the house, he should coordinate the work with an excavator (if underground) and should coordinate with the utility company to assure the new service is installed in a timely manner.

Service entrance. Typically, the utility company is contacted to determine a feasible location on your wall for the service head. There is some latitude in the location of this entrance head, but the utility company wants it in the shortest line possible to the service at the street, assuming the utility company pays for the line and installation to the service head. There is some variance in these responsibilities from city to city (find out what your responsibility is). You usually have a choice between a wall-mounted entrance head and an eave-mounted one; select the one that fits best with your design.

EXCAVATION AND CONCRETE WORK

Excavation is a general term. It means removing earth. Excavators dig trenches

Power mixers can be small enough for convenient hand mixing, or large enough to serve professional needs.

from the street to the house for mechanical, plumbing, and electrical services; they scoop out earth for walks, driveways, foundation footings, and floor slabs.

It is assumed that you do not know the construction work sequences of the various trades and the way the different trades work together. The safest way to avoid coordination problems with excavation is to have each subcontractor provide his own excavation, and to have them contractually obligated to coordinate with each other. If the subcontractors are responsible for their own excavation, they should have no complaint about the excavation needed (if any) for their services.

In times when there is much residential building going on, excavators are easier to find than in periods of slack building. Excavators supervise the equipment operators. In slack building times, excavators tend to thin out and you may have to settle for an equipment operator (bulldozer operator) whom you can supervise yourself.

Doing the Excavation Yourself

You may wish to be "the excavator." If so, you should be sure the subcontractors understand that you are looking to them to help you avoid duplication of effort and that you expect them to coordinate with each other. This should point out the need for a good set of plans: with a good set of plans, you can have meetings with all your subcontractors before any major work is undertaken so that everyone knows the schedule — this should reduce coordination problems between the subcontractors.

Equipment Use

You probably should not attempt to use the heavy machinery for excavation unless you have had experience with it. Bulldozers are typically used to excavate for floor slabs and other wide, shallow excavations. Backhoes and power shovels are used for foundation and other trenches. Shallow trenches (18 inches or less) and floor slabs can be dug by hand, if you have the time and the back for it. Use a pointed shovel to take out the bulk of the earth and a square shovel to level the bottom of the excavation.

Concrete Subcontractors

There are concrete contractors who specialize in pouring foundation footings and foundation walls. Others specialize in pouring floor slabs. This is in periods of intense residential building. However, you should not have trouble finding a concrete contractor to do any concrete work you have: walks, drives, foundations, floor slabs, whatever. The yellow pages will have a range of concrete contractors, but it is a good idea to call an architect or landscape architect for a reference. Concrete contractors frequently will do their own excavation and some of them will clear lots in preparation for concrete pouring.

Concrete is one of the elements of construction that a careful amateur can do and save money, so you may want to consider doing all the concrete work yourself. Whether you do it yourself or hire it done, be sure you coordinate the concrete work with the other contractors or you will end up breaking out already-poured concrete in order to place plumbing lines.

FRAMING CONTRACTORS

The framing contractor, like the excavators and concrete contractors who specialize in foundations and floor slabs, tends to disappear in slack building times. You should strongly consider doing your own framing, because framing is one of the simplest elements of residential construction. Mistakes made by amateurs in wall and partition framing usually can be corrected quickly and without much expense.

If you contract the framing done, a small general contractor is your best choice. Or, as an alternative to hiring a general contractor or doing all the framing yourself, hire a carpenter with residential framing experience to work with you.

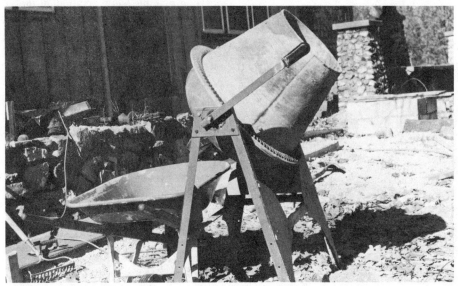

A portable cement mixer is a help in an extensive concrete pouring job. However, position your wheelbarrow carefully so that your concrete does not overshoot the wheelbarrow.

Cement, sand and gravel are heavy and are delivered in large, heavy trucks. Be sure that your driveway can support the trucks. Do not let trucks drive over your lawn.

3
Works Plans

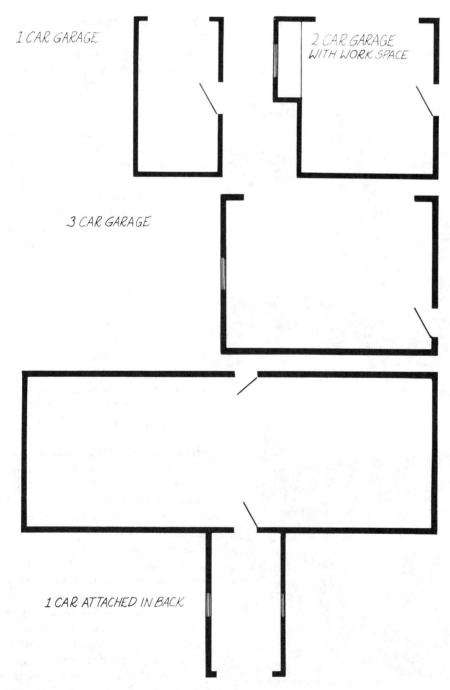

1 CAR GARAGE

2 CAR GARAGE
WITH WORK SPACE

3 CAR GARAGE

1 CAR ATTACHED IN BACK

For the most usable arrangement, consider the floor plan of the existing house. These drawings use a scale of ⅛ inch equal to 1 foot.

HOUSE PLANS

It cannot be overemphasized how important the house and site plans are. The plans are a recording of all the planning and decision-making. Their creation must precede the expensive business of construction. Costs of materials and labor reach record highs every day. Taking short-cuts on this vital planning link in the building process can become very extravagant in the long run. Every experienced, honest contractor prefers to work with a thorough, well-detailed set of plans.

WHERE TO GET THE PLANS
Consulting an Architect

The most qualified person from whom to get the plans is an architect. He is also usually the most expensive — on the front end. However, a complex job may require the services of an architect.

For small jobs, you can hire an architect by the hour. The rates may sound high, but the architect will be able to do your plans with speed and accuracy. The architect can do both design and working drawings if you wish, or you can employ him just for his design services. If nothing else, it is recommended that you employ an architect for the design and then you can draw up the plans. In either case, you must have your needs and ideas fully detailed before going to the architect; work out sketches on graph paper. Otherwise, you will waste valuable time and money while he leads you through the preliminary planning.

Should you try to do your own design? Probably not, unless you have had experience in home design. It usually is better to save the money by doing work yourself, relying on a really good set of plans. With a good set of plans and the aid of contractors along the way, you can save hundreds to thousands of dollars, and probably come out with better work than if you had hired it all out, because you probably will be more conscientious than other workers would be.

Other Plan Sources

There are ways to find a good design, other than just hiring an architect. The drafting services, as an alternative to an architect, are a good choice. You can best locate a drafting service by calling a reputable local builder and asking for a recommendation. Builders often use drafting services because builder homes are usually quite similar in design and construction. Builders themselves will sometimes sell or even give you a set of stock plans. You also can buy stock plans. You might also buy a set of stock plans and have the architect modify them to suit your needs.

As a general procedure, it will be helpful for you to go to a drafting service to look over their plans available, as well as to check the magazine racks and library for published plans. Since there is a certain amount of research you must do, familiarizing yourself with a number of plans will make you a more informed decision maker when, and if, you talk to an architect. When you know exactly what you want, and you have those desires down on a complete set of plans, you will find that dealing with contractors is a much simpler and more pleasant affair.

PLANS AND THEIR PURPOSES

The following list again uses HUD as a guide to the type and amount of information you need, drawn on a scale of ¼ inch = 1 foot.

(1) Floor plan of each floor, including the basement.
(2) Plan of garage, carport, and any nearby terraces or porches.
(3) Separate foundation plan if structure has crawl space; a section through the building will suffice for a slab foundation.
(4) Framing plans, indicating floor and ceiling members, girders, columns, piers; show sizes, spacing, and direction.
(5) Partition locations: give door sizes; showing which way the doors swing.
(6) Equipment locations and sizes — plans showing kitchen cabinets, closets, storage shelving.

(7) Electrical equipment locations and identifications using symbols to show switches, outlets, fixtures, and so forth.
(8) Heating system plan (usually on a separate drawing, but possibly on the floor plan or basement plan) including: system layout and duct plan, piping, registers, radiators, and so forth — all located and sized.
(9) Cooling system plan, which can be shown right on the floor plan if you have room. Otherwise, put it on a separate sheet; show the system layout, ducts, registers, compressors, coils, and so forth.

For the heating plan, locate the heating unit and room thermostat. Indicate total calculated heat loss of the addition (if it's a dwelling). If a duct or piped distribution is used, show calculated heat loss of each heated space.

For the cooling system plan, indicate the heat gain numbers, including the estimate of heat gain for each space that is conditioned. Give the brand, model number, and BTUH capacity of the equipment or units per any ARI or ASRE standards that may apply. For stated local design conditions, give the BTUH capacity and the total KW input. For room and zone conditioners, give the location, installation details, and size.

Drawing Exterior Elevations

Here are basic guidelines for drawing up the exterior elevations.

(1) Draw the main elevation at ¼ inch scale. Other elevations may be drawn at ⅛ inch = 1 foot, if they contain no special details.
(2) Show the front, rear, right side, and left side elevations; show the elevations of any courtyards.
(3) Show sections through stairs and landings, stairwells. Indicate headroom clearances and show framing methods. Use a minimum scale of ¼ inch = 1 foot.
(4) If you use roof trusses, draw details,

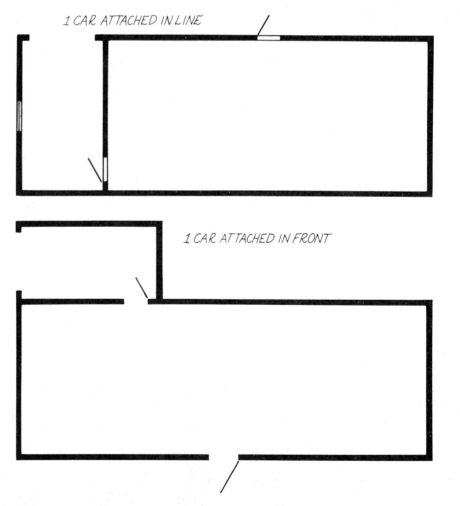

1 CAR ATTACHED IN LINE

1 CAR ATTACHED IN FRONT

An attached garage addition should be placed for convenient access through the house, taking into account foot traffic patterns.

including stress or test data and show connections. Use a minimum scale of ⅜ inch = 1 foot.

(5) Draw sections through all fireplaces and show the fireplace in elevation.

Use a minimum scale of ⅜ inch = 1 foot.

(6) Draw sections through the kitchen cabinets, showing the shelving; draw elevations. Use a minimum

scale of ¼ inch = 1 foot.

(7) Draw sections for any special conditions such as structural details, special millwork, any critical construction point. The minimum scale

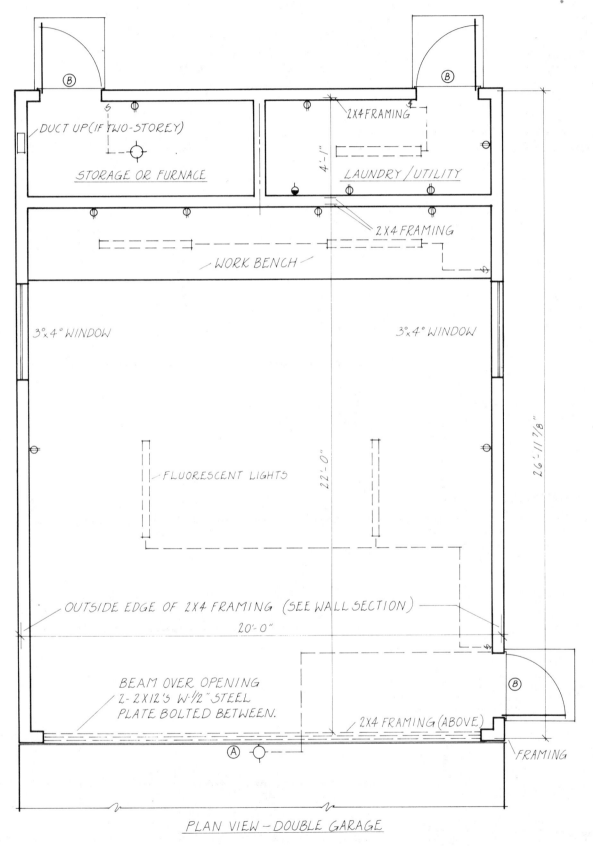

PLAN VIEW — DOUBLE GARAGE

Shown is wall partition layout, kitchen equipment, and lighting plan, with four 4-foot surface-mounted fluorescent fixtures with 2 lights each.

should be ⅜ inch = 1 foot.

The above is not meant to be taken as a complete listing of HUD requirements, but it should aid you in providing the technical detailing that will be asked of you if you plan to do your own drawings. If you are not interested in HUD-approved financing, the above list will be of less interest to you. However, if your drawings meet the HUD requirements (check with your local HUD office for a copy of the Minimum Property Standards handbook), they also will meet the requirements of lending institutions.

SAMPLE CONSTRUCTION PLANS ONE-STORY DOUBLE GARAGE

Planning the construction steps before you start will save you money, effort, and time. It may also help you avoid injury due to incorrect handling of materials or physically over-taxing yourself. Planning also assures that the completed project satisfies your needs. Builders and carpenters who have built dozens of garages can often do them without plans. But you will find that even professionals prefer plans,

if for no other reason than they can post the plans at the construction site so that the workers can check with the plans instead of having dozens of impromptu conferences. The following considers a simple and typical garage: the one-story frame building has a concrete slab floor, siding, and an asphalt shingle roof.

The Floor Plan

Begin with a floor plan, such as that shown for a typical double garage with the storage areas entered from outside. There is enough space inside to park two cars and still have a workbench across the back. There is a side entry door so the family can enter and leave the garage without having to open the big overhead door. There are two windows to provide ventilation and some light, although the work light is an overhead fluorescent.

The floor plan will include: dimensions for the length and width of the building; locations and dimensions of interior-wall partitions; placement of doors and windows. The floor plan enables you to estimate the amount of materials you need for

the interior and exterior walls.

Section Through the Building

When you have completed the floor plan, you need a section through the building. The section through the building shows ceiling height, wall and foundation details — it is a slice through the building. The section through the building is more help-

This classic-style detached garage requires only the carpentry offered in this book, but uses siding and doors that dress up its lines.

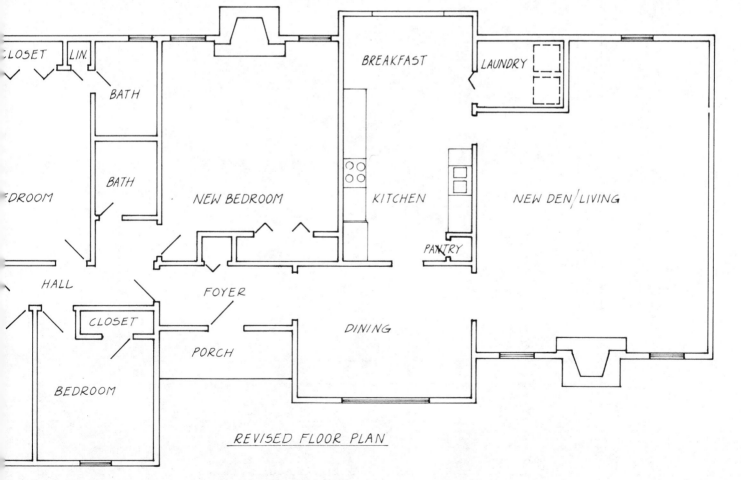

REVISED FLOOR PLAN

This plan started with the floor plan on page 13 and converted the double garage to a new den/living area; the old den became a bedroom with a fireplace.

ful for construction illustration than for materials estimating. Once you have a floor plan and a section through the building, you can plan the foundation.

Foundation Plan

The foundation plan for a one-piece slab and foundation garage is very simple. The dimensions are arrived at by studying the floor plan. The foundation is based on your floor plan. The foundation must support anything you show on the floor and must be designed accordingly. Study the floor plan for dimensions.

In this example, the slab length and width dimensions are measured from outside edge of exterior wall frame to outside edge of exterior wall frame *plus* the thickness of the wall sheathing, which in this case was estimated at ½ inch. That dimension will vary according to the sheathing you use. Note that the sheathing rests on the slab while the finish siding extends down past the top of the slab (see the

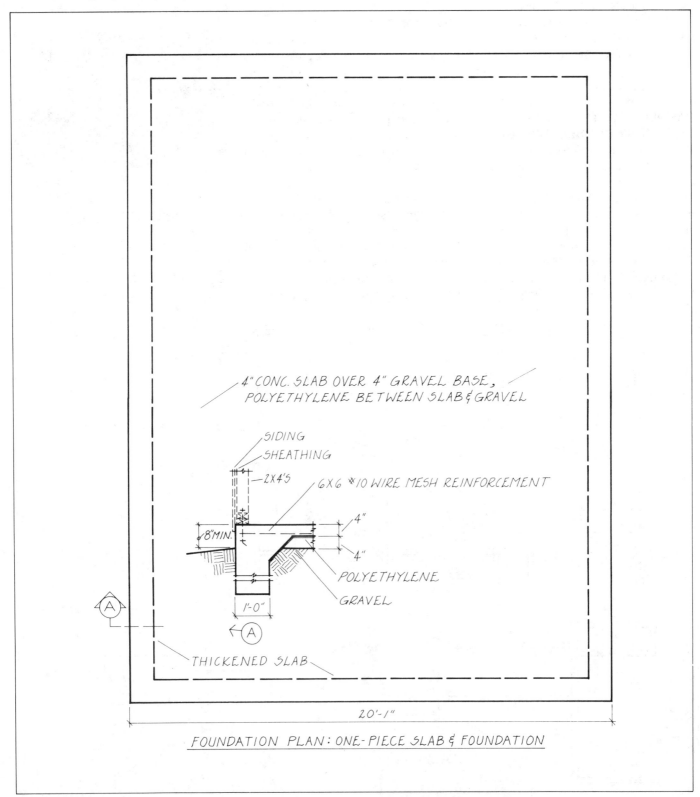

4" CONC. SLAB OVER 4" GRAVEL BASE, POLYETHYLENE BETWEEN SLAB & GRAVEL

SIDING
SHEATHING
2X4'S
6X6 #10 WIRE MESH REINFORCEMENT
8" MIN.
4"
4"
POLYETHYLENE
GRAVEL
1'-0"
THICKENED SLAB
20'-1"

FOUNDATION PLAN: ONE-PIECE SLAB & FOUNDATION

A foundation plan should show materials, and dimensions. The thickened slab perimeter anchors the slab to prevent frost heave.

thickened slab edge detail). This kind of planning and attention to detail will save you problems later.

Framing Plan

Next, draw the framing plan. The illustrations shown include: right side wall framing plan (right as you face the front of the garage; the left side is the mirror image view of the right side), the front wall framing, and the rear wall framing. The interior partitions will be of similar construction: 2x4 studs 16 inches on center. The sill plate is a continuous line of 2x4s (although one 2x4 is typical for sill plates, we suggest two for extra support, but this is optional); head plates are doubled 2x4s; ceiling joists are 2x6s placed at least as often as shown — one at every rafter is preferable; the ridge is a 2x8. The gables are supported by the ridge and by the ex-

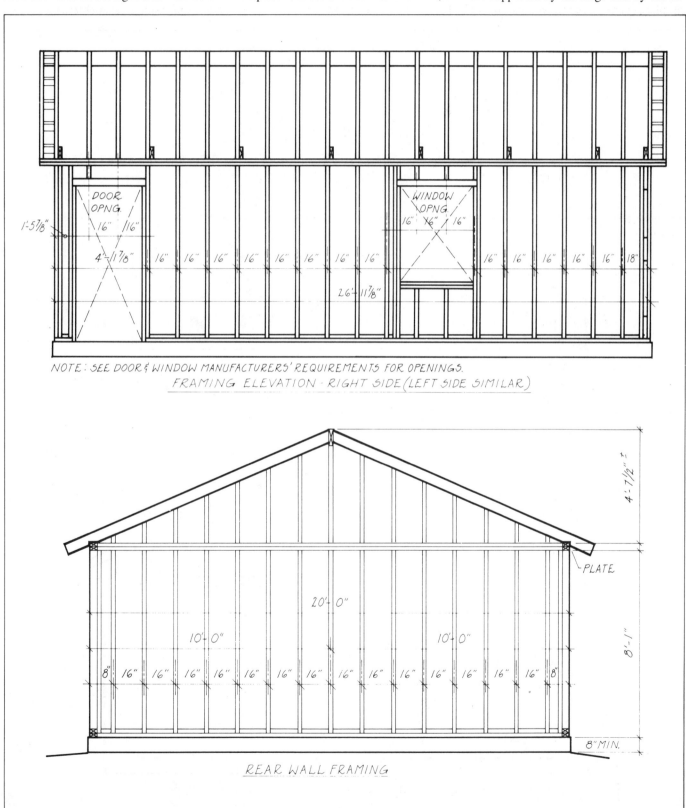

NOTE: SEE DOOR & WINDOW MANUFACTURERS' REQUIREMENTS FOR OPENINGS.
FRAMING ELEVATION · RIGHT SIDE (LEFT SIDE SIMILAR)

REAR WALL FRAMING

Stud walls here are recessed on the slab to allow for sheathing and finish paneling. Stud wall and gable members are 2x4s; rafters are 2x6s; the ridge is a 2x8.

tension of the head plates. They receive 2x4 blocking 16 inches on center. From the framing plan, you can estimate all the structural lumber you need.

Sheathing Plan

You do not really need a separate "sheathing plan" *per se* because you can figure how much sheathing material is needed by working from the framing plan, which will in most cases show both sheathing and finished siding at the building front. You should follow the manufacturer's instructions for the installation of whatever sheathing and finish siding you choose. The illustrations show the finished right side with entry door and window, the finished rear, and the finished front. The particular siding shown is texture 111 (T-111), an exterior plywood siding typically available in 4x8,9, and 10 foot panels. It is grooved in a manner to simulate individual boards. There are many finish sidings available; a more thor-

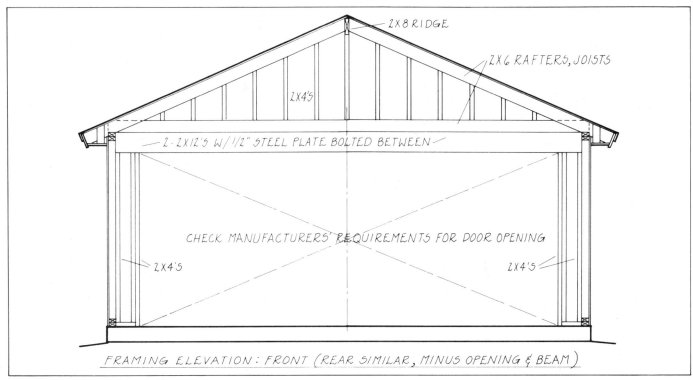

Typical framing is 2x4 stud walls with a double 2x4 plate on top, and at the sill if code requires it.

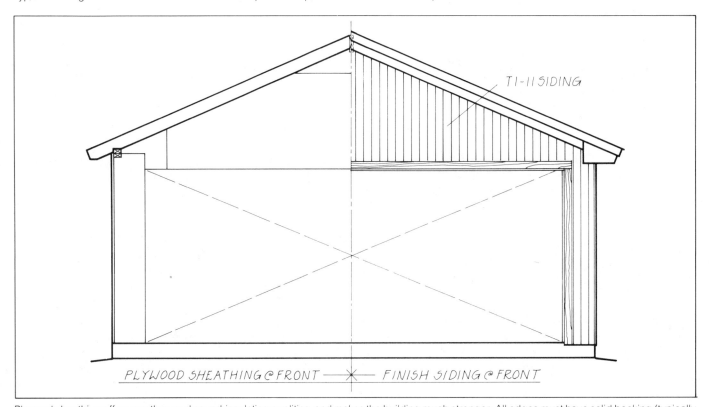

Plywood sheathing offers weather- and sound-insulating qualities, and makes the building much stronger. All edges must have solid backing (typically 2x4s).

ough discussion of them is given in the next chapter.

Heating and Cooling Plan

The heating and cooling of your home or addition starts with a plan, like the plumbing and electrical sections do. But the heating and cooling plan must be drawn early in the planning process due to the physical area required for the furnace and duct work. The heating and cooling plan will show the location, brand, and model number of the furnace, if one will be added. It will show its heating and cooling capacity and its heat loss and gain, based on the amount of insulation in the walls, ceiling, and insulation on the ducts. From the furnace location, it will show the duct runs and sizes and the grill locations and sizes. When you have the heating and cooling plan (it is here assumed that the heating ducts will be sized to accommodate cooling also), sit down and discuss the work program with your subcontractor.

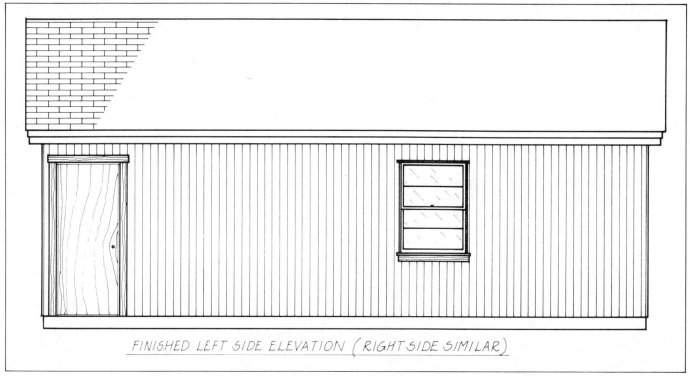

FINISHED LEFT SIDE ELEVATION (RIGHT SIDE SIMILAR)

This garage has a vertical installation, since a horizontal application would make the long, low building appear even lower.

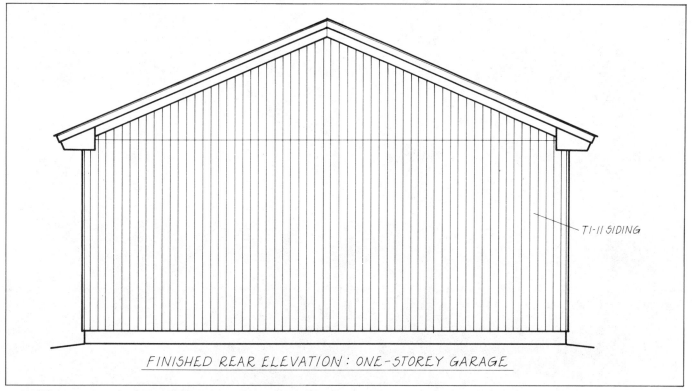

TI-II SIDING

FINISHED REAR ELEVATION: ONE-STOREY GARAGE

Siding material may be applied horizontally, diagonally, or nearly any way you choose. Joint treatments vary with the various applications.

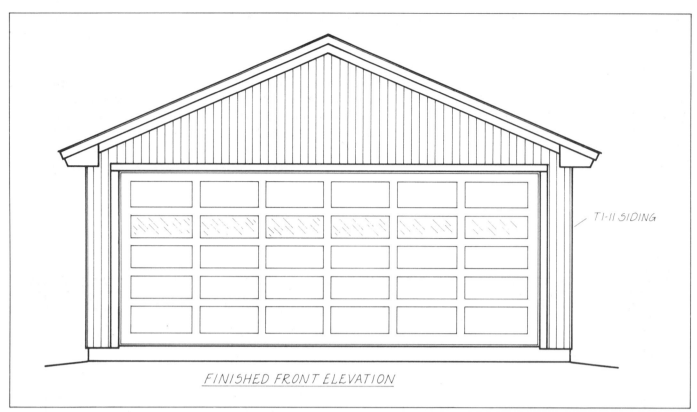

FINISHED FRONT ELEVATION

TI-II SIDING

The front view of the garage revolves around the overhead door. When you have selected the door, you can dimension the framing around it.

Redwood siding offers one of the most attractive links between the architectural styles of an existing house and a new garage.

Electrical Plan

The floor plan shows the location of wall outlets, switches, light fixtures, and so on, but it does not show which circuits these items are on or the route of the circuits back to the distribution box(es). The electrical plan does all this. But even the electrical plan may be too schematic for someone unfamiliar with wiring diagrams. It may be helpful to do more graphic sketches of the circuitry. The illustration shows a typical residential circuit. It would also be helpful to show dimensions on this diagram: height above floor level of the convenience outlets and wall switches, location of the ceiling lights within the room spaces, and so on.

All the items in the accompanying chart must be planned for; they should be located on the floor plan, with circuitry shown on the electrical plan. Then the service wiring must be located at the framing to properly receive the appliances.

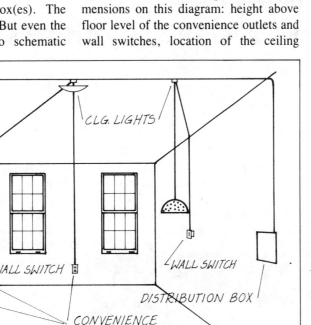

This is a typical general purpose residential wiring circuit; local codes specify distance between convenience outlets.

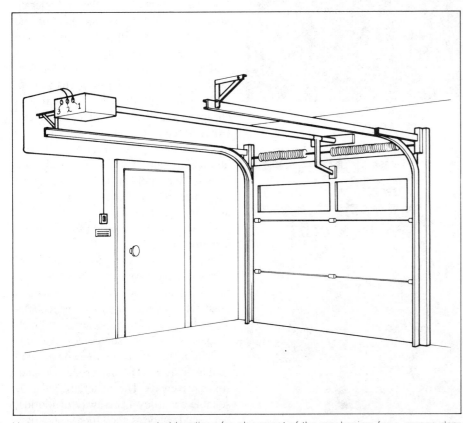

Here are common, recommended locations for placement of the mechanism for a garage door opener, and for the accompanying components.

ELECTRICAL DEMAND

Appliance	Power Usage
Automatic clothes washer	4.0 kw
Dishwasher	.6
Electric range	8.0
Built-in electric oven	3.6
Built-in cooking top (4 units)	4.5
Electric clothes dryer	3.4 to 6.3
Electric water heater	1.5 to 3.4
Food freezer	.6
Food waste disposer	.4
Water pump	.4
Attic fan	.4
Electric bathroom heater	1.3
Central heating system	.5
Room air conditioner (each)	1.0

ELECTRICAL SCHEDULE

Symbol	Remarks
	Ceiling fixture
	Wall mounted
	Recessed light
	Fluorescent fixture
	220 Receptacle
	Garbage disposal
	Exhaust fan
	Wall receptacle

DOOR SCHEDULE

Mark	Remarks
A	18'x7' Overhead door.
B	2'8"x6'8" Flush, solid door. Exterior grade.
C	2'6"x6'8" Flush, hollow door. Interior grade.
D	2'x6'8" Louvered folding door.
E	2'6"x6'8" Flush, hollow folding door.
F	Pair — 2'6"x6'8" Louvered folding doors.
G	2'4"x6'8" Flush, hollow door.

WINDOW SCHEDULE

Mark	Remarks
1	2'6"x3' Double hung, aluminum.
2	5'x4' Window greenhouse

4
Materials: Wood and Concrete

Since all wood is so expensive, and selection can be confusing, the following discussion about yard lumber and plywood is offered in order to help you understand more about lumber grading and usage. It is, however, a general discussion and you should work with local experts — building department officials, HUD, and material suppliers — to decide on the best materials for your particular project.

Vertical siding on this residence gives some visual interest to an otherwise plain face on this house. The siding is used on the stair rails and on the inside walls of the carport.

Wide plank siding on this residence is used to face the garage door. The house overhang is repeated at a slightly lower level on the garage. The door is a straight-lift overhead type.

MATERIAL AND GOOD DESIGN

Select materials with your total site and even the total neighborhood in mind. For example, if every drive in the neighborhood is concrete, your driveway probably should be concrete too. This is not to discourage innovation or creativity. It is to suggest that "different" is not necessarily "better." There is no point in making your project different only for the sake of contrast. An architect the author knew once observed that if the design is different from anything you have ever seen, it may be because it is a new and better design; however, on the other hand, it may be because a lot of other people already thought about the idea and rejected it. If you carefully study the function and economy of materials, creativity will often take care of itself.

If you have a large wooded lot, you might want to consider an asphalt driveway. The asphalt drive typically is cheaper and easier to install than concrete. Going a step further in your thinking, you might decide to press an earth-tone gravel into the asphalt, to soften its appearance. Such a drive would blend well into natural surroundings and would be simple, cheap, and effective. The same drive, on the other hand, might be out of place in a suburban development.

The best designs for homeowners will be an effective compromise between function, aesthetics, and economy. As another practical example, think of the cobblestone driveway. Cobblestone — or "metro pavers" — are sometimes available free from the city if the homeowner will haul them away. This can produce a handsome driveway. The material would be suitable for a level driveway in Florida, but would not be as good for a steep driveway in Wisconsin or North Dakota, where the surface would be more difficult to keep free of snow and ice than would asphalt or concrete.

YARD LUMBER

Yard lumber (lumber used for typical residential construction) comes in two main grades: select and common. These two grades are further broken down: select grade lumber comes in grade A, B, C, and D; common grade lumber comes in grades 1, 2, 3, 4, and 5.

Select Grade Wood

Grade A select. This is almost perfectly clear wood; no knots, or defects interfere with the appearance of the grain. You pay a premium for wood of this quality. Grade A select can be finished naturally with shellac or similar clear finishes, or it may be simply waxed.

Grade B select. This grade is slightly lower than Grade A in quality, although it is almost perfectly clear wood grain. Grades A and B select are used mainly for construction of cabinetry, tables, door frames, decorative trim — interior uses for which fine quality wood grain is important.

Grade C select. Slightly below Grade B select, Grade C usually requires paint as a finish.

Grade D select. The lowest level, Grade D, is just enough higher than #1 Common to warrant being considered a grade wood. Grade D select requires a paint finish. Grades C and D select could

Do not buy boards with pith lines — they will warp. Pith lines occur in boards which have been cut from the center of a tree. They appear as brown lines.

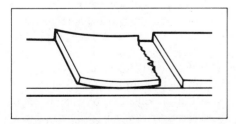

Boards should lie flat. To select boards that are true, sight down the length of the edge. A little warpage is allowed, but nothing drastic should be tolerated.

be used for painted woodwork around doors and windows (depending in part on personal taste and preference), or for painted shelving.

Suitable usage. The above grades have a ''face'' and a ''back''. The ''A'' veneer, for example, may have A on the face and B on the back. Such a grade would be used for cabinet use or other uses where the finish appearance is important. A typical grade for floor underlayment or other base uses is CD interior. Each grade is usually available in interior or exterior grade. Use the appropriate grade for your project. There is no point in spending extra money for exterior grade plywood if interior grade will be good enough. Conversely, do not use interior grade where the wood will be exposed to the elements. Other typical grades include: BB exterior, used for concrete forms; AC exterior, used for siding or soffits; CC exterior, chosen for sheathing.

Wood is one of the more expensive materials for home projects, but *all* materials in your project designs should be selected with a view to specific needs rather than a preset list of requirements.

Common Grade Lumber

Common lumber used for utility construction, such as wall studs and concrete formwork, is most often No. 2 common. Common lumber is not usually good for finished woodwork such as door frames or interior woodwork (unless you want a rustic appearance). Common lumber comes in Grades 1, 2, 3, 4, and 5. No. 1 Common and No. 2 Common are good enough that they can be used without waste of lumber — that is, the knots are tight and there are no other faults bad enough to waste some of the lumber in using it. Grades #3, #4, and #5 are low quality grades suitable only for rough usage such as stakes, or support members for concrete formwork, etc., where the purpose of the lumber is to temporarily support straighter lumber of better grades.

Hardwoods vs. Softwoods

You will be concerned with two types of timber with your building projects: softwoods and hardwoods. Softwoods are cone-bearing trees, hardwoods are leaf-bearing trees. Knowing this will enable you to separate the tree types in the woods, but probably will not help you identify the two types in the lumber yard.

What will gain your attention between softwoods and hardwoods while at the lumber yard is their relative costs. Softwoods, like pine, generally grow faster than hardwoods. Therefore, they are cheaper. This means that softwoods are generally used for floor, ceiling, and roof framing, and where fine-grain appearance is of less importance than economy. Hardwoods are sometimes used for doors and windows and interior trim, but rarely for framing. You might choose to use hardwood for cabinets, bookcases, and similar projects, but it will be expensive. Handsome finish work can be done with softwoods. Hardwood is frequently used for finished flooring material. Select the most economical and aesthetically pleasing type of wood for your specific needs — this will require that you spend some time browsing around lumber yards.

Lumber Characteristics

Nominal and actual lumber sizes. Lumber sizes are given nominally, for simplicity. A 2x4, for example, is not 2 inches x 4 inches, once it has been milled. It is 1½ inches x 3½ inches. This difference in nominal size vs. dressed size is not important when you are figuring some-

You can buy Common lumber instead of Clear, and cut clear, usable sections from it. Even if you buy double the amount, you are still likely to come out ahead.

Vertical sawn boards are less desirable, but less expensive, than flat sawn boards.

Flat (quarter) sawn boards are tight grained — good for finishing and tooling.

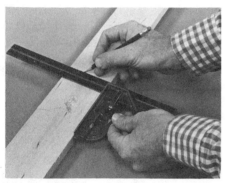

Use a combination square for square, 45-degree angles, depth of cuts, and level.

Portable electric drills, hand braces, and their bits, are the basic hole-boring tools.

thing like framing material quantities for a wall of your garage, because you will consider the wall framing dimensions from outside corner to outside corner, and then arrange the "2x4" studs from center to center (typically 16 inches on center).

However, the size difference between nominal and dressed lumber should be kept in mind where exact dimensions are called for. For example, when you are installing ducts and other mechanical equipment, plumbing, and electrical service in the wall spaces between the 2x4s, you must remember that you do not have 4 inches of clear space. You have only 3½ inches. In general, you must consider the exact size of the lumber whenever a manufactured item comes in contact with your framing or other lumber work: door, windows, other prefabricated items. The more precise the work, the more you must consider the actual, dressed sizes of lumber rather than the nominal sizes; examples of such precise work include: cabinet work and door thresholds.

LUMBER SIZES

Nominal	Dressed
2x4	1½x3½
2x6	1½x5½
2x8	1½x7⅜
2x10	1½x9⅜
2x12	1½x11⅜
3x4	2½x3½
4x4	3½x3½

These are *typical* sizes, but there can be some local variations. Ask what the dressed sizes are when you buy lumber.

How lumber cuts affect grain. Grain is important in the appearance of naturally finished woodwork like cabinets, baseboards, door and window trim, and so forth. The way the wood has been cut will influence the way the grain appears on the surface of your boards. You will be primarily concerned with these cuts: vertical grain, flat grain, mixed grain — and occasionally, spiral grain.

Vertical grain. This lumber is sawn at approximately right angles to the annual growth rings of the tree, leaving the rings at an angle of 45 degrees or more with the surface of the board or piece of lumber.

Flat grain. The lumber is sawn approximately parallel to the annual growth rings, leaving the rings at an angle less than 45 degrees with the surface of the board or piece of lumber.

Mixed grain and spiral grain. The mixed grain is a combination of vertical grain and flat grain. Spiral grain is formed by a deviation in the slope of grain in the tree itself, when the fibers in a tree become twisted in a spiral manner around the trunk — instead of being vertical, as is normal.

How to Cut Lumber

Some professional carpenters still get by with only a handsaw to do their lumber cutting. Most of them use circular power saws to do the bulk of the work and handsaws for incidental work.

Power tools. The rotary power saw is a commonly used lumber-cutting saw. It cuts faster and requires less physical effort than a handsaw.

If you plan to use a rotary saw, investigate the accessories that may help you with your specific tasks. There are "radial arms" that slide along the edges of the lumber being cut, holding the saw in place. And you can tilt the saw to make slanted cuts. There are other accessories for drilling, sanding, and shaping wood.

Rotary saw blades are available with many edges, for different uses. Some manufacturers of rotary saw blades produce as many as 16 different blade edges, each having a specific use.

Handsaw. There are a variety of handsaw lengths and tooth coarsenesses. Select the length with which you can saw comfortably. Then choose the blade coarseness to match the type wood you are cutting. For example, the "general use" handsaw can be used for cutting nearly any species of 2x4, and wood members both larger and smaller than the 2x4.

A sharp handsaw will slice through framing lumber and plywood with surprising ease and speed. The handsaw can be used for crosscuts (cutting across the wood grain), and for rips (cutting with the grain).

Blades. Usually, each handsaw and each rotary saw blade states on the package what kind of wood and other materials the blades will cut. But if the usage is not clear, ask your building materials supplier what the local builders use.

Cutting techniques. On all cutting, always draw a pencil line of your cut on the lumber before you saw. When you saw, cut on the outside edge of the pencil line. Otherwise, the width of the blade can add up to dimension problems with your lumber. When working with small pieces of lumber, cut them out of the larger piece. Avoid carrying the larger pieces around on the job unnecessarily.

Building Materials Suppliers and Local Availability

It will serve you to find a reputable building materials supplier, one who has knowledgeable employees, employees who know local building practices, not just clerks who dispense products from a "warehouse of materials." If you get blank stares when you ask about local building practices, what the builders use for certain jobs, you are in the wrong store. The building department, an architect, or a builder can recommend a building materials supplier to you. This is a business made up of specialists and the specialists, including the suppliers, should be thought of and used as resources.

Local availability. Grading rules for lumber vary from region to region around the country and even somewhat within the same general geographic regions. So, if you live in Georgia and you want to build a garage in your backyard, it is of little consequence to you what the lumber species, grades, and usages are in California, and vice versa. Freight on lumber, at this writing, is reported to account for as much as 40% of its cost. Few of us are willing, or able, to bear the kind of expense involved in "importing" wood from other regions to do jobs as large as a garage.

WORKING WITH PLYWOOD
Types of Plywood

There are two basic types of plywood:

exterior and interior. The type and method of gluing is important. Exterior plywood (generally used where a waterproof plywood is needed) uses hot-pressed adhesives that are insoluble, moldproof, and durable to hold the wood together. Exterior type plywoods are glued together in such a manner so as to resist nearly any conditions that would not destroy the actual wood itself.

Interior plywood may be cold-pressed as well as hot-pressed, and uses adhesives that will withstand some wetting — such as the occasional wetting that occurs during construction — but will not hold up under continual or long-term wetting.

Veneer grading. Both interior and exterior plywood are subject to grading. They come in several grades, typically A, B, C, and D.

"A" veneer. This has a smooth surface with no knots, holes or openings; usually it is painted. The "A" grade veneer may contain repairs. These repairs are smooth patches shaped like tear-drops with points at each end; you can spot them easily, but they will be neatly done. They will, however, become obvious if you stain the wood rather than paint it. Use the "A" grade where the wood will be the finish surface, or where a particularly smooth wood surface is needed.

"B" veneer. The "B" veneer has minor defects, and sometimes is patched with round plugs of wood. "B" plywood is typically used for roof and wall sheathing, concrete forms, and other utility uses.

"C" veneer. The "C" veneer can contain 1-inch knotholes, 3/16 inch splits that taper to a point, and other minor open

defects in the surface. The "C" grade is used for sheathing under plywood surface paneling. It may be used for some exterior finish panel projects where the relatively rough surface will not be a problem: possibly as fencing material where closely spaced battens (8 inches to a foot, approximately) over the plywood surface would draw attention from the defects. It is the lowest grade plywood usable in concrete formwork in which the concrete comes in contact with the plywood surface.

"D" veneer. The lowest grade, "D" veneer, contains 2½ inch knotholes, splits up to ½ inch that taper, and other defects. It is not used for concrete formwork where it will come in contact with the concrete. Nor is it used where its surface will be the finish surface, unless a very rustic appearance is desired. It is suitable for rough utility construction and as backing for better plywood grades.

Veneer core plywood has plies that are alternating layers of thin sections of wood and compressed wood chips.

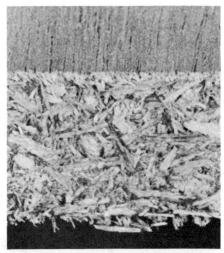

Plywood with a core of bonded wood chips is less desirable than lumber core material. It has a compacted-sawdust look.

PLYWOOD GRADES AND USES

Grade	Face	Back	Plies	Uses
A-A EXT.	A	A	C	Outdoors; cost may limit use to projects when both sides show
A-B EXT.	A	B	C	Outdoors when both sides show
A-C EXT.	A	C	D	When only one side will show
C-C EXT.	C	C	C	Best for framing construction
B-B EXT.	B	B	B	Utility plywood; for some concrete forming, walks, and other rough use.
A-A INT.	A	A	D	Best panel; for cabinets, built-ins, and other construction where both faces will show
A-B INT.	A	B	D	A little less than A-A
A-C INT.	A	C	D	Good face, fair back; for paneling where one side will show.
B-D INT.	B	D	D	Utility grade; for rough projects such as underlayment for flooring
C-D	C	D	D	Sheathing grade
CDX	—	—	—	Sheathing grade; usually for exterior use. panels may be used indoors

Types of Plywood Siding

Rough-sawn plywood panels. These have a saw-roughened finish. They are available with or without grooves, and in lap sidings as well as in strictly panel form. The panels typically come in ⅜ inch, ½ inch, and ¾ inch thicknesses. There are a variety of qualities available, from "clear" or "premium" grade to knotty. The panels can be stained or painted or left to weather naturally.

Fine-line siding. This type of siding is available in the same sizes and with characteristics similar to the rough-sawn pan-

With a radial or table saw, the good side of the plywood faces upward, toward the blade. Use a sharp combination blade or a fine-toothed one without much set.

Use a sabre saw to cut irregular curves and shapes. Place the front of the sabre saw platform against the face of the panel, and tilt the blade downward.

When using a portable power saw, keep the good face of the plywood down.

els. It gets its name from shallow grooves sawn about ¼ inch on center and about ¹⁄₃₂ inch wide. The fine lines give a striped effect.

Brushed siding. Available in the sizes and with the same characteristics of the panels described above. These panels have had part of the surface wood removed so that the grain itself stands up in relief. The effect is to accent the natural wood.

Overlays on plywood siding. Various overlays are seeing more use. Metal overlays are popular; exposed aggregates in a variety of surface textures and colors can be found. There are other coatings available, which vary with the different manufacturers.

Other Siding Materials

In addition to the plywood sidings listed above, there are many types and configurations of solid wood sidings, vinyl siding and metal sidings. These can be seen at most any large building materials supply store.

Hardboard sidings are also available — in many of the same sizes, and with the same textures and configurations as the plywood panels and solid wood sidings. These sidings of medium density hard-

board can be bought in plain panels ⁷⁄₁₆ inch thick and 4x8 or 9 feet in size. They are also available in reverse board and batten, horizontal lap, and vertical groove configurations. You can buy them plain, factory primed, or factory stained. There are a wide variety of colors: greens, browns, golds, grays, whites, and yellows, to name a few. One of the most interesting hardboard finishes is simulated stucco. These stucco panels can be installed with the ease and speed of installing plywood panels and they look like stucco.

All siding should be installed per the manufacturers' instructions. Before you buy the siding, you should familiarize yourself with the specifications and guarantees applicable to the material.

CONCRETE
Estimating Amounts Needed

When you have completed the foundation plan, you can estimate the amount of concrete you need. Concrete is usually sold by the cubic yard, occasionally by weight. Either way, you need to know the cubic volume your job requires. For the double garage in this text, the slab dimensions are 20 feet 1 inch x 27 feet ⅞ inch. The slab is 4 inches or .33 foot thick. Then there are

This attached garage combines brick with board and batten siding to match the house. The Z-braced barn doors give access to upper level garage storage and provide decorative focus.

the thickened edges to figure. Multiply 21 feet x 28 feet x .33 and you have 194 cubic feet. Divide by 27 (one cubic yard) and you have 7.1 cubic yards.

Now figure the footing requirements similarly. If the footing for the one story garage, which is a thickening all around the edge, is about 1 foot wide by 1 foot deep on a 21-foot by 28-foot garage, (for example's sake) you would follow these steps:

(1) multiply length of the slab times the depth times the width of the footing (22x1x1) = 22;
(2) multiply 28x1x1 = 28;
(3) multiply each by two 56 + 44 = 100;
(4) divide 100 by 27 = 3.7.

This would give you about 3.7 more cubic yards. So you would need 11 cubic yards in all. If in doubt, order an extra yard. (Check with the building department for required footing depth.)

Choosing the Right Concrete

The type of concrete you use is important and will vary according to the job, the weather, your work schedule and the amount of available labor. Concrete is a mixture of cement, aggregate, and water. The most-used cement today is portland cement. The three most common types of portland cement are Types I through III, and air-entrained.

Type I. This cement generates considerable heat during curing and is therefore good in colder weather, where the heat helps prevent freezing. This characteristic will, of course, work against you in hot weather. Type I is the most frequently used type of cement.

Type II. Because it generates less heat in curing than Type I, this cement is used when pouring in high temperatures.

Type III. With its early strength and fast set up, this cement is useful in cold areas and temperatures because it cuts down on the cost and bother of keeping the concrete protected against cold during the curing process. If possible, of course, it is best to wait until moderate weather to build.

Air-entrained portland cement. Air-entrained cement is recommended for very cold regions. It has an agent that causes the finished concrete to be filled with millions of tiny air bubbles. These air bubbles permit water to freeze and expand without damaging the concrete. It is very

useful in areas where severe frost is a problem. The "bubble agent" can be added to Types I, II, and III portland cement.

Aggregate and water for best concrete strength. The strength of concrete comes from the structural makeup of the aggregate, bonded together by the cement paste. The coarsest aggregate in most concrete for residential purposes is about 1½ inches in size. Around these coarse pieces are smaller pieces, grading down in size to sand. The voids between all this aggregate should be completely filled with cement.

Cement paste is just that: a high-strength paste that holds the crushed stone, gravel and sand together. The right mix of these elements and water is crucial. To insure against organic matter in the water, the water should be drinkable. The amount of water used also is important. Too much water will make the cement paste too thin to hold the aggregate together. Not enough water will leave tiny pockets of dry aggregate and will weaken the concrete.

Tools for Concrete Preparation

Shovels and hoes are necessary for moving the material around in the forms, as well as a garden hose and water supply for

cleaning tools. You should also have a pair of high rubber boots for wading around in the material. If you do any large jobs at all, like a patio or floor, sooner or later you are going to have to get right in the "mud." Always be careful not to let your skin come in contact with wet cement; it can cause skin burns. There are also a few specialty tools: some of them you may wish to purchase, some you may wish to rent, and some you can make yourself.

Building a measuring box. One tool you can make quite easily is a measuring box. This is actually a bottomless box that has handles on its sides. It measures 12x12x12 inches on the inside to provide a measured cubic foot of material.

Wheelbarrow and mortar box. You will need a wheelbarrow to move the material to the form. A small garden wheelbarrow is not good enough; you need a large, sturdy contractor's wheelbarrow, preferably one that has wooden handles and a large pneumatic tire. If you mix the material yourself and plan on mixing only small batches, you can do the task in a wheelbarrow, a special mixing tub, or on any flat, level surface. Or you can use a mortar box. These come in several differ-

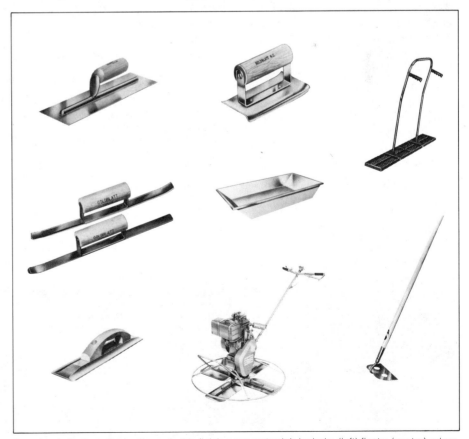

From top to bottom, the tools needed to finish a concrete slab include: (left) floats; (center) edger, mortar box, power trowel; (right) tamper, hoe.

ent sizes, the smaller ranging from an 11x23x42-inch box that hold 6 cubic feet of material to one that is 11x35x82 inches and holds 15 cubic feet. For hand mixing, you will also need a mortar hoe.

Power mixers. A much faster method is to utilize a power mixer, which will be required if you are adding an air-entraining agent. (An air-entraining admixture is mandatory in areas with severe winters and frost heave.) Mixers come in a range of sizes, from a small 1½-cubic-foot wheelbarrow size that can be rolled to the job to a large 6-cubic-foot mixer that is pulled behind your automobile. You can rent mixers from most tool rental yards in larger cities. Most mixers come equipped with an electric motor, but you can also find them with gasoline motors for use in more remote locations. Incidentally, if you rent a gasoline-powered unit, make sure you have the rental people start the motor to see that it operates easily.

If you live some distance from a larger city, or if you plan on doing quite a bit of concrete work, you may prefer to purchase your own mixer. A unit that will do most home jobs quite well holds 2½ cubic feet. The stationary type costs just a little over $300. A portable trailered unit, which can be towed behind an automobile, will cost around $500. (These costs are based on January, 1981, prices.) This tool can become an invaluable item for anyone who plans to do considerable amounts of masonry work, especially since it can be used to mix mortar as well as concrete.

Mixing Concrete by Hand

If you mix the concrete by hand, you can

The best kind of wheelbarrow for concrete work has a pneumatic tire and wooden handles.

cut the cost of concrete drastically. But it is slow and difficult work. For a large project such as this, we suggest ready-mix or use of a power mixer. Mixing your own concrete becomes more and more difficult as the size of the job increases. You could hand-mix your own concrete for a double garage, but since you and the helper could only mix about a yard at a time, it would be a slow process and you would become fatigued before you started screeding the slab.

Combining the materials. First, mix the sand and cement together by spreading the sand over the platform. Then cover the sand with cement. Spread another layer of sand over the cement. Now place the remaining cement over the sand. Layering the materials like this cuts down on the shoveling. Usually, you and one helper should not mix more than about one cubic yard at a time.

Face your helper across the materials and, working from the edges to the center, turn the materials evenly. Add the aggregate, mixing as you did before, working the aggregate in as evenly as possible.

Adding the water. Work out a bowl-shaped depression in the center of the mixture and add a measured amount of water. Turn the dry materials into the water. Repeat this process, adding measured amounts of water until the water has been used and the mix is appropriate for the job.

The platform must be watertight and no water must be allowed to run off the edges of the platform.

Silt testing. Any rule on aggregate sizes is fairly loose because you will probably have to use whatever types and sizes are most common in your area. Most building and masonry supply dealers will have the most commonly used sizes and materials on hand. The most important thing about the aggregate is that it should be free of silt and debris, for these can not only ruin the appearance of the job, but weaken it as well. To test for the cleanliness of the aggregates, place about 2 inches of aggregate and sand in a fruit jar. Then pour water over the materials and shake gently. Allow the material to settle and the water to clear. If there is more than ⅛ inch of silt on top of the aggregate, it should be washed. This can be done quite easily — dump the aggregates onto a clean, hard surface, such as an existing concrete slab, and hose the material down. Rake the material around some to make sure all of it is clean.

How much water is the correct amount? Measure the amount of water just as accurately as the solids. Turning on the hose and adding water until you feel you have the right amount can often result in a disaster. If you get too much water and do not have enough cement to add to it to correct the situation, you can ruin an

TABLE 1. PROPORTIONS BY WEIGHT TO MAKE 1 CU FT OF CONCRETE

Maximum-size coarse aggregate, in.	Air-entrained concrete				Concrete without air-entrainment			
	Cement, lb.	Sand lb.	Coarse aggregate, lb.*	Water, lb.	Cement, lb.	Sand, lb.	Coarse aggregate, lb.*	Water, lb.
⅜	29	53	46	10	29	59	46	11
½	27	46	55	10	27	53	55	11
¾	25	42	65	10	25	47	65	10
1	24	39	70	9	24	45	70	10
1½	23	38	75	9	23	43	75	0

*If crushed stone is used, decrease coarse aggregate by 3 lb. and increase sand by 3 lb.

TABLE 2. PROPORTIONS BY VOLUME*

Maximum-size coarse aggregate, in.	Air-entrained concrete				Concrete without air			
	Cement	Sand	Coarse aggregate	Water	Cement	Sand	Coarse aggregate	Water
⅜	1	2¼	1½	½	1	2½	1½	½
½	1	2¼	2	½	1	2½	2	½
¾	1	2¼	2½	½	1	2½	2½	½
1	1	2¼	2¾	½	1	2½	2¾	½
1½	1	2¼	3	½	1	2½	3	½

*The combined volume is approximately ⅔ of the original bulk.

entire batch of concrete. The best bet is to fill a large tank or drum with water and dip water out of it as needed. Again, use a bucket that has a known capacity so you can accurately measure the amount of water you are using.

Probably one of the biggest problems with the ingredient proportions is the amount of water required. In fact, the strength of the concrete will depend on the amount of water used. If too little water is used, there won't be enough to provide a good fluid state that can be worked easily and will ensure that each and every solid particle is coated and bonded together. You should use as much water as possible without creating a problem with the workability and smoothness of the concrete. Too much water results in concrete that is unworkable and hard to set up. The cement particles will float up to the surface and, worst of all, weaken the slab.

In most instances, professional masons consider 6 to 7 gallons of water the correct amount of water per bag of cement, depending on the dampness of the sand and the size of the aggregate.

Testing and Correcting the Mix

Too much water, or too little. One problem that you will soon figure out is that the more water is added to the mix, the easier the mix is to work with, and also the easier it is to pour into the forms.

Testing the mix: the slump test. When you have mixed the concrete to your satisfaction, you can test to see if it is correct by making the slump test. You can use a professional tool called a slump cone, or create your own by removing both ends from a coffee can. Fill the cone

in three layers. After each layer, tamp down 25 times with a stick to be certain there are no air pockets. After tamping the third layer, scrape the concrete level across the top of the cone. Then lift the cone. The concrete will settle. Set the cone beside the concrete and measure the difference between the two heights. A large slump indicates a wet consistency. A slight slump indicates a stiff consistency. The material should slump down to about half (but no less) its original height if you have the correct amount of water and ingredients.

The settling test. Another test is based on the stiffness of ridges in the concrete. Pull the concrete up in a series of ridges with the hoe. If the ridges slump back down and cannot be seen easily, there is too much water. If you cannot create distinct ridges, there is too little water.

Poor mixing. Make sure you have mixed all the ingredients properly and thoroughly, scraping them from the sides and bottom of the wheelbarrow or mixing box. The concrete mix should be an even color. Light or dark streaks indicate poor mixing.

Remedying a poor mix. If your mix is too wet, it doesn't have enough sand and aggregate for the amount of cement paste. Add 5 to 10 percent more of sand and aggregate, mix well, and test. Repeat this until the mix is correct. Keep careful notes of the added amounts; when you make the new batch, you will follow the revised figures for sand and coarse aggregate.

If your mix is too stiff, it has too much aggregate. Do not try to remedy the situation by addition of water alone. Instead, add a cement-water solution that has pro-

portions of 2 to 1. Unfortunately, in most cases even this will not work and you will have to start all over again with decreased amounts of sand and coarse aggregate. Experiment, keeping track of the decreased proportions, until you have a satisfactory mix. You may have to prepare several batches before you produce the right mixture.

How to Use a Power Mixer

Mixing with a powered mixer prepares concrete much easier and faster than does hand mixing. Position the mixer close to the sand and gravel pile. With the mixer turned off, add the amount of dry ingredients needed. Then turn the mixer on and allow it to run in order to mix the dry ingredients thoroughly. Then pour in a little water, allow it to mix a few minutes, and add more water a little at a time until you have added the whole amount already decided on for the mix. Once the material has been properly mixed, turn the mixer over and dump the concrete into a wheelbarrow and start over as needed. As you can see, in this situation two people can really do a better job than one. One person keeps the mixer going while the other moves the concrete to the form, dumps it, spreads it out and gets ready for the next pour. .

Using Ready Mix

This is delivered to your door already mixed and in larger quantities than you

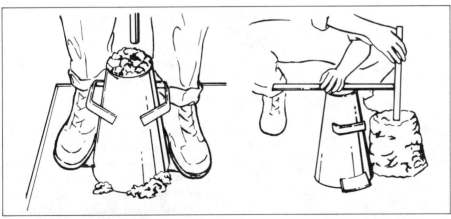
A slump cone is 12 inches high, with 8 inches at the base and 4 inches at the top. Set it on a firm surface. Hold it down by placing your feet on cone projections. Fill with 3 layers of concrete; tamp each 25 times before adding the next one. Level off the concrete. Lift the cone and allow the concrete to settle. Place the cone beside concrete to measure. A large slump indicates a wet consistency; a slight slump, a stiff consistency.

Measure concrete ingredients carefully by weight or volume, as close to the site as possible.

can easily or quickly mix yourself. Ready-mix or transit-mix concrete has definite advantages — it is often more economical than the total cost of the individual ingredients, and air-entrainment can be provided.

Transport and access. There are several possible limitations, however, that must be considered before ordering ready-mix materials. The first is whether or not the truck can get to the forms. Most trucks have chutes that can be attached to enable the operator to move the concrete as much as 20 feet, but that is about the limit. If the truck cannot get close enough, you will have to move the material in wheelbarrows to the final location. If there is any doubt about your situation, and if you are dealing with a fair amount of materials, it would be wise to have the concrete dealer

come out and look at your situation.

You also should be aware that concrete transit trucks are extremely heavy. Fill areas around new house construction, or even around older homes, may be too soft to support the weight. The result is often a stuck truck.

If you will have to move the concrete some distance by hand, this must also be explained to the dealer, since his truck may be at your site longer than normal. Some dealers may even charge for this extra time. You should also specify to the contractor what you are actually building as well as the aggregate size and the maximum amount of water per cubic yard. If you wish additives such as air-entrainment, this must also be noted.

How to order and schedule. After determining that you can utilize the trucks to

haul the material, the next step is to figure the amount of concrete needed and to order it from the dealer. If at all possible, specify the load to be brought early in the morning; this will give you plenty of time to work it properly.

In almost all instances the truck will bring a bit more than is needed. Since the truck may have to be rinsed and dumped, you should have an area available in which to dump the excess. If just a little is left over, it can be put in a wheelbarrow and kept until the pour is completed — in case you need it. After the forms are filled, you may need a shovelful or two in places that looked full during the pour.

Preparing for the delivery. Soak the form and the subgrade with water the evening before you make the pour — or moisten the subgrade just before the pour. This will prevent dryness in the soil and the forms from pulling moisture too quickly from the concrete, which makes it stiffen too quickly. In some instances, the subgrade takes up too much water from the concrete and causes a low spot in the slab.

The morning the mix is to arrive, make sure that you have properly prepared the site, and that you have all tools on hand. It is a good idea to have a couple of friends for a large pour, as it takes a great deal of work to spread the large amounts of concrete required for a patio or a long sidewalk.

Since concrete is such a heavy building material, it's best to break up large jobs into smaller segments. You may take longer to build the project, but the job will definitely be easier on you. For instance, divide each portion of a patio into smaller segments that are poured one at a time. Allow one to cure; then remove the form from that section before you pour the next.

Using Transit Mix
An alternative to the ready-mix delivery is a U-Haul delivery of concrete. This may be available on a trailer that you pick up and haul to your home. The trailer is equipped with a device to keep the concrete mixer during transit. Or the unit may be a pickup truck that has the concrete mixer mounted on the bed. The truck is easier to handle than the trailer because a trailer loaded with concrete is difficult to back into place. Also, some of today's smaller cars may have a problem hauling the heavy concrete load. The average load for each of these is one cubic yard.

If a concrete driveway is large, decorative control joints may make the expanse interesting.

5
Grading and Drainage

Grading and drainage affects all the things we build — concrete slabs, carports, garages — any structure that lays on the earth or penetrates it. Drainage is affected by the type soil you build on or in; different soils have different capacities to soak up water. Drainage also is affected by the way you shape, or grade, the finish surface of the soil. So a brief discussion of soil will be helpful to you.

SOIL
The ground is made up of many types of soil; these can vary considerably short distances. For example, you may be living on clay or rock strata and a neighbor several houses down the street may have sandy soil. Rain soaks into these different soils at different rates, depending on how loose they are. Clays are tight, finely grained soil. Sandy soils are looser. The difference between these soil types is something like the difference between coffee grinds — water runs through a coarse grind quicker than it does through a fine grind. Therefore, drainage is not just directing water along the surface (grading), it is also allowing for the ability of the soil to let water come through it.

CLIMATE AND WATER
During the different seasons the amount of precipitation and the temperatures will vary. Take precautions to assure good drainage to protect your structures, especially in areas of extreme cold. Everyone knows that water expands when it freezes. You must prevent water buildup under and around concrete slabs, drives, foundations, or along the earth side of retaining walls and other structures. Generally, the way to protect your structures from drainage/cold weather problems is to keep them as dry as possible.

Drainage Requirements
To keep structures dry, you must aid underground drainage as well as aiding surface drainage by way of grading (manipulation of the soil surface). Aiding underground drainage may involve removing soils with high clay content and replacing them with sandy soil. Aiding underground drainage almost always entails the use of gravel and/or sand, materials that drain well because of their looseness. Concrete drives, walks, floor slabs, foundations, and other structures in contact with the earth are typically protected by building them on a bed of gravel. This bed of gravel prevents accumulation of water under or next to the structure. The water could freeze and damage the structure. Even without freezing, an accumulation of water will cause interior moisture problems such as mildew.

Frost Heave
Frost heave is not fully understood, and it is certainly not predictable. What is clear

Control of water runoff is very important. This drainage surface is next to a retaining wall. This avoids water wear on the wall.

is that frost heave is different from mere expansion due to freezing. Frost heave is most dangerous to structures in soils with high clay content. The freezing of soils with high clay content results in dramatic expansion of the soil that can literally force fence posts out of the ground, crack concrete foundations and concrete slabs and seriously damage any structure. There is no "cure" for frost heave, but there are a few ways of dealing with it that minimize its effects.

One way to deal with frost heave is to improve drainage — below ground as well as surface drainage. As stated above, gravel and/or sand are the typical materials used to aid underground drainage. Install gravel and/or sand as a base for concrete slabs, drives, and walks. Use gravel under foundations to keep water from building up next to your structures.

If you are building on soil of high clay content, you may have to remove some of the clayey soil and replace it with looser, sandy soil. This removal may assume large-scale proportions. For example, it may be necessary to remove the clayey soil under a building slab completely down to the frost line or below the frost line. (The frost line is the depth of freezing of the soil — your building department can tell you what the usual frost line is for your locality.) This clayey soil would then be replaced with sandy soil. Another way to protect structures from frost heave is to bring the footings below the frost line.

Both these treatments can be impractical in areas where the frost line may be as deep as the height of the outside walls are above ground. The above- and below-ground drainage for the projects in this book are for typical conditions in moderate climates. For areas of extreme cold, where frost heave is a serious problem —

and an expensive one to deal with — you need to consult with a civil engineer and/ or with your building department for local standards required to protect specific structures against frost heave.

Existing Drainage

Most of us in suburban developments inherit the soil and drainage patterns the developer provided. This is both good and bad. The good part is that developers are required to provide drainage that ensures all the house lots drain properly. Therefore, drainage problems are rare in most suburban developments. However, developers are only required to meet minimum standards for drainage. They rarely do more; this is the bad part of taking what the developer gives. Developers do not often spend money on special items like catch basins, retaining walls, or other terracing and drainage devices for interesting and aesthetically pleasing lawns. This is not necessarily a criticism of developers. The developer of speculative housing — the way most homes are built — is required to provide drainage so that the house is safe. He does that. To do more — to spend money on "custom" landscaping — is asking him to gamble his investment on what the unknown buyer might like.

Catch basins, retaining walls and swales. The developer will try to avoid catch basins (a concrete basin that collects water like a miniature manhole and runs the surface water through underground lines to a disposal point) and retaining walls (a wall that holds earth, allowing you to create multi-levels in your lawn to aid surface drainage) because they are expensive. Typically, the developer will use swales to aid surface drainage. Swales are simply shallow depressions in your lawn — very shallow ditches — that guide water to other points than would be possible with the natural configuration.

Planning for Changing Yard Grading

If you are adding a carport, garage, room addition, or any structure that affects surface drainage, study the existing drainage patterns. This can be done simply; observe your yard drainage during a rain. The heavier the rain, the better. If you are adding only an item or two — a new garage or carport and drive, for example — conform to the existing drainage pattern as much as possible. But if you know that over the

years you will be altering your home and lawn radically, it is best to plan the whole project and drainage pattern in advance. Then place the new elements in accordance with the total plan. You may need a landscape architect for planning of this scope.

Recognizing existing problems. If you already own your house and you have a drainage problem, you would be wise to contact your building department. Usually, they can tell you how to approach the developer to get the condition corrected or advise you how to correct it yourself. It is simple enough to verify that you have a drainage problem: if the lot stands in pools after a rain, or if the house and garage have mildew problems, or if your patio is overrun during the rains, your yard has a problem that needs to be corrected.

Correction devices. There also are often cases where the drainage pattern you inherited is far from adequate for the landscaping and building plans you have in mind. Then utilize surface drainage and landscaping aids such as: retaining walls of varying heights to help you terrace steep slopes; dry wells to help drain trouble spots (a dry well is a hole filled with rock — see your building department about dry wells) and catch basins. Retaining walls allow you to raise, lower or level areas. Dry wells may keep otherwise difficult spots dry. Catch basins drain low areas.

Creating a protective contour. The first consideration in drainage is to keep

the house and the access routes to it safe from flooding or excessive water runoff. To accomplish this, a protective slope like an apron is created around the house. Protective swales may be used in combination with these slopes. Design of these protective measures depends upon your particular lot and locality. If you do not use a landscape architect for planning your contours, consult with HUD and the building department and have them go over your plans with you.

Directing the water. Avoid grades that direct water toward foundation walls or garden walls. This water can be harmful to the foundations of any structure. Water trapped against the foundation walls of your house can cause moisture and mildew problems in the house, any crawl spaces, or basement. Slope new paving so

At the end of a natural slope that is braced by a retaining wall, you can create a berm and cover it with grass.

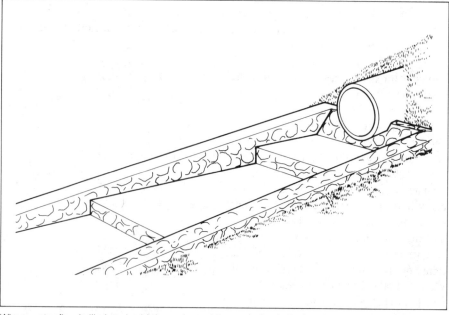

Where water flow is likely to be high, such as at the end of a drainpipe, a concrete lined swale with steps will control and direct runoff. This avoids erosion problems.

runoff is directed to existing drainage aids such as swales, ditches, drives, catch basins, and dry wells.

Frost heave precautions. In areas subject to frost heave, drainage is more critical than in some moderate climates because buildings, walls, paving, and fencing can be damaged or destroyed by the frost pressure. If you live in an area where temperatures become extremely low, check with your architect or building department.

Installing catch basins. When catch basins must be used, do not install them where overflow would run into the house. Plan the overall drainage and grading so that if the basin should overflow, the water would run into the existing drainage course — away from the house.

Dry wells. If you use a dry well to drain problem areas, check with the building department to determine the depth of the ground water table. The bottom of the dry well should always be above the water table at any time of the year. However, the bottom of the dry well must project into a level of porous soil capable of absorbing the water from the well. Keep dry wells well away from buildings and foundations of other structures. Check with local experts — a landscape architect, civil engineer, the building department, or HUD, if you have questions about requirements in your locality.

Utility lines. Check with the utility and phone companies for location of existing underground lines. Install or move any underground lines or equipment before you begin paving.

HOW TO REGRADE YOUR PROPERTY
Doing it Yourself

You can do most residential grading with a few hand tools, some stakes, and a line level. Grading — for the typical suburban lot — is usually a matter of flattening, smoothing, and sloping the soil to drain away from the house, garage or carport, or other projects to lower disposal points, to the street or to both. A grid system, made by stretching string a foot or so above the area to be graded, is helpful in creating the desired slope.

The desired rate of the slope away from the house, drive, and different use areas varies according to the particular lay of your lot. If you employ a landscape architect, his plan will provide for adequate

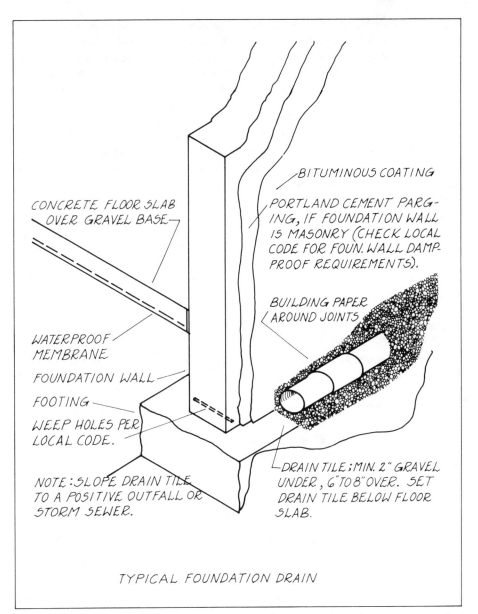

CONCRETE FLOOR SLAB OVER GRAVEL BASE

WATERPROOF MEMBRANE

FOUNDATION WALL

FOOTING

WEEP HOLES PER LOCAL CODE.

NOTE: SLOPE DRAIN TILE TO A POSITIVE OUTFALL OR STORM SEWER.

BITUMINOUS COATING

PORTLAND CEMENT PARGING, IF FOUNDATION WALL IS MASONRY (CHECK LOCAL CODE FOR FOUN. WALL DAMP-PROOF REQUIREMENTS).

BUILDING PAPER AROUND JOINTS

DRAIN TILE; MIN. 2" GRAVEL UNDER, 6" TO 8" OVER. SET DRAIN TILE BELOW FLOOR SLAB.

TYPICAL FOUNDATION DRAIN

A good foundation drain directs water to a storm sewer. The purpose is to relieve any pressure that may build up from ground water and threaten the integrity of the foundation.

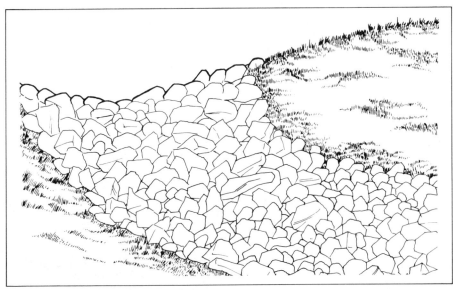

A swale is a natural ditch. When erosion of the swale becomes a problem, you can line the swale with rubble to protect the soil from being carried away.

drainage of all areas. If you do not use an architect, the building department or HUD can advise you about minimum slopes to handle your particular project.

Very generally, the protective slopes should drop vertically about 6 inches for 10 feet of horizontal run of the slope. Both these figures are minimums — that is, you should have sloping ground away from your house or garage for at least 10 feet and it should drop at least 6 inches in this horizontal distance. This is for grassy areas. Other materials, such as concrete, asphalt, or gravel, require different slopes. Concrete and similar surfaces need about 1/16 inch drop per foot of horizontal run. Again, these are general figures and they will vary with your locality.

Example Project

As an example of a typical project, let us suppose you wanted to regrade your front yard so that it would drain toward the street.

Preparing the soil. First, loosen the soil with a double-ended pick. This has a pick at one end and a blade at the other. You can use a long-handled, pointed shovel to fill the obvious depressions and level the mounds. If it is necessary to use a wheelbarrow to move the dirt, rent one with a pneumatic tire and sturdy framing.

Finding the slope. Next, set up a grid system to help guide the grading. Place a stake at the foundation wall of one corner of the house. Place another stake at the edge of the sidewalk nearest the house, on a line perpendicular to the house but in line with the first stake. Attach a string to the foundation-wall stake at the point at least 8 inches down from the inside finished floor elevation. Stretch the string to

the stake at the sidewalk and attach it there, leveling it with a line level. Make sure the string is not touching the ground anywhere. If it is, dig a trench under the string so it does not touch the ground. Measure up from the top surface of the sidewalk to the string. This tells you the vertical rise. Measure the distance between the stakes, and you will have the horizontal run. Repeat this staking process at the opposite corner of the house.

Setting up the grid. Stretch a line between the stakes at the sidewalk edge. Attach it to the point where the first strings are tied. Now you have described a string boundary around the lot. Drive stakes at six-foot intervals around the string boundary. Connect the stakes with strings to form a string gridwork over the lot. Check the strings for level with a line level.

Moving the soil. Move around the lot within the grid, shoveling and raking the soil so that it slopes down to the sidewalk at the desired rate. The string grid provides you with a handy slope check at many points on the lot; use a yardstick to check the distance between the string and the soil. When you have created the desired slope, tamp the soil to minimize uneven settlement.

How to Control Erosion

If your lot has steep natural grades, you may have an erosion problem. Each time it rains, you may lose part of the soil on the steep slope. If so, you must protect the soil itself — that is, prevent erosion. Stopping erosion starts by slowing down the surface water. There are several ways to do this.

Using ground covers. You can plant a ground cover: sandwort, thrift, Dianthus, Juniper, Pachysandra, and Taxus are good

ground covers that prosper in many parts of the country. Your garden center can recommend ground covers that thrive in your locality. Explain where and why you want to plant the ground cover, and the garden center will tell you the best for each location and use. Most ground covers grow thickly, squeezing out most weeds and presenting a neat, uniform coverage. Ground covers may not be enough to prevent erosion on very steep slopes. If not, you may have to modify the slope itself.

Using stones. Stones are one of the cheapest and simplest materials to help prevent erosion on steep slopes. All you have to do is line the slope with stones large enough to stay in place when the water runs over them. Most stones have a relatively flat side so laying them is not a problem. Use a pointed shovel and scoop out enough earth so that the stones are set in securely. The number and sizes of the stones you use depends on the steepness of the slope and the amount of water that flows over it. Stones allow you to experiment fairly easily. Put down what looks like enough and then add more if you need them. A 4-to-6 inch layer of stones set 2 inches or so in the ground will usually take care of most erosion problems.

You may want the entire surface covered uniformly with stone. However, you may prefer to set the stones apart somewhat and plant a ground cover between them, softening the appearance of the slope with the plants. A ground cover and stone combination is a good-looking solution to the problem of erosion.

Using baffles. Baffles slow down surface water and prevent erosion. A baffle may be any structure that will slow the flow of surface water. It may be built of

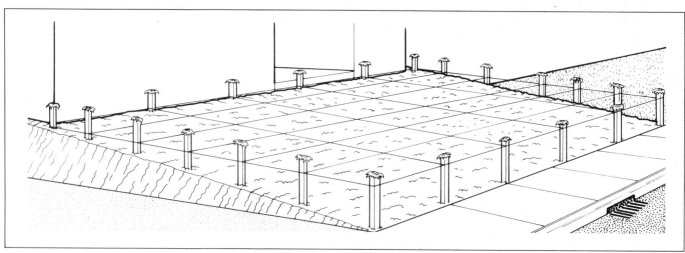

A stake and string grid provides a good, level guide for measuring the slope when you are regrading an area by hand.

any appropriate material, relative to your needs and design appearance: pressure-treated wood landscaping timbers, cross ties, stone, masonry — or some combination of these and other materials.

To use a cross tie as a baffle, lay the tie on the slope perpendicular to the flow of the water. Deciding how deep to scoop out the earth for the tie to be secure is a matter of judgment. However, as a rule, burying the tie about halfway should be enough. Appearance enters into the decision. If you find the ties unsightly, you may want to bury them a little deeper — but remember, their purpose is to slow water, so the more they protrude, the better. The number of ties you need is another matter of judgment. Consider the steepness of the slope and the amount of water that runs over it. You can experiment: lay some ties; add more if you feel the first set is not doing the job. It is simple enough to determine whether you have enough ties by observing the water flow during a rain. You also can test by using a garden hose to see how the ties slow the water. Lay the ties end to end across the slope.

After looking at the slope and considering what the visual effect will be, you may decide you want to combine cross ties, stones, and ground covers to slow down surface water and prevent erosion. This combination can be one of the best-looking solutions.

Terracing a slope. Still another way to slow down surface water on steep slopes is to build terraces. You do this by digging, cutting, filling and manipulating the surface. Unless you have serious problems with your soil, the only tools you need are a pick, pointed shovel, garden rake, and wheelbarrow.

Work the slope until it resembles a set of giant steps. Plant these ''steps'' with grass or another ground cover to slow down the surface water.

Creating swales. Swales — shallow depressions, gently sloped ditches or lined and steeply sloped cuts — may be created in your yard to direct and control runoff. The nature of the swale depends on the slope, your yard plans and the amount of water you must control. For example, a mild slope might be handled by digging a swale as little as 2 inches deep and 18 inches wide.

Take the dirt you scoop out and lay it along the down side of the swale, patting it with the shovel to form a lip along the

swale to keep water from running over the downside edge or front of the swale. Swales should be laid *almost* perpendicular to the direction of water flow so that the water is trapped and then runs out of the swale in the direction you choose.

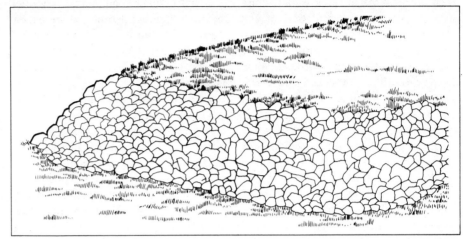

A relatively gentle slope may become subject to erosion during rainy periods. To protect the slope, cover the bank with rubble set into the soil.

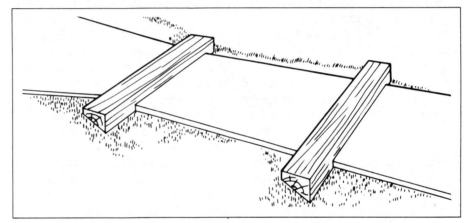

Baffles break up the flow of water down a slope. In this case baffles serve as riser faces in a stepped ramp to direct water away from the step edges.

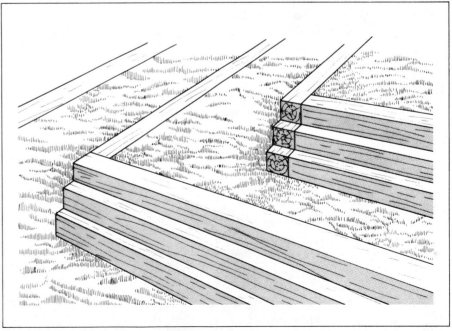

Terracing a lawn with landscaping timbers or railroad ties creates low retaining walls to slow runoff that might otherwise erode the sloping ground surface or wash away plantings.

Dry Wells

In most cases, creating a dry well calls for professional help. Why use a dry well? There are areas that are impossible to drain economically by manipulation of the ground surface. For example, when several natural swales (the swale formed by the intersection of two planes of land) come together to form a low spot, they create a basin. In cases like this, the only way you may be able to get rid of standing water is by digging a dry well. A dry well is simply a well, or pit, filled with coarse gravel or masonry rubble. The hole allows water to run down through it quickly. The size of the dry well depends on the amount of water that it will have to absorb and the depth of the water table. The building department and HUD can tell you how deep the water table is in your area, and they should have construction standards for the dry well. The bottom of the dry well should be above the seasonal high of the water table.

Round off the edges of swales because sharp corners erode faster than smooth ones. Take the earth you removed for the swale and form a lip, or slight berm, at the lower edge of the swale. Pat the berm smooth and compact with your shovel.

Drainage ditches and swales often run almost perpendicular to the flow of water down slopes. This way, the swales catch and hold the most water and change its direction. Sometimes it is necessary to run swales or ditches in the direction of the water flow. When this is the case, line the bottom of the swale with stone or rubble — set deep enough so the water does not pull it out — to prevent erosion of the swale or ditch.

Frost heave precautions. In areas subject to frost heave, drainage is more critical than in some moderate climates because buildings, walls, paving, and fencing can be damaged or destroyed by the frost pressure. If you live in an area where temperatures become extremely low, check with your architect or building department.

Installing catch basins. When catch basins must be used, they must not be installed where overflow would run into the house. The overall drainage and grading plan should be done so that if the basin should overflow, the water would run into the existing drainage course — away from the house. It is advisable to have a catch basin system designed by an engineer.

Building Retaining Walls

Retaining walls require careful attention to structure, reinforcement, drainage, soil, and weather conditions. They often require a building permit and are expensive and difficult to build. If built incorrectly the wall will fail — collapse — causing considerable trouble and further expense.

Retaining walls that are a height of more than 3 feet require professional guidance (especially detailed plans from an architect or civil engineer). Otherwise, the building department may require that you remove it. It could fall, if not adequately designed and installed, possibly injuring someone. The depth of retaining wall footings below ground, the amount of reinforcing necessary — the whole structural design — include many variables that that are frequently beyond the ability of even the advanced handyman. Seek professional help. However, for walls 3 feet 0 inches or less, where the grade is level at the wall top, are much simpler and are within the capability of most homeowners.

Timber retaining walls. For mild slopes that go to a level grade at the wall top, a timber retaining wall can be built easier than nearly any other retaining wall, even by one man. Labor is always a considerable expense — in cost if you contract labor and in time if you do it yourself. The timber wall described addresses both

these items. And there are no forms to build as in a concrete wall. For mild slopes, no reinforcement is needed but for

A railroad tie retaining wall was installed to secure the steeply sloping ground between the house and lower-level sidewalk.

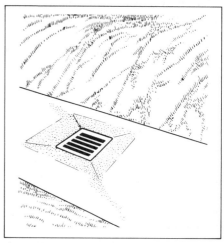

In an area exposed to a great deal of runoff or where ground slopes lead to standing water, a catch basin may be installed.

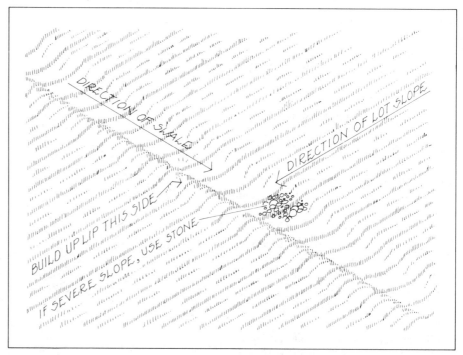

A swale may be manipulated to control runoff and prevent erosion. Here the swale intersects the direction of the runoff, using a built-up ridge and stones to control speed and direction.

more difficult conditions the wall could be reinforced like a counterfort retaining wall. Shown is the wall with 6x8 posts at 8 feet on center. The posts measure 8 feet long and have been embedded 4 feet in the ground and surrounded with concrete. The wall is really just a massive fence that retains soil.

The horizontal members are 4x6 timbers spaced approximately ⅜ inch apart. The spacing is maintained by simply leveling the first or bottom course of timbers, then laying a shim of ⅜ inch lath on each end of the member before laying the next one on top. Check each member for level using a spirit level and by frequent visual

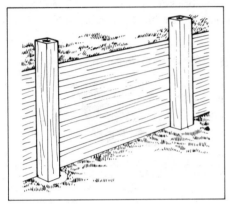

A timber retaining wall may be more suitable to a setting than a stone wall. Well secured, a wall may be as much as six feet high.

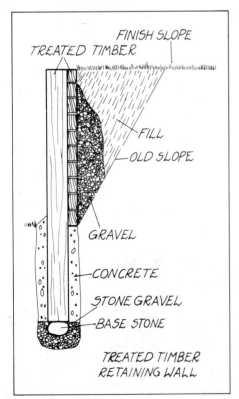

TREATED TIMBER RETAINING WALL

Timber posts must be set in concrete on a base that provides excellent drainage. Excellent drainage must be provided at the fence, too.

checks from a distance. The panel timbers are nailed to the posts from the fill side. In general, the horizontal members simply follow the line of a sidewalk or a lot line. Usable lawn area can be increased. Use "Wolmanized" timbers — a trade name for the pressure-treating process of the Koppers Company. Each timber absorbs .40 pounds per cubic foot of chromated copper arsenate. The chemical will not leach out into the soil and the wood can be painted or stained, if desired.

Adding weep holes. It is necessary to reduce soil pressure against retaining walls by providing drainage (weep) holes, or by installing drain tile the length of the wall at the bottom of the backfill. Drain pipes through the wall are typically spaced 10 feet or less apart and approximately 8 feet above finish grade on the lowest side.

Filling in with gravel. Add gravel the length of the wall; it should be deep enough to reach above the weep or drainage holes. You will have to dig away enough soil to give yourself space to work comfortably when you pour the footing for your retaining wall and then to build the wall itself. Before you add the fill to bring the grade up to the top of the wall, shovel in gravel the length of the wall until it is approximately a foot above the weep holes (the gravel should be approximately 4-6 inches thick). Where there is no serious frost heave, and drainage is the only problem, shovel gravel around all the weep or drainage holes. Add the gravel before you start filling soil against the wall when you have completed it. Shovel the gravel in a few inches below the level of each weep hole and up above it a foot or so and let the gravel slide down around each side of the weep hole. Check to see that the weep hole is surrounded by gravel — at least 6 inches on each side and at the top and running several inches below the weep hole. Then shovel the soil in to the top of the wall.

Gravel for frost heave. Where frost

This retaining wall has large weep holes to relieve the water pressure in the soil.

heave is a problem, install gravel 4 to 6 inches thick for the full height of the wall. Do this by using a 4x8 sheet of plywood as a temporary form for the gravel. Have someone hold the plywood about 6 inches from the inside face of the wall and shovel in gravel a foot or two deep. Then bring the soil up to the same level on the other side of the plywood. Lift the plywood almost to the top of the gravel and bring the gravel and soil up until the soil holds the gravel up against the wall. Finish the length of the wall in the same way. You will need only the one sheet of plywood and one helper.

For long walls of masonry, expansion joints should be designed and located by a professional to avoid cracking. The timber retaining wall drains particularly well due to the space between the timbers in the panels. Combined with liberal use of gravel, this wall should never present a drainage problem.

Slanting the wall. All high retaining walls are likely to lean slightly when the fill is placed. Also, whether they really lean or not, high retaining walls may give the illusion of leaning, perhaps because of the difference in grade. To counteract this unsettling appearance, it is good practice to slant the wall slightly toward the fill. A slope inward of ½ inch per foot is typically used. For a wall 4 feet above grade, then, the difference in plumb at the top would be 2 inches. You can measure this distance by setting up a plumb bob with line and measuring the distance from the plumb line at the face of the wall to the point at which the wall slanted. For a timber wall, for example, set the posts in place so they are plumb. Then move the top in the appropriate distance from plumb. One way to do this would be to set a tripod of three 2x4s on which to set the plumb bob and line so that the line is flush with the face of the post. Then, simply push the post back the right distance and secure it in place until you can pour the concrete around it. When all the posts are like this, secure the panels.

Corbeling brick. If you want to slant a brick retaining wall inward (such as a wall 4 feet above grade), you can move each brick course in slightly as you go up. A 4-foot wall should slant in about 2 inches at the top. There are 18 courses of brick in 4 feet, so if you corbelled each course in ⅛ inch (starting with the first course above the base course), the wall would slant in

$2\frac{1}{8}$ inches at the top. It is suggested you not corbel any given course in more than $\frac{1}{8}$ inch and do not slant the bricks like this except for the top 4 feet of the retaining wall. If the wall were 4 feet 8 inches, go up 8 inches with regular coursing, then start corbeling the course.

Angling concrete block. Concrete block is not as easy to slant inward because the block coursing is taller and you would have to push the block courses back too far — you should not expose the block cells — to get the slant you need at the top.

One solution for a 4 foot wall is to use larger blocks than you really need at the bottom and smaller ones as you go up. For example, use 12-inch wide blocks for the first two courses, then two courses of 10-inch blocks, and the last two courses of 8-inch block. The blocks would be solid core and the fill side of the wall would be flush, so that the viewed side would "step" up, giving the desired slant effect.

Stone walls. It is harder to slant walls of brick and block than those of stone. The stones are solid, with no cells to consider

and it is easy to make the bases a little larger and slope the wall inward as the courses are laid.

Areas of extreme cold. Retaining walls of 3 feet or less retain little soil and are not subjected to the forces of the higher walls. In areas of extreme cold, however, it is suggested you gravel all the way up the inside face of these walls and set all posts and/or footings on a minimum of 4 inches of gravel — check with your building department for code requirements. A variety of materials and configurations may be used. Depending on the design of your total landscape, you can choose the material that fits best: concrete block, concrete brick, clay brick, stone, brick veneer on concrete block, or railroad ties.

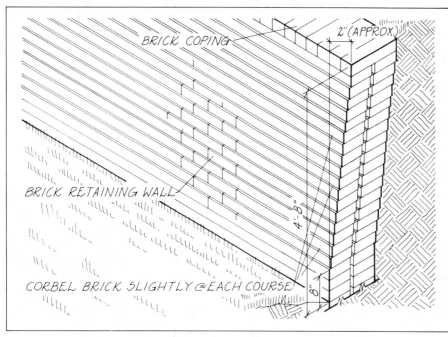

To avoid the illusion that the wall is leaning, narrow the thickness of the retaining wall. The distance you can corbel each brick course depends on your project and building codes.

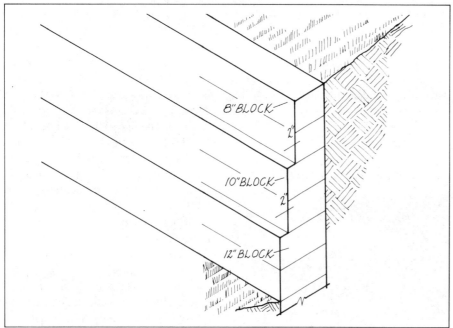

Solid concrete block is easier to corbel than hollow block, because there are no cells to expose. The corbelling will produce a "stepped" appearance.

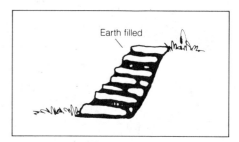

This stone retaining wall follows the line of the slope and uses a series of bond or tie stones for structural strength.

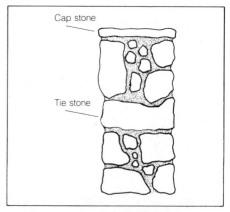

The stability of a free-standing stone wall comes from the regular placement of bond or tie stones that reach across the width.

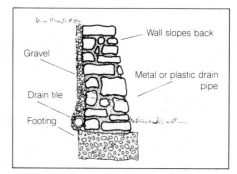

A stone retaining wall against a straight cut of earth must be wider at the base than the top and have both weep holes and drain tile.

6
Footings & Foundations

The foundation requirements for a single and double garage differ only in their size and the quantities of materials needed. We will give the details for building a double, detached garage; you can adapt the specifications to build a smaller, one-car garage if desired.

SETTING UP REFERENCE POINTS FOR A CONCRETE FOUNDATION
Using the String/Arc Method

The first step is to locate the corners of the building relative to your house. From one corner, such as a corner closest to the house, measure 30 feet in a straight line away from the house. Stake both the 30-foot mark and the corner near the house (Corner 1 and Point R in the illustration). The assumption here, for example's sake, shows the front of the garage parallel to the street in a typical tract house layout, with the garage at one side of the house and behind it.

Finding the garage corners. From the end of the 30-foot distance (Point R) use a string with chalk at the end to describe an arc with a fifty-foot radius, as shown. Draw this arc on the ground. If you have an existing lawn, it may be helpful to temporarily lay pieces of polyethylene on which to chalk the radii and the arcs. From the first corner of the garage corner, use string to mark a 40-foot radius. Stake the intersection of the two arcs. This gives a triangle (Point R, Corner 1, and the arcs' intersection) that is a multiple of the 3-4-5 triangle, and assures square corners.

From the stake at the intersection of the arcs, stretch a line back to the first corner. Run string from Corner 1 to Point R. Use nails in the center of the stakes to hold the lines taut. Now measure along line 1-2 and 1-4 for the front of the garage for Corner 2, and one side for Corner 3. Stake corners.

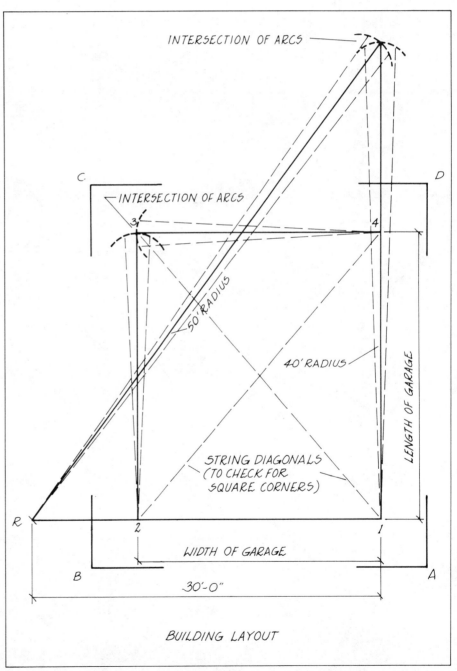

On the ground, or on protective sheets of polyethylene, draw arcs from Corner 2 and Corner 4. The intersections of the arcs will indicate where the stakes should be placed for Corner 3. Check diagonals to ensure a square layout.

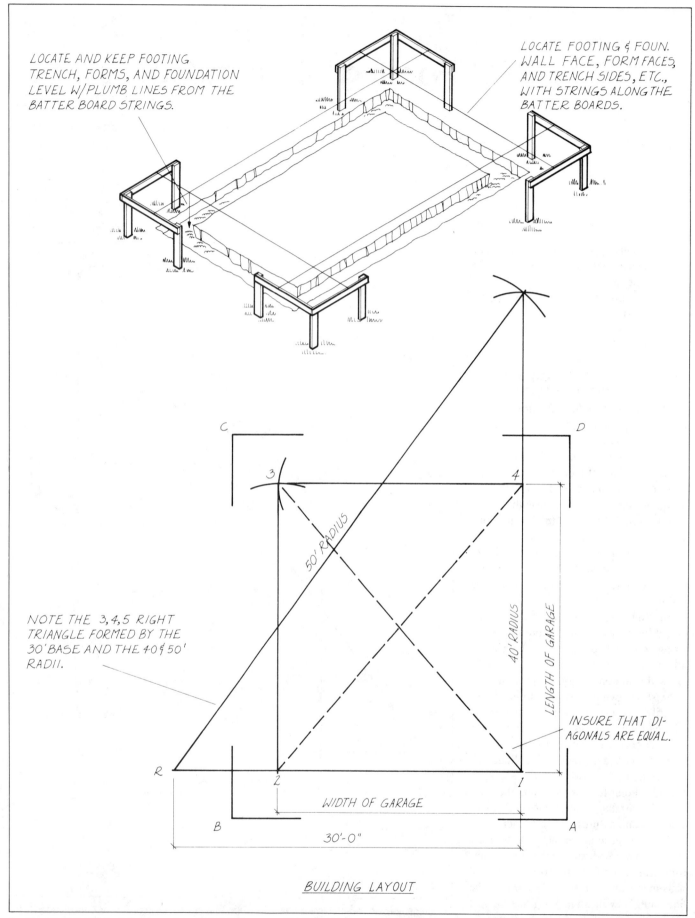

LOCATE AND KEEP FOOTING TRENCH, FORMS, AND FOUNDATION LEVEL W/PLUMB LINES FROM THE BATTER BOARD STRINGS.

LOCATE FOOTING & FOUN. WALL FACE, FORM FACES, AND TRENCH SIDES, ETC., WITH STRINGS ALONG THE BATTER BOARDS.

NOTE THE 3,4,5 RIGHT TRIANGLE FORMED BY THE 30' BASE AND THE 40 & 50' RADII.

50' RADIUS

40' RADIUS

LENGTH OF GARAGE

INSURE THAT DI- AGONALS ARE EQUAL.

WIDTH OF GARAGE

30'-0"

BUILDING LAYOUT

A garage can be laid out simply and accurately, using no sophisticated instruments. The layout shown calls for an accurate 3,4,5 right triangle large enough to measure the building lines. Batter boards are set up to provide an accurate system of reference lines.

Chalk an arc, on the ground, from Corner 2. Use a string that is equal to the length of the side of the garage. From Corner 4, stretch a line equal to the length of the front of the garage. Draw an arc. The intersection of these two arcs marks Corner 3. Stake this last corner.

Stretch diagonals across the stakes (dotted lines in the illustrations). If the lines are equal, the building layout lines are square. You may have already noticed that the thirty foot side, the forty foot side, and the fifty foot radius form a 3,4,5 right triangle. This is a simple way to lay out square corners. A fast check of the corners, in addition to the diagonal check, is to make up a 3,4,5 right triangle from wood. (See page 61.)

Using A Transit-Level

For any work requiring some precision — foundations, slabs, walls, and so forth — you need accurate reference lines. No building or construction project will be perfect, but if the reference lines are not very accurate, the normal inaccuracies and tolerances inherent in building will be multiplied as you work. The result is sloppy-looking projects and sometimes unsound ones when errors occur in structural components such as the footings and foundation walls.

The transit-level measures accurate horizontal angles and measures differences in elevation. It also gives straight, level reference lines. With this reference information you can lay out foundation footings that are square at the corners and level; you can fix grades, and lay drives and walks that slope as you want them to.

Preliminary measurements for the first corner. To lay out the one-story garage in this text, begin by measuring the exact distance from your house to the closest corner of the garage. (You may instead measure the distance from a property line or any other known point.) Exactly where the garage (and the first corner) is located is a matter of design preference and of building codes; the building code specifies how close you can build to other buildings and to adjacent property lines. The corner itself can be located by measuring from the house corner with a surveyor's metal tape. The tapes are commonly available in 50, 100, and 150-foot lengths. A 50-foot tape will be sufficient for a garage and for most other residential work. Remember to be careful when using metal tapes near power lines.

Once you locate the corner of the garage, stake it with a 2x2 stake. The stake is a rough location device. After you stake the location of the garage corner closest to the house, measure the distance again and pinpoint the precise corner location on the top of the stake with a pencil. Then drive a nail (4 to 6d) in the stake to register the point. Now you are ready to locate the other corners with the transit-level, relative to this first corner. But first, here is a brief discussion of the transit-level.

How the transit-level works. Refer to the diagram for identification of the transit-level components. The transit-level is essentially a telescope that can be utilized to accurately measure horizontal and vertical angles. A 20 power telescope makes a sighted object appear 20 times larger; an 18 power telescope will make the object appear 18 times larger; and so forth. The telescope pivots at its center to measure vertical heights, but you will not be concerned with this aspect of the transit-level for the projects in this text. The uses you are more interested in are measuring horizontal angles (to figure corners for foundations and concrete slabs). The undercarriage rotates to allow the telescope to measure horizontal angles.

The transit-level is equipped with a spirit level, which has four adjustable screws to enable you to level the instrument. When speaking of "the transit", or "the instrument", one usually means all the parts described above that fit on the tripod. The tripod legs are adjustable and assure a steady footing on level soil and most slopes. Directly under the tripod head there is mounted a plumb-line hook.

This is one of the more common builder's transists available on a rental basis.

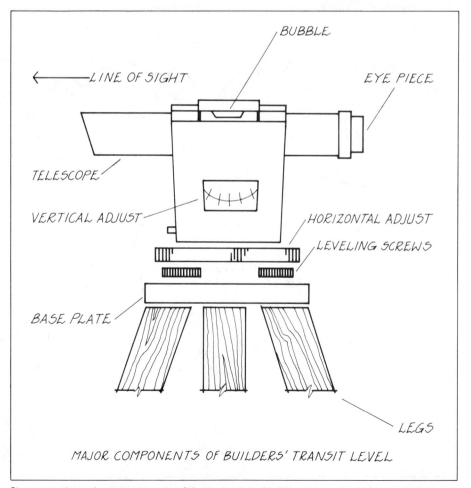

MAJOR COMPONENTS OF BUILDERS' TRANSIT LEVEL

Shown are the various components of the common builder's transit-level, which can aid in layout and elevation measurement.

With a plumb-line and plumb bob on the hook, you can center the transit over a reference point such as the corner stake of a building.

How to use the transit-level. To set up the transit, set it over the corner stake with the legs at least 3 feet apart. If you are working on a hill, one leg should be uphill with the other two on the downhill side. Adjust the tripod legs so the base plate of the transit (the plate that attaches to the tripod) looks level to you, with the center of the base plate apparently centered over the nail in the stake.

Attach the plumb-line to the tripod hook and let the plumb bob hang just over the nail in the stake without touching it. Press the tripod legs firmly into the soil, keeping the plumb bob over the nail. The tripod legs have foot pedals close to the pointed ends to help you push them into the soil. With the transit centered over the reference corner stake, you are ready to level the instrument.

The instrument is leveled with a spirit level that is mounted on the instrument. Four leveling screws permit leveling the bubble accurately. The four screws are mounted 90 degrees apart and, by turning two of them at a time, in opposite directions, you move the bubble one way or the other. This may sound more complicated than it is, because the leveling screws work about the same as turning the water faucets in the bathroom shower. The best way to learn is to rent the transit-level to get some hands-on practice adjusting the screws a few times before you use it for the garage.

Next, turn the telescope 90 degrees and level the bubble again (with the opposite pair of leveling screws you used before). Leveling may cause the plumb-line and plumb bob to move off center. If so, re-center the plumb bob over the nail. Now, check the leveling of the instrument again. Do not be surprised if you have to repeat this whole leveling and centering process several times; this is normal. But, if you cannot get the instrument leveled and centered after several cycles of these "accuracy bracketing" attempts, you may have to have the bubbles adjusted. This is a job for the supplier. The safest way to handle the transit-level, in this regard, is to have the supplier (typically a drafting materials/blueprint store) go through the process with you before you leave with the transit-level to be sure the instrument does not need internal adjustment.

The transit-level is an aid in accurate layout of your garage or building project; it is not a planning or design tool. You should already have an accurate, detailed plot plan showing the location of the project on the site. The transit-level is not a substitute for drawings and measurements.

Finding approximate locations of garage corners. Before you use the transit-level, find the rough locations of the garage corners as depicted on your site plan. Use a metal tape, measuring from known points. Mark the corners with stakes that are lightly hammered in.

Laying out the first corner of the garage. Level and center the transit over the accurately located first, or reference corner. Focus the telescope along the line of one side of the garage. Have an assistant with a leveling rod (the leveling rod is a kind of large, graduated scale or ruler) stand just beyond the roughly located side corner of the garage. Instruct him (as you

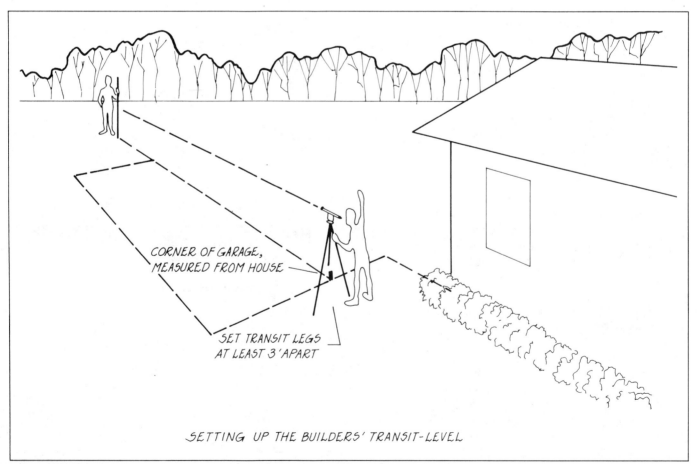

CORNER OF GARAGE,
MEASURED FROM HOUSE

SET TRANSIT LEGS
AT LEAST 3' APART

SETTING UP THE BUILDERS' TRANSIT-LEVEL

Set the builder's transit over the first corner stake, typically the one closest to the house. Place the legs at least 3 feet apart. Then adjust the transit exactly over the center of the stake, using the plumb bob at the bottom of the base plate.

look through the telescope) to place the leveling rod so that it is exactly in line with the line of sight of the telescope. You will have to give directions until he has it where you want it. With the rod in place, have him hold a plumb bob on a line as it hangs above the rod to locate the line of sight for the side of the garage. Mark this point on the ground and stake it. Since this stake is beyond the actual corner of the garage, you have to measure off the distance from the reference corner toward the stake; use a metal tape. Move the stake to the exact corner spot and pencil mark the top of the stake, using the tape again. Record the point with a 4 to 6d nail. If this sounds like tedious work, it is. But it is necessary. What you are doing is moving from rough dimensions to very fine, accurate ones. Regardless of how you lay out building projects, this kind of meticulous care is needed, if your projects are to look professional.

Laying out the remaining corners. Now turn the transit-level 90 degrees, focusing along the front line of the garage. Repeat the layout procedures discussed above for the front of the garage. Move the transit-level to the second corner of the front of the garage and sight along the second side of the garage. Remember to relevel and recenter the transit-level when you move it. Repeat the above layout procedures.

Checking for square. Once the four corners of the garage are staked, with nails accurately locating the exact corners, check for squareness at the corners. Use a large carpenter's square, or stretch a line across the diagonals of the building corners. If the corners are square, the diagon-

als will be equal. Another method calls for 3,4,5-foot triangle to measure squareness of the corners.

Finding differences in elevation. To set up batter boards or forms, or to establish drive slopes, or do anything that involves accurately determining differences in ground height from some beginning point, proceed in a manner similar to the above. From a beginning point, like a corner of the garage, find another corner and stake it. Sight along the leveling rod at the distant corner to get the elevation. If it reads 6 feet and the beginning corner stake reads 3 feet, then you have a difference in elevation of 3 feet.

The illustration on page 60 shows a reg-

ularly sloping grade. You can measure any number of points, dozens if you need to, between the two stakes. In this sense, the transit provides an invisible, perfectly level reference line from which you can establish level lines on the ground (for footings, tops of foundation walls, and so on), using the leveling rod for measurement.

Do you need to use a transit? Transits are not difficult to learn to use. They are quite expensive and you will probably want to rent one unless you have extensive building to do. The bigger the job, the more valid is the use of the transit. You probably will be able to master the use of the transit quickly in order to lay out your

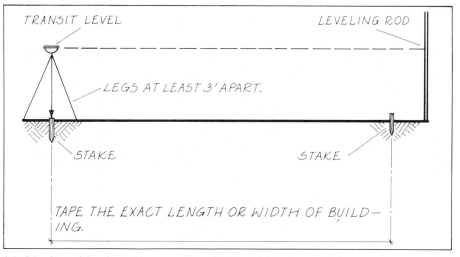

A builders' transit level provides you with perfectly straight reference lines.

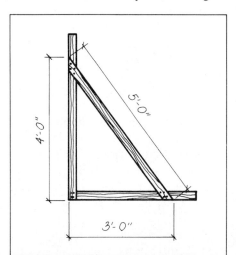

Shown is a basic 3-4-5 triangle; it can be built in any multiple of these dimensions.

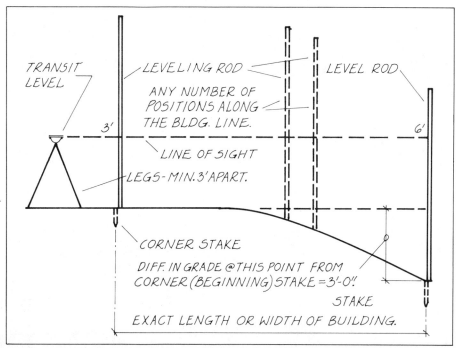

The transit level and leveling rod offer an accurate means of establishing level reference lines for footings, foundation walls, trenches. Set the legs firmly and note the differences in the leveling rod readings as you move the rod along the building lines.

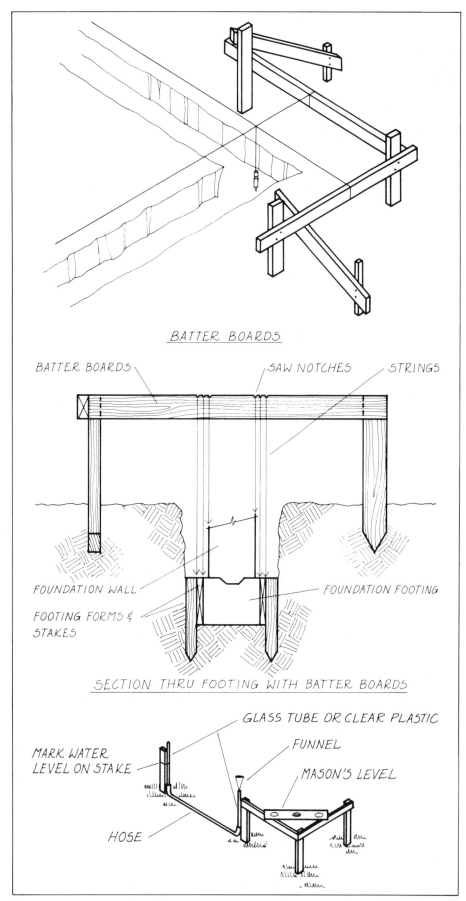

BATTER BOARDS

BATTER BOARDS   SAW NOTCHES   STRINGS

FOUNDATION WALL
FOOTING FORMS &
STAKES
FOUNDATION FOOTING

SECTION THRU FOOTING WITH BATTER BOARDS

GLASS TUBE OR CLEAR PLASTIC

MARK WATER
LEVEL ON STAKE
FUNNEL

MASON'S LEVEL

HOSE

One leveling device consists of just a hose, some glass or plastic tubing, a funnel, and a level. Secure the tubes to the two points you want level. Pour the water until it reaches the height you need and is the same height at both ends. Also shown are corner batter board setups and the relationship between the batter boards, foundation, and footings.

garage, set up the batter boards, and so on. However, the hose-and-water technique, discussed in "Setting Up Batter Boards" below, is just as accurate and probably nearly as fast to use. Do not feel like you "just have to" use a transit.

For garage expansions and room additions, a transit is less of an aid because all of the reference points — foundation, floor, and so on — are already there and all you need to do is to extend them.

Setting Up Batter Boards

Batter boards are a field convenience. They allow you to record horizontal reference points — such as faces of footings or foundation walls — far enough away from the digging and working so that you don't lose the points. Otherwise, you may spend your time constantly relocating the working area. Batter boards will help you locate (and keep track of) buildings, walls slabs, walks, or anything else that must be built with some precision.

To place batter boards, first locate Points A,B,C, and D (as indicated on page 58). These are 4 to 10 feet from Points 1,2,3 and 4, respectively. Points A,B,C, and D will be the intersections of lines stretched parallel to the building outline, 4 to 10 feet out — six feet, for example, is ample for a garage. You may also locate Points A,B,C, and D by extending the diagonal measuring lines beyond Points 1, 2, 3, 4 by 4 to 10 feet. Drive stakes at Points A,B,C, and D.

Drive 2 more stakes at Point A — one on each side — so the three stakes form a corner. (The illustration shows stakes with batter boards attached.) Nail a horizontal member (usually a 1x3) to Stake A and to one of the stakes next to it. Level the board with a spirit level. Nail a second horizontal member to Stake A and the new stake on the other side. Using a spirit level, level the second board with the first.

Now stretch a line from the horizontal members at Point A to the corner stake at Point B and level the line with a line level, marking the level position on the corner stake of Point B. Attach the other horizontal members, leveling them each to the other with a spirit level, like you did the first one. Repeat the process for Points C and D.

The hose-and-water technique. There is an alternate method for the above process. Attach the horizontal members at Point A, as described above. Level the boards with a spirit level. Then, using a hose and two glass or plastic tubes as shown, you can transfer any vertical point from Point A to Point B. Funnel water into the tubes until the water reaches the desired level at Point A. The water level at this end of the tube will be duplicated at Point B. This ''hose method'' is desirable where the distance between the two points is great enough to cause a line to sag.

Locating the horizontal and vertical dimensions. With the batter boards set up, you can accurately find and mark any horizontal dimension accurately — both sides of the foundation footing, foundation wall, or forms. Hang a plumb bob from the lines to find all the vertical points — the bottom of the excavation trench, the top of the footing, or the top of the foundation wall. Notch the locations of the footing faces and the foundation wall faces on the batter boards with a saw, and note them with a pencil. Once these points are registered, remove the string. You can replace them later if you need them. This is suggested for large dimensions where over a period of time, the line might sag. Next you will dig the footing trenches and excavate for the slab.

Slab Excavation

Tools and machinery. In many areas of the country, the slab and footings for a one-story garage can be poured in one piece.

The footing and slab excavation can be done satisfactorily with hand tools, but it is slow and difficult. Small back hoes and trenching machines can be rented, but operator skill is required. When digging out footing and slab dirt, you do not want to remove any more dirt than you have to. If you take out too much, it will be necessary to fill the unnecessary void with concrete — never build on fill when you can avoid it. When you cannot avoid it, get a professional to help you with proper fill. A small mistake with excavation machines can cost you the money and time you were trying to save. One alternative is to hire a small contractor to do the excavation for you. Equipment suppliers can be helpful in selecting the machinery you need and finding good people to operate it.

Footing trenches. When digging footing trenches, dig so the bottom is level, at the correct depth. Check frequently by hanging a plumb bob from the batter board strings. Ask your building department

about the required depth of footings for your area and for information about frost heave and local methods of dealing with it. (Note that concrete block is not an acceptable foundation wall material in areas where frost heave is a problem.)

The building outline discussed above, outlined by the lines connecting Points 1 through 4, is the typical starting point for recording reference information on the batter boards. From the foundation plan, you can see how all the different lines

relate to each other. For example, in a foundation with a concrete block or poured concrete foundation wall, the footings will be the widest component. The trenches dug for the footings will extend outside the line representing the building line. For a one-piece floor slab and foundation, the outside edge of the slab is also the outside edge of the footing trench. See the foundation plan below to understand how the excavation relates to the footing trenches.

The foundation wall should extend beyond both faces of a concrete block wall, whether or not there will be an additional masonry (or other) veneer.

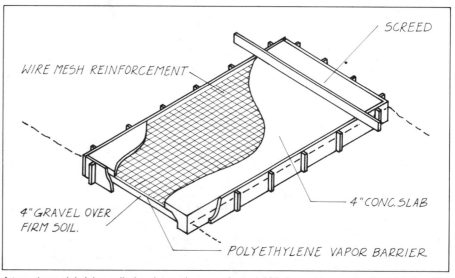

A turn-down slab (also called an integral or one-piece slab) is formed by pouring the slab, foundation wall, and footing all in one pour. The turn-down slabs require less formwork than for separate pours of foundation and footing (discussed in Chapter 9).

Building the Forms

Where firm soil is available, the earth itself may be used as a ''form'', omitting any wooden ones. But it is safer and probably easier to build wood forms.

Stakes and strings. First, place alignment strings on all the batter boards. The string line representing the outside face of the footing will also represent the inside face of the form.

From the intersection of the lines hang a plumb bob to the excavation floor. Drive a stake there. Pull up the line with the plumb bob so the plumb bob hangs just over the stake without touching it. Have someone pencil mark the exact point on the stake. This process very accurately locates the outside corner edge, or face, of the footing. Drive a 4 to 6d nail into the pencil mark on the stake, letting a quarter inch or so of the nail stick up so you can attach a string to it. Repeat this staking and nailing procedure for all four corners. Then stretch string from nail to nail, outlining the outside edge (face) of the footing. This marks the inside face of the forms.

The corner staking you have just completed is just to hold in place the string that represents the outside face of the footing. The corner stakes will be removed after the next step, which is to drive the form stakes that support the footing forms.

Driving the form stakes. The form stakes should be 2x4s that have been sharpened on one end. Their length should be equal to the depth of your particular footing, plus another foot. In most cases, the stakes will be about 2 feet long. This length will allow you to pound the stake about 1 foot (use a 5 or 10 pound sledge hammer) into the ground, allowing some of the stake to be left above the form. The stake will later be cut flush with the form.

Drive the form stakes firmly into the ground, beginning a few inches from any corner and proceeding around the string outline. Place stakes on both sides of each corner, not more than a few inches from the corner. The spacing of the stakes around the form depends on the form material you are using. If you are using 2 inch lumber for forms, you can space the stakes

at about 3 feet on center. If you use ¾ inch plywood for forms, you will need more stakes, placed about 18 inches on center. When driving the stakes, remember that the string line is the outside edge of the footing; therefore, you need to place the stake far enough from the string to allow space for the footing form. The safest and easiest way to deal with this problem is to cut a length (about a foot) of the form material and place it so it touches the string (as the real form would do). Then drive the stake so it touches the outside face of the lumber piece.

Once all the form stakes are driven, remove the string. Then choose any stake and on it mark the point to which the top of the footing reaches. From that point, stretch a line to the next stake and level it with a line level, marking the form position on the stake. Proceed in this manner, locating the footing form top on all the stakes and marking them with pencil. Install the form boards, frequently checking for level with a spirit level. Then cut the stakes off flush with the top of the forms.

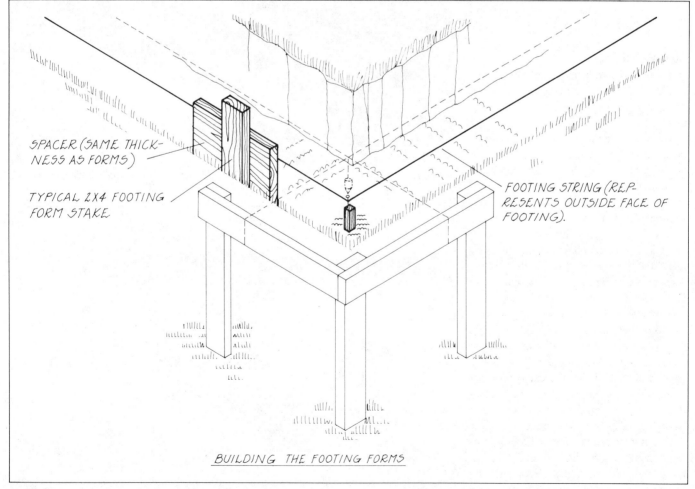

SPACER (SAME THICK-
NESS AS FORMS)

TYPICAL 2X4 FOOTING
FORM STAKE

FOOTING STRING (REP-
RESENTS OUTSIDE FACE OF
FOOTING).

BUILDING THE FOOTING FORMS

Once the footing strings are in place, you can begin building the forms. You will need outside forms only for a one-piece slab. Use boards as spacers to represent the thickness of the form boards.

Reinforcing. If you are using a one-piece slab and footing, set the reinforcing in place using small stones or steel rods to hold the wire mesh off the ground. For most cases, 6x6 #10 wire mesh is satisfactory. But if you have an unusually heavy load somewhere in the garage (a car does not fit into this category) you should consult with an architect or engineer. In a four-inch slab, the reinforcing should be toward the bottom half of the slab, but not touching the ground.

Pouring the Concrete

Tools for placing the concrete. You should use a special concrete hoe or a square-ended shovel for placing the concrete in the forms. Use a concrete rake for tamping down small jobs and a vibrator for very large jobs. (Do not use ordinary garden tools when you work with concrete — they can separate the water from the rest of the mixture and ruin the project.) You will also need 2x4 boards to use as screeds or strike boards. These pull the excess concrete off the forms. The boards should be straight and lightweight and should measure about 1 to 2 feet longer than the width of the form.

Placing the concrete. For a one-piece slab and foundation, the foundation will probably not be very deep. Before the concrete is poured, dry ground should be moistened with a hose. Otherwise, the ground will pull moisture from the concrete, which will weaken the concrete. Try to place the concrete as close to its final position as possible. Do not dump it in one spot and move it. Spade and tamp the concrete to prevent air pockets. Level the concrete by placing a 2x4 screed across the forms and, with one other person, working it back and forth.

Tools for finishing the concrete. You will need several tools for finishing concrete. These include floats and darbies, which you can purchase or make out of wood. Floats provide an even but fairly rough finish. The final smooth finish is applied with metal trowels, several different kinds and designs are available. You will also need an edger for finishing the edges of walks and patios, as well as a groover for cutting the control joints. The blade on the groover must be one inch deep (or one fourth of the thickness of the slab). If you need to trowel a large area, you can usually rent a power trowel. Broomed finishes call for a stiff-bristled

shop broom or a special concrete broom, which you can buy.

Floating the surface. The first step in finishing is floating the surface of the concrete. This can be done with a bullfloat or darby, followed by a hand float if necessary. The bullfloat is used on large surfaces, such as patios or floor slabs. The float removes excess water from the surface and knocks down the small ridges left by the screeding operation. It leaves the pour smooth and level.

Push and pull the large bullfloat back and forth over the concrete. At the end of each stroke, lift the float and move it over to make another parallel stroke. When pushing it forward, tilt it a little so the front edge is raised; when pulling backward, tilt the back edge up just a little to prevent the edge of the float from digging into the concrete. This is the hardest part of the job for most novices, but one that will come with practice.

Placing the sill bolts. Before the concrete sets, install the sill bolts. Let the concrete become just stiff enough to support the bolts without their sinking into the concrete. For a one-piece slab and foundations, and for other foundations with concrete foundation walls, locate the ½-inch sill bolts a maximum of 8 feet on center, embedded in the concrete at least 6 inches. The sill bolts should have 2 inch washers (or the equivalent, like large nuts) on the end, embedded in the concrete. A threaded end, with which to secure the sill plate, is left protruding. The sill bolt should stick up enough (be long enough) to go through the sill plate (which is of one or two 2x4s). There should be enough length for the nut and washer to secure the sill plate; select the bolt lengths accordingly.

Sill bolts for masonry foundations. For masonry foundation walls, use the same bolt and washer configuration as above, but embed the bolt at least 15

When the sheen of surface water is gone, float the surface to remove excess water and to smooth down ridges from screeding.

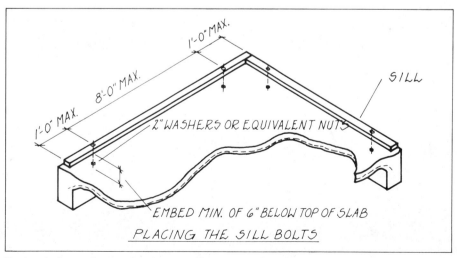

To place bolts, you first need to plan your sill; that is, you must know the points at which the 2x4s butt. Then you can place the sill bolts appropriately along the sill.

inches. Fill the masonry cell or cavity with grout, placing the grout around the bolt. The bolt spacing should not be more than 8 feet.

Sill bolts in cured concrete. As an alternative to the bolt systems above, you can let the concrete cure and then secure the sill plate with steel studs, which are similar to nails. These are installed with a power driver. Steel studs are spaced a maximum of 4 feet on center. This alternative is not acceptable in all localities; it is for concrete foundation walls only, not masonry.

Whatever the installation system, there should be a bolt no more than 12 inches from every corner, both directions from

Use a star drill to make holes in a concrete slab. Rotate the drill as you hit it with a mason's hammer.

Holes also can be drilled with a carbide-tipped masonry bit. The bit must be big enough for the anchor, not just the screw.

the corner. There always must be at least 2 bolts per sill length.

When to start finishing the surface. After you have leveled ("floated") the slab with the wooden screed, allow the concrete to set slightly before you do any further finishing. If you start finishing the concrete too soon, you will bring too much of the water in the mix to the surface. Too much cement will be floated away and the result will be a weakened pour. On the other hand, if you wait too long, the concrete will set up so firmly that you cannot work or finish it at all.

Because of the variations in humidity, climate and even the concrete mix itself, there is no way to say exactly how long you should wait. A large pour on a cool, humid day will probably take several hours to stiffen enough to finish. A good rule of thumb is to start the finishing process as soon as the sheen of excess water is gone and the concrete can withstand foot pressure. Another indication is the texture; the concrete surface should feel like gritty sand under trowel pressure.

Troweling. If you want a really slick, hard finish, smooth the concrete with a steel trowel. Apply it in the same circular motion as the float, and, as with bullfloating, keep the edge lifted slightly with each pass so you do not cut into the surface of the concrete. Sprinkling the surface with a bit of water will help provide an even slicker finish, but do not overdo it. Use slight pressure on the trowel to get the best finish; trowel until the surface feels silky

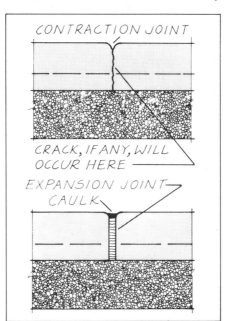

Control joints are shallow; expansion joints reach through the concrete, to the base.

smooth without any gritty feel of sand.

Once the troweling has been completed, go back over the edges and grooves to lightly clean off any excess moisture and cement that might have been forced down into them. You can use a hand brush for this. Be careful to keep the edges of the tools from cutting into the freshly troweled cement.

How to create a broomed finish. In some instances you may prefer a lightly broomed finish. The roughness resembles that of a floated finish, but a broomed finish has quite a bit more tooth.

In most instances, the brooming is done after floating the slab. Brooming may be done with almost any broom. However, a stiff bristle, push-pull, shop broom works the best. You can also purchase special concrete brooms. The hardest problem is working the broom without digging the bristles into the surface and marring it. The best method is to pull the broom across the surface. Lift it after each stroke and move to the opposite side. Pull across again. For the best results, broom the surface at right angles to the traffic pattern rather than in the same direction.

Cutting joints. After finishing, cut control joints in the concrete. These do not prevent cracks; they are simply weak points that you make in the concrete so that the inevitable cracks will occur in or near the control joints. Local weather conditions influence the placement of the control joints. Sometimes you can simply divide the two-car garage into quarters. To be safe, add more control joints rather than less, similar to those shown in the illustration. Cut the joints between one-fifth and one-fourth the depth of the slab.

Control joints are cut with a grooving tool. To provide a straight line, place the tool against a 2x4 guide strip tacked across

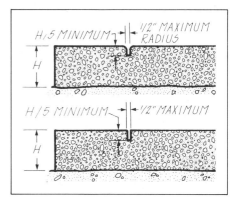

Control joints may have curved or straight finishes and ½ inch widths. Depth varies but a guide is ⅕th the thickness of slab.

the top of the forms or a plank laid on the concrete. There are two types of groovers, a hand groover and a walking groover. The former is the one most commonly used for home masonry. You push and pull the tool along, forcing the V-shaped bottom to cut through the wet concrete and form the joint. On large pours, the walking groover is easier to use. However, if you hand-groove, you will need to support your weight with knee pads or flat pieces of plywood on the concrete. Remove them as you progress.

An edging tool can also be used to cut control joints, but you will have to make two passes, since it only finishes on one side at a time.

Finishing masonry foundation walls. For masonry foundation walls, the top of the footing can be flat and the foundation wall built up from it. Before the masonry is built up, smooth the concrete footings for masonry foundation walls with a wood float. In areas of extreme cold, concrete block is often unacceptable as a foundation wall. In these areas, and two two-story construction, it is advisable to use concrete foundation walls.

Installing isolation joints. Where one concrete structure butts another, such as where the driveway butts the floor slab, or where a garage slab butts the steps, you need an isolation joint to allow expansion of the different materials. Isolation joints differ from control joints in that they go all the way through the slab; they are not just grooves. Half-inch-wide joints are recommended. Cut them so they reach just up to the surface. Then place the strip of asphalt-impregnated cane into the groove; caulk it.

Curing the concrete. Concrete requires time to cure after it has set. Do not assume that because the concrete is hard, it has cured. It will take a week to a month for your concrete to reach full strength. Let it cure at least 7 to 10 days before you build on it. During this period, keep the concrete moist by sprinkling it very lightly or covering it with damp sheets of burlap or other cloths. Curing temperatures range from 40°F to 70°F. Watch the weather and do not pour concrete if the weather will conflict with your curing schedule. Leave the forms on as long as you can — they help hold moisture in and protect the edges of the slab. Curing compounds are available to aid curing. However, nothing can substitute for sufficient time.

WOOD FOUNDATIONS

The wood foundation system is a stud foundation wall sheathed with exterior-grade plywood. The foundation wall sets on a wood "footing plate" which takes the place of the typical concrete footing. This plate, in turn, sits on a bed of gravel or crushed stone. All the wood elements are chemically pressure-treated to protect them against termites and decay. Although it sounds strange to hear of wood being used below ground, the system reportedly has been accepted by the Federal Housing Administration, the Veterans Administration, Farmers Home Administration, The Basic Building Code, The Standard Building Code, and the Uniform Building Code. None of these organizations is noted for making hasty decisions. It would, nevertheless, be wise to check your local code before assuming that wood foundations are accepted by the codes in your area.

Advantages

All-weather wood foundations are relatively new and may be of particular interest to amateur builders because of their relative ease of installation and cost savings.

Wood foundations can be installed in weather during which it would be impossible to carry out concrete work. The elimination of concrete foundation walls and footings is good news for people with no previous experience in concrete work. Advocates say there are materials cost savings as well, because the poured concrete foundation walls can be eliminated.

Place sill bolts when the concrete is stiff enough to support the bolts without their falling over, but before it gets too hard.

Wood foundations are suitable in areas that are not subject to extremes of weather.

For framing, use 2x10 studs (or the size required by codes).

A slab may be poured before or after the foundation is in place.

After the foundation, slab and first floor joists are secured, backfilling can begin.

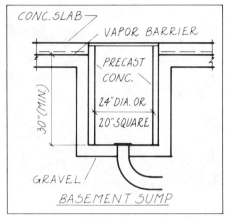

CONC. SLAB
VAPOR BARRIER
PRECAST CONC.
24" DIA. OR 20" SQUARE
30" (MIN.)
GRAVEL
BASEMENT SUMP

You can build a simple basement sump, like the one shown, using a precast concrete box or a pipe set into a bed of gravel.

Wood foundation walls create a crawl space (or if you dig deep enough, a basement) that is convenient for duct work. The stud wall cavities can house electrical conduit and plumbing; the wall cavities can be insulated.

Unless slab edges and concrete foundations are insulated, a considerable amount of heat is lost. The stud foundation wall can be effectively insulated in the same manner as for the building's exterior walls. There may be some energy savings with wood foundations; wood is a better insulator than concrete.

The pressure-treated wood foundations and construction illustrations shown will

help make you aware of a conceptual alternative to poured concrete and concrete block for foundations. Foundations are extremely important; professional design is more important for a wood foundation than for most other elements of the structure. The actual building of this type of foundation, however, is something you can do yourself in order to save considerable money. The wood foundation system will probably be easier for you than working with concrete and/or masonry.

Basement sumps. It is sometimes necessary to build a basement sump. Whether or not you need a sump, and its exact configuration, varies with the ground conditions.

Installing the System
Excavate the site as deeply as required. You can even dig out enough for a basement. When the excavation has been completed, install the plumbing lines along with provisions for foundation drainage.

After the plumbing lines are in place and the earth has been graded to drain (and the drainage system provided — sump or whatever is necessary), lay a 4-inch bed of gravel. If there will be no basement, lay a vapor barrier directly on the gravel. If there is a basement, lay 4 inches of gravel. Then place on the gravel, a vapor barrier and a 4-inch reinforced concrete slab. For crawl spaces, gravel is laid in the same manner as for concrete footings.

Foundation walls. The foundation walls typically are constructed of 2-inch thick wood members. The width of the members, and spacing, is determined by the design requirements of the structure, height of fill, soil conditions, and weather. For a one-story garage in a moderate climate, the foundation wall is similar to a typical stud wall, except for the weatherproof materials. Since the system is so new, try to contact your building department for specific foundation design requirements. However, you may find that local builders know more about the system at the moment than does your building department.

Footings. Typical footings are of 2x6s or 2x8s, assuming supporting soil of 3,000 and 2,000 pounds per square foot, respectively. The footings are laid on a gravel base. The footings must be wider to support a masonry veneer, if you use it. If building a two-story garage with brick veneer is higher than 16 feet, extra support

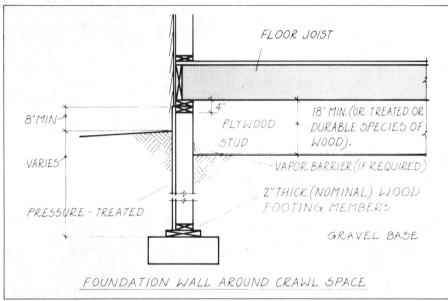

FLOOR JOIST
8" MIN.
VARIES
PRESSURE - TREATED
4"
PLYWOOD
STUD
18" MIN. (OR TREATED OR DURABLE SPECIES OF WOOD).
VAPOR BARRIER (IF REQUIRED)
2" THICK (NOMINAL) WOOD FOOTING MEMBERS
GRAVEL BASE

FOUNDATION WALL AROUND CRAWL SPACE

Manufacturers say pressure-treated wood foundations have been accepted by many leading institutions and by HUD. One of its advantages is that it is less hampered by bad weather.

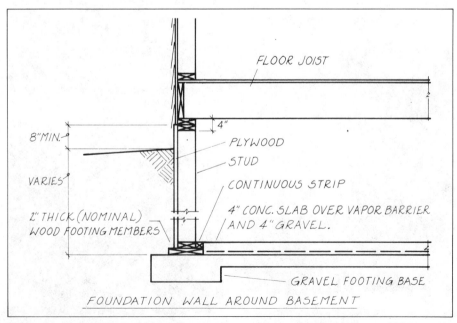

FLOOR JOIST
8" MIN.
VARIES
4"
PLYWOOD
STUD
CONTINUOUS STRIP
4" CONC. SLAB OVER VAPOR BARRIER AND 4" GRAVEL.
2" THICK (NOMINAL) WOOD FOOTING MEMBERS
GRAVEL FOOTING BASE

FOUNDATION WALL AROUND BASEMENT

Since pressure-treated wood foundations require a crawl space under the floor, you may want to consider building a basement — the cost would be less if you used masonry foundation walls.

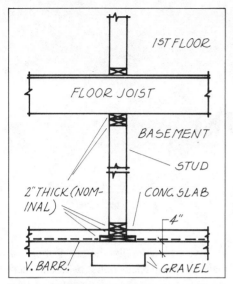

2"THICK (NOM-
INAL)

1ST FLOOR

FLOOR JOIST

BASEMENT

STUD

CONC. SLAB

4"

V. BARR.

GRAVEL

Pressure-treated lumber has made wood foundations possible.

provisions must be made. There would not, of course, be 16 feet of brick on a one-story structure.

Gravel bed. The depth of the gravel bed is three-fourths the width of the footing. Concentrated loads, such as columns, require greater depths and widths of gravel. These considerations should not significantly increase cost and you should, therefore, be generous with the gravel.

Extra support. Some additions may require a support in the crawl space (a crawl space is the space between the bottom of the floor system and the ground; the depth of the space varies) or basement for the floor joists. One way to build the supports for the floor joists is shown. The example support is a stud wall (2x4s 16 inches on center is typical, but consult with an architect for your particular design loads). The wall rests on a 2-inch thick wood footing plate, which in turn rests on a thickened slab. All the wood members — the studs, top and bottom plates — should be pressure-treated. Reinforcement may be required in the thickened slab (the amount of reinforcement needed varies according to the weight on the support wall).

For more information about wood foundations, contact the American Plywood Association, in Tacoma, WA, or the National Forest Products Association, in Washington, D.C.

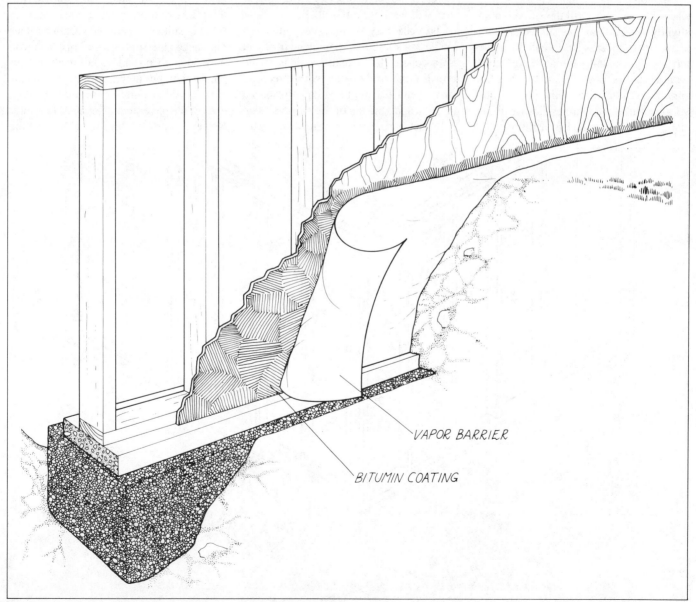

VAPOR BARRIER

BITUMIN COATING

Shown is a wood foundation wall with an adhesive application of polyethylene sheeting for below grade. The basement floor can be poured anytime before backfilling.

7
Framing & Exterior Finishing

PUTTING UP WALL FRAMING
Building the Side Walls

Sill and plate. Start with a side wall. Lay 2x4s along the slab edge and locate the sill bolt positions, marking them on the slab with a pencil. Drill the sill bolt holes slightly larger than the sill bolts themselves. The sill bolts are ½ inch in diameter, so drill the holes about ⅝ to ¾ inch with a hand or power drill. Check to be sure the outside edge of the sill is where you want it — sometimes flush with the slab, sometimes pulled in a distance. In the case of the text example, the sill is ½ inch in from the slab edge to provide space for the sheathing. Make any corrections in the location of the sill bolt holes before you erect the wall, otherwise the corrections will be more difficult.

The code may or may not call for a double 2x4 sill, but I recommend it. If you use a double sill, toenail the ends of the top sill piece to the studs with three 10d nails (each end) and three equally spaced 8d nails along the top of the sill. Nail size and spacing requirements also may vary locally, but generally the sill is held in place with ½-inch bolts as mentioned above and as discussed in the slab section in Chapter 6. Generally, the studs are nailed to the sill plate (or ''sole'') with three 10d or four 8d nails (toenailed). In some localities, where the sheathing does not anchor the studs to the sill plate, you may have to provide additional support (check with building department or an architect). When building the plate, butt the ends of the plate stock over a vertical stud. However, for a doubled plate, stagger the

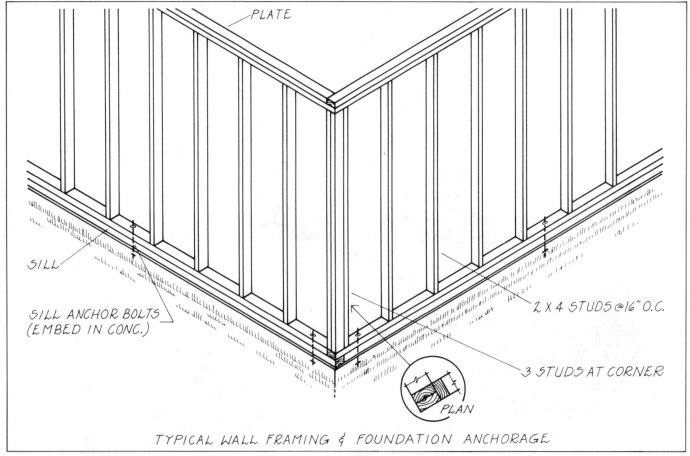

PLATE

SILL

SILL ANCHOR BOLTS
(EMBED IN CONC.)

2 X 4 STUDS @ 16" O.C.

3 STUDS AT CORNER

PLAN

TYPICAL WALL FRAMING & FOUNDATION ANCHORAGE

Framing for a garage must be sturdy 2x4 construction. A double sill (bottom) plate is used and is secured to the foundation with anchor bolts that were set into the foundation when it was poured. The bolts are no more than one foot from a corner; standard spacing is 8 feet on center.

vertical joints of the butt ends in the doubled plate. Do not align the joints of both layers of wood over the same stud.

Studs. Studs should be spaced 16 inches on center. Mark the stud locations on the sill, using a square. Lay the top plate against the sill and mark the same stud locations onto the top plate.

Openings for windows, doors, vents. If there are windows, doors or other openings in the framing, you may want to adjust the spacing and build the rough openings while the framing is on the ground (the ground must be flat where you

build the framing). To vary the stud spacing for the door and window openings, you must plan ahead. For example, you often will have cases where there is less distance left between the last stud and the opening. It might be, for instance, 8 inches between the last stud and the opening. This is a total of 24 inches (8 + 16 inches on center). In these cases, you can place two studs at 12 inches, rather than placing the last stud as usual. If the opening without the last stud were 28 inches, the studs would be 14 inches apart. In any case, do not rearrange the studs so that any

of them are greater than 16 inches on center.

As an alternative, build the framing with the studs at 16 inches on center, and ignore the openings until the assembly is erected. If you do it the second way, you will have to cut out studs for the rough openings. However, the framing will be in a convenient position while you work, and the stud sections you cut out can be used for blocking at the eaves and the gables. The accompanying illustration shows a typical door and window opening. The door and window rough openings are fairly standard, but always check the manufacturers' *exact* rough opening requirements for your particular door and windows. Shown are a few window styles and sizes out of the wide range that is available.

Always use a square to draw a line on all studs before you cut them; cut the studs while they are on a level surface. Any inaccuracy in the framing will be carried through the building: crooked framing becomes a bulge in the finished wall, and walls out of plumb show up as crooked eaves. Do not take short cuts.

Wall assembly. To assemble the wall frame use two 16d common nails at each joint. You can check for square with the frame, just as you did with the building layout: check the diagonals; if they are equal, the frame is square. When you have

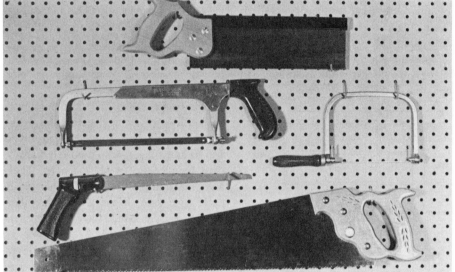

A back saw (top) is for a mitre box, a hack saw for metal, a coping saw for curves, a keyhole saw for openings in plywood sheets, and a crosscut saw for 2x4 or other stock.

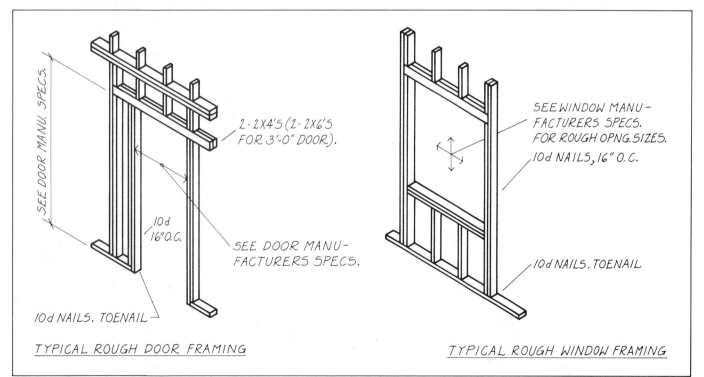

Windows require double framing. Use doubled headers above the opening, doubled jamb (or jack) studs on the sides, and a double sill.

verified that the frame is square, nail two 1x6s diagonally from each end, toward the center of the frame. This will hold the frame square while you are erecting it; you may want to notch the 2x4s and let the 1x6s remain as permanent braces.

Installing the wall frame. With the frame square and braced, stand it on the sill. Do not try to do it alone. You need at least one other person, preferably two people. One person will have to nail temporary braces to hold the frame in position until the other walls are attached, while two people hold the frame upright and in position. The braces can be 2x4s, nailed close to the top of the frame and secured at the ground with stakes, several feet out from the slab edge. Put the sill nuts on the bolts and finger-tighten them. Level the frame on the slab. Only minute adjustments should be necessary; check with a

spirit level to achieve level and plumb.

Leveling the frame. If the frame is square but is still not level on the slab, the slab is not level. Level the frame by driving shims under the sill from both sides. The shims are tapered. Tap them toward each other from opposite sides of the sill. They "feather" together beneath the sill. Drive them in flush with the sill edge all along the space that needs to be raised. Your local building department may require that you use only enough shims to level the sill, and then flush the gap with concrete. A typical mixture is 1 part cement and 2 parts sand, but check with the building department for their suggestions if you have a leveling problem with your wall frames.

Fastening the frames together. This step is essential to the stability and strength of the garage. When all the

frames have been erected, plumb the corners before you nail them together. Plumb by hanging a plumb bob from a string secured at the top of the frame at the corner, an inch or two away from the end stud. The string will be straight, hanging beside the stud. Now, adjust the framing so that the distance between the string and the stud is the same all the way down, from the top to the bottom. When the distance between the string plumb line and the stud is the same at all points, then the stud is plumb. Use the wall braces you used to hold the frame up in the beginning to keep the walls plumb until you can nail the corners permanently. This means that the wall braces will have to be adjusted from their initial position. Plumbing the frame is an important and sometimes annoying process if your studs are not straight.

Creating corners. The corners should be made up of not less than three 2x4s. These corner 2x4s are nailed to each other and to any filler blocks used (short 2x4s used for blocking) with 16d nails. They are a maximum of 24 inches on center in each wide face of the 2x4s. The filler blocks, if used, should have at least three 16d nails in them.

When you have the square frames level and plumb and nailed together at the corners, tighten down the sill nuts.

THE ROOF AND CEILING
Installing Ceiling Joists

Use 2x6s for the ceiling joists; in the example given, the joists are 20 feet long. The spacing for this garage (joists at every fourth rafter) is adequate, but if you plan to floor the joists for overhead storage, space the ceiling joists 16 inches on cen-

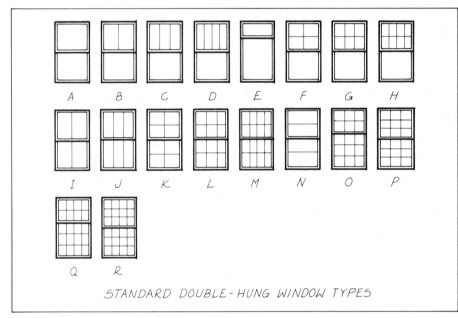

STANDARD DOUBLE-HUNG WINDOW TYPES

Windows come in a variety of patterns to complement various architectural styles.

STANDARD DOUBLE-HUNG WINDOW SIZES

Height of Opening	Width of Opening									
	1'-4"	1'-8"	2'-0"	2'-4"	2'-8"	3'-0"	3'-4"	3'-8"	4'-0"	4'-4"
2'-6"	ABFN	ABFN	ACGN	ACGJN						
2'-10"	ABFN	ABFN	ACGN	ACGN	ACGJN	ADHJN	ADHN			
3'-2"	ABFN	ABFN	ACGILN	ACGILN	ACGIN	ADHIJN	ADHIN			
3'-6"	ABFN	ABFN	ACGILN	ACGILN	ACGIN	ADHIJN	ADHIN	ADHN	ADHN	
3'-10"	ABFN	ABFKN	ACGIKLN	ACGILN	ACGILN	ADHIJLMN	ADHIN	ADHN	ADHN	
4'-2"	ABFN	ABFKN	ACGILN	ACGILN	ACGIN	ADHIN	ADHIN	ADHN	ADHN	
4'-6"	ABFN	ABFKN	ACGIKLN	ACGIKLN	ACGILN	ADHILMN	ADEHIMN	ADEHLMN	ADEHN	ADEHMN
4'-10"	ABFN	ABFKN	ACGIKLN	ACGILNO	ACGILN	ADHILNQ	ADEHIMN	ADEHIMN	ADEHN	ADEHN
5'-2"	ABFN	ABFN	ACGIKLN	ACGIKLN	ACGILN	ADHILMN	ADEHILMN	ADEHIMN	ADEHN	ADEHMN
5'-6"	ABFN	ABFN	ACGIKLN	ACGINOP	ACGILND	ADHILNOQR	ADHINOQ	ADEHIMNQ	ADEHN	ADEHNQ
5'-10"	ABFN	ABFN	ACGKN	ACGIKN	ACGIKLN	ADHILN	ADHILMN	ADEHIMN	ADEHN	ADHMN
6'-2"	—	ABFN	ACGN	ACGIN	ACGINO	ADHIN	ADHINQ	ADHN	ADHN	ADEHN
6'-6"	—	ABFN	ACGKN	ACGIKNOP	ACGIKLNOP	ADHILNOPQR	ADHILNOPQR	ADHMNQR	ADHN	ADHMNQR

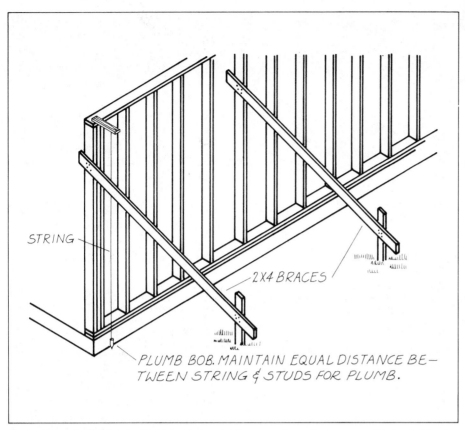

STRING

2X4 BRACES

PLUMB BOB. MAINTAIN EQUAL DISTANCE BE-
TWEEN STRING & STUDS FOR PLUMB.

Stud walls are built flat and raised into place, a job for several people. Be sure wall is level at the top and sits plumb. Do not tighten sill anchor bolts until the wall is true.

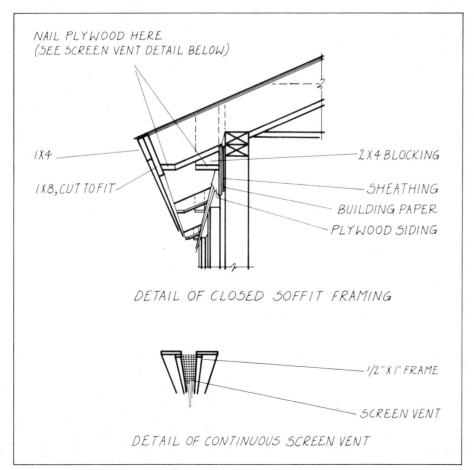

NAIL PLYWOOD HERE
(SEE SCREEN VENT DETAIL BELOW)

1X4

1X8, CUT TO FIT

2X4 BLOCKING

SHEATHING

BUILDING PAPER

PLYWOOD SIDING

DETAIL OF CLOSED SOFFIT FRAMING

1/2" X 1" FRAME

SCREEN VENT

DETAIL OF CONTINUOUS SCREEN VENT

A closed soffit gives a completely finished look to a garage, but you must provide soffit ventilation. A continuous screen strip is a good method for doing this and is attractive.

ter. The joists also should be spaced 16 inches on center if you plan to install a ceiling in the garage or a second story. The extra joists are needed to support the ceiling material, typically plywood or sheetrock. For a second story, check building codes to see if heavier joists are needed. You will need to know your eave detailing before you begin. The eave detailing inherently involves the rafter slope, so you will have to know that too before you can cut the joists. Shown is the eave condition for the example project.

Cutting the joists. Note that the ceiling joists end flush with the outside edge of the wall plate and that they are cut flush with the rafters. They have the same slope as the rafters. The slope of the rafters is 4 inches of vertical rise for every 12 inches of horizontal run.

You can measure the slope of the rafters onto the joists while they are still on the ground, then draw it on and cut the joists before you put them up. Or, you can put them up with square ends and line up the cuts with a string. Do this by locating the cuts on a joist at each end of the garage. Then stretch a string between them and locate all the cuts along the intermediate joists. The latter method of joist cutting probably offers better assurance of lining the joists up accurately and providing a true surface (joist ends all in same plane).

The cuts for the rafters (eave extensions) can be done this way also. But again, cutting the joists in place can be awkward for the inexperienced carpenter, because you will be perched on the joists while you are doing the cutting.

Nailing the joists. Start the ceiling joists at the first stud back from the corner at either end of the garage, toenailing the joists to the wall plate with three 10d nails. Nail temporary bracing across the tops of the joists as you go along to keep the joists vertical. This bracing need not be heavy — 1x6s will do. You can leave the bracing there, if you do not put flooring over the joists. If you instead use 2x6s for the bracing, they would give you enough support for a "platform" on which to sit as you install the joists. In the example project, a closed soffit is used with a continuous screen vent for ventilation.

The Ridge and Rafters
Building the ridge. The ridge is a single 2x8, but you will need two 14-foot lengths to create it. So there will be a joint

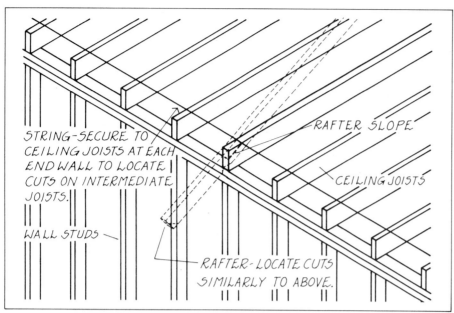

Ceiling joists and rafters must be notched so the roofline will be smooth. Use a string guide to locate beginning point of identical cuts on ceiling joists.

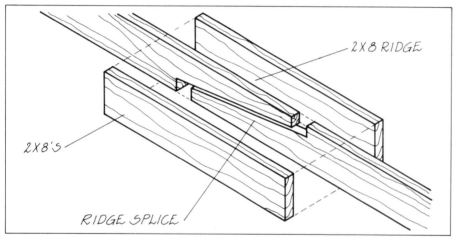

A ridge board must be spliced to create a board long enough to reach the entire length of the garage. Cuts are held and supported by a bracing board nailed to either side of the splice.

where the two lengths of 2x8s come together. Where the joint occurs is not too important, but typically it will be somewhere close to the center of the garage. The best joint can be made by splicing, or angling, the 2x8s together where they meet, rather than just butting the square ends together. If the splice is, for example, 3 feet long, fit the 2x8s together and toenail them with 10d nails 6 inches on center, staggered on each side of the splice, and on each side of the ridge. Then nail a 4-foot length of 2x8 centered on the splice on each side of the ridge. Nail these supports with 10d nails, staggered (one high, the next one low) at 6 inches on center.

Figuring out the height of the ridge. The ridge should be at the proper height to gain the slope you desire — 4 inches high in a 12-inch run for this example. The easiest way for most people to find the height of the ridge is graphically: do a very accurate drawing of the rafter/ridge/eave relationship and then take measurements from the drawing. The illustration shows a section through a one-story garage and is for illustrative purposes. For this reason, the lumber sizes were drawn nominally. Although you may not be able to do your own drafting for building a garage, you can do enough to figure the roof slope and eave dimensions. Of course, you could also request such a drawing from the drafting service or wherever you get your plans — a drawing that shows more detailed dimensions than architects and other professionals normally show on drawings.

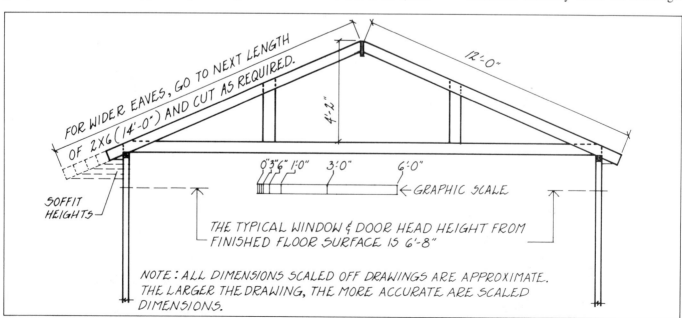

A scale drawing will tell you what your garage roof slope and peak will look like and give you a guide for measuring materials.

Assuming you want to work out the drawing yourself, draw the members their exact size as for the drawing shown. The 2x6 rafters then are actually 5½ inches wide. The 2x8 ridge is actually 7⅜ inches deep. And the 2x6 ceiling joists shown are actually 5½ inches deep (shown vertically, in the drawing).

In the example garage, the distance between the outside edge of the wall plate to the exact center of the garage is 10 feet. Note that the rafter bottom edge hits exactly on the inside top edge of the double 2x4 wall plate (3½ inches wide). It is notched over the wall plate before it continues out over the plate to form the eave. If you have an adjustable triangle, set it for the slope you want (5 inch rise for 12 inch run in the text example) and, using the inside top edge of the wall plate as the starting point, draw the bottom edge of the rafter until it reaches the center line of the garage. Then measure 5½ inches perpendicularly from the bottom of the rafter to find the top of the rafter. Draw the top of the rafter to the garage center line.

If you do not have an adjustable triangle, and you probably do not, then measure off (you *must* have an architect's scale to do these drawings, as well as a medium-sized drafting triangle; either a 30-degree or 45-degree triangle will do) any 12 units from the inside top corner of the wall plate. Count toward the center of the garage and indicate the 12th unit with a pencil mark. From that point, measure up by 5 units (you can use ¼ inch as "the unit"). The slope made by connecting

these two points is 5 inches of rise for 12 inches of run, and it is also the slope for the bottom of the rafter. When you have a drawing utilizing dressed lumber sizes as described above, you can then measure the ridge height and the eave dimensions right from the drawing.

Fastening the ridge. Temporarily secure the ridge at each end of the building, at the proper height. Use 2x4s as braces, or substitute wood scraps of equal strength. Do not be concerned, for the

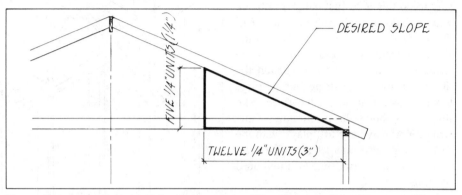

The scale drawing will give you the rise/run relationship so that you will be able to use the rafter or carpenter's square to measure and mark the rafter boards for your garage roof.

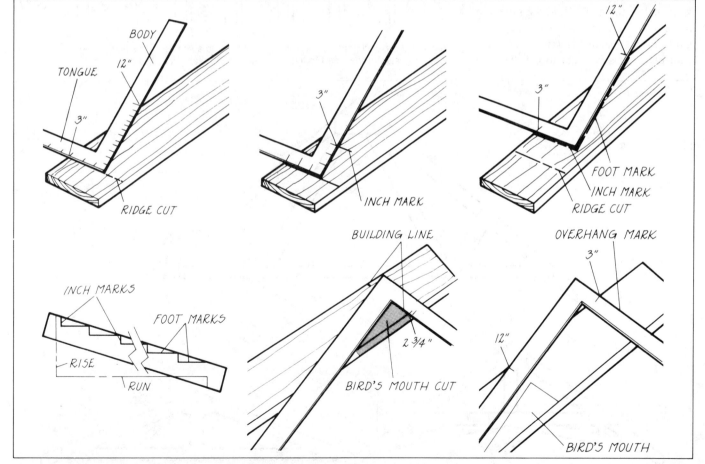

Cut the rafter with a rafter or carpenter's square. The cut for the ridge is marked by aligning the square with the foot mark on the arm and the rise per foot on the tongue. Measure any odd inches of distance first, then measure the feet by moving the square along the board and marking. When you reach the point even with the building line, turn the square over and align the inside of the tongue with that point, keeping the 3 and 12 inch marks against the lower edge of the board. For a 1-foot overhang, mark as shown in last drawing.

moment, about the sag in the ridge member, but doublecheck to be sure the height of the ridge at each end is correct. Do this by measuring straight down from the ridge top to the top of the wall plate at the ends of the building.

Go to the center of the ridge and brace it up with 2x4s, leveling it with a spirit level. Doublecheck for levelness along the ridge by attaching a string about two inches up from the top of the ridge (the narrow, horizontal side) at each end. One way to do this is to first nail a 2x4 block wide-side down on the ridge and then nail the string flush to the block. Stretch the string tight and measure along between the string and the top of the ridge to be sure the distance between the string and the ridge top is constant all along the ridge. The illustration shows the positioning of the string. You may have to ''play'' with the 2x4 bracing in the middle; and some more if necessary at intermediate locations until the ridge is level.

Cutting the rafters. When the ridge is level, cut a set of rafters for one end of the building (you get the dimensions from your scaled drawing). Hold the rafters in place to be sure they fit. Use them as a guide to cut where the rafters meet the wall plate. It is best not to cut the eave

edges of the rafters until all the rafters are nailed in place. Then figure the cuts for the ends with a string as previously discussed for the ceiling joists.

Attaching the rafters. The rafters should be toenailed to the wall plate with four 10d nails (two on each side). The rafters should be nailed to the ceiling

joists. The number and size of nails needed to secure the rafters to the ceiling joists depend on the slope of the rafters. For a 5 in 12 slope, as used in the text example, five 16d nails are adequate in most instances. Spread the nails over the area formed by the rafter lapping the ceiling joist. The nails should not be closer to the

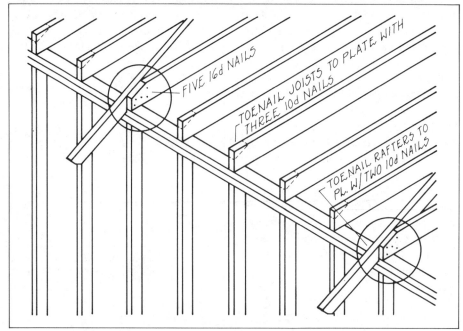

The nailing of the ceiling joists and rafters must provide a secure connection to the top plate. The rafters and joists are toenailed to the plate and then directly nailed to each other.

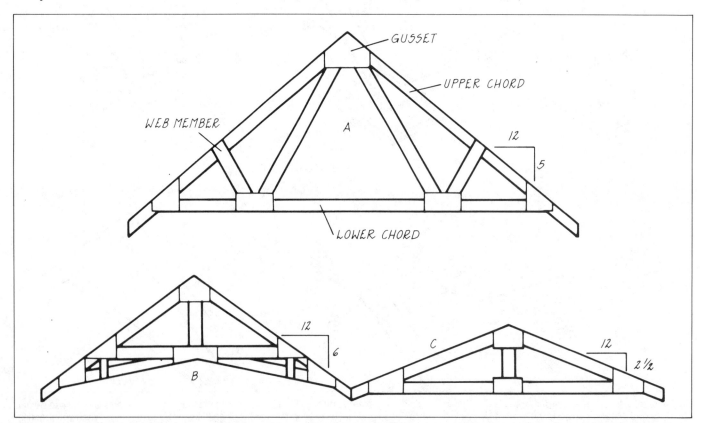

Prefabricated trusses provide a broad clear-span roof structure with great strength. There are trusses for various pitches. A and C are for flat ceilings; B is for cathedral ceilings. A truss structure will allow the largest possible open interior space.

end of the ceiling joist than about an inch. Remember, in this example, and in all the text examples, the specifics of the projects (such as nailing), are *typical* solutions for average conditions; for this reason, if you work out the drawings yourself, check them with a professional.

Secure a pair of rafters at each end of the wall. Then move to the middle and secure another pair. Fill in the intermediate areas. Next, remove the ridge bracing. Trim the rafter ends to accommodate the eave condition you have and install the fascia board and trim (1x8 fascia and 1x4 trim in the text example).

When to Use a Prefabricated Truss

Disadvantages. Prefabricated roof trusses are not the roof panacea they may at first appear to be. First, they have to be built somewhere. This means an added cost if you buy them ready-made. If you make them yourself, you have to first make a jig and get set up to do them. Installing the roof in the conventional manner usually makes more sense than prefabricating the trusses yourself. If you buy prefabricated trusses, you will need more help to set them in place because they will be much heavier than any of the single members — whether ceiling joist, roof rafter, or ridge member — that you would have handled in conventional roof construction. When you set them in place on the wall plates, you will also need some kind of scaffolding to work from; using ladders to install roof trusses is gamblers' work. Another negative aspect to use of prefabricated trusses is that they are not as flexible in use as the conventional methods. If your roof has hips, or any unusual feature, trusses become less feasible.

Advantages. Trusses are a good choice where you have a large, simple building to roof and you can realize labor savings by taking advantage of mass factory product methods. Trusses are also desirable for simple structures such as the garage example in this book, if getting the garage constructed faster is worth the extra cost to you of the trusses. They make most sense where you have long spans to cross and you want the space open below, with no wall partition.

How to find them. Local availability will limit your truss selection. Shipping costs often make them impractical for garages. Look in the yellow pages to see if there are any local suppliers. There are some companies that specialize in building components such as trusses, wall panels, other components. If your area has no such contractors, try some building contractors; they sometimes build trusses as a sideline, or they may build them for you as cheaply as the specialists. However, be sure they guarantee their engineering and meet code requirements. Lumber companies also sometimes build component parts. Show your floor plan to your lumber supplier; he may be able to advise you whether to build with trusses or not. If you have no local source, check Sweet's Catalogue, available at most libraries.

Trusses require the same attention to construction detail and planning as do manufacturer requirements for doors, windows, and other wall frame openings.

If you cannot find prefabricated trusses made to your requirements at a favorable cost, you will have to settle for working out the eave details around the trusses.

Installing a Prefabricated Truss

Marking for truss location. You will need scaffolds to erect the trusses. Rent two scaffolds adjustable to about 6 feet high. Standing on the scaffold, put a pencil mark over the studs on which the trusses will rest. Typically, the trusses will be 24 inches on center. This will insure that the truss weight runs from the stud directly to the foundation, instead of relying on the wall plate to transfer the weight.

How many trusses will you need? The number of trusses will depend on the length of your building and whether or not

Plates hold boards firmly in truss construction. The "W" bracing transfers the roof load to the walls and gives stability. There are no interior obstructions in a truss-roofed building.

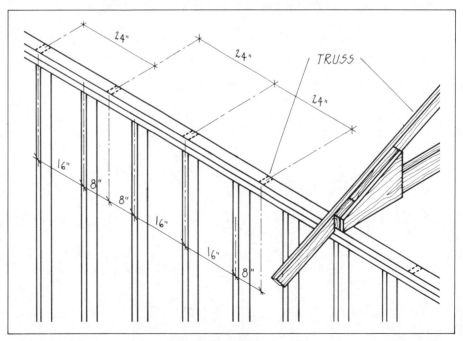

If studs are 16 inches on center, and the trusses are placed every 24 inches, every other stud will have a truss above it.

the building is a multiple of the stud spacing (16 inches). For example, in the garage shown, if you started with a truss over the corner studs at one end of the building, you would use 14 trusses to get to within approximately 9 inches of the opposite end corner studs. You could use a truss at that corner (making the total 15 trusses) or you could build rafters at the corner (the cheapest way). The best procedure is to work out your floor plan and wall framing plan and take it to the truss supplier, who will be able to analyze your needs quickly.

Adding framing anchors. When you have marked the truss locations on both sides of the wall, you can begin installing the trusses. Steel framing anchors are a convenience, especially for the inexperienced, because they have nail holes already positioned in them. Also, they are more secure than toenailing the trusses. Strong fastenings are especially important in high-wind areas. If you use steel framing anchors, locate and nail the anchors in place on the wall plate first, then nail on the trusses (10d nails are typically used).

Raising the trusses. To raise the trusses, you will need at least two helpers. Put the scaffolds inside the garage, one at each wall, under the points at which the trusses will rest. With one person on each scaffold and one person on the floor, lift the truss onto the wall plates. It will probably be most convenient to lift the truss with the peak down, so that the scaffold workers can lift the ends with the floor person as-

sisting by lifting at the peak. When the ends are on the wall plates, the floor person can help rotate the truss into position, using a length of 2x4 to push the peak up when it gets beyond his reach.

Fastening the truss. With the two scaffold workers holding the truss in position, the third person can toenail the truss to the wall plate (four 10d nails, two on each side), or nail the truss to the framing anchor. Temporarily secure the first truss by nailing lengths of 2x4 to the truss and wall framing. Be sure the truss is well-secured, since someone could be seriously injured if it fell. Plumb the first truss using a level. Double check to be sure the overhang is the same on both sides of the wall plates.

String alignment. Attach a string to the end of the truss and run it to the end of the building. Nail a 2x4 to the end plate, the same distance out from the wall as the end of the first truss. Secure the string to the 2x4. This string will help you keep the ends of the trusses lined up.

Installing the remaining trusses. Install the second truss as you did the first one. Check the spacing at the tops of the trusses to be sure they are all equal at the top and bottom. Always check the trusses for plumb as you install them. Temporarily secure the second truss to the first one, using several 1/6s nailed across the tops of the trusses. Remember that when you are using trusses, the roof sheathing bonds the

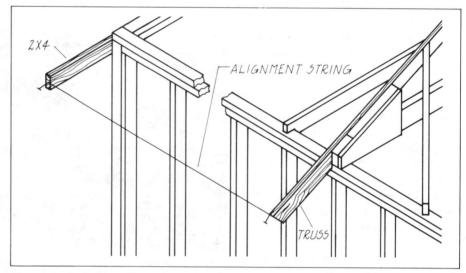

Alignment string helps position trusses, so ends line up. Attach string to first truss and stretch to 2x4 set at same distance from the wall.

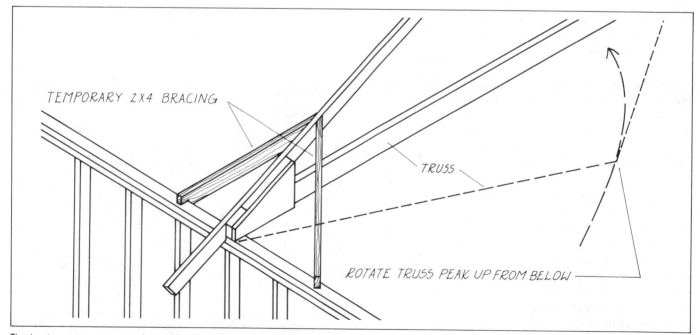

The best way to put trusses in position is to lift them onto the wall, then rotate the peak up. Temporarily brace truss at each end with 2x4s.

whole structure into a rigid unit. Since there is no ridge member to hold the trusses together until the sheathing is in place, you are depending on the temporary 1x6s to hold the trusses together against winds. Place all the trusses in this manner until you have only the gable trusses still to put in position.

Gables. Although it is not necessary for the gables to extend beyond the end walls, it is desirable. The extension gives added weather protection and improves the structure's appearance. The extended gable gives a shadow line, helps define the roofline, and seems called for to match the overhang at the side. If you want the gable to extend more than the overhang at the sides (which is not recommended) remember that the more you extend the gable, the more blocking and support will be necessary to hold the extra weight.

Sheathing. Install the roof sheathing as soon as possible, removing the temporary 1x6s as you place the sheathing. There are code variations concerning the thickness of exterior plywood roof sheathing — know the requirements for your area. Typically, ⅜ or ½ inch sheathing is used for moderate climates and ⅝ inch for areas of heavy snow. Plywood is recommended unless you are using wood roofing.

EXTERIOR FINISHING
Plywood Wall Sheathing
Plywood wall sheathing is sometimes required by local codes, sometimes not. It is always a good idea to use it if you can work it into the budget. Plywood greatly strengthens the structure, provides insulation, and offers noise resistance. Although finish-plywood manufacturers claim that their products can double as sheathing and

finish, the resulting construction is simply not as strong.

Installation. Plywood sheathing panels can be installed vertically or horizontally along the wall studs. For extra sheathing stiffness, some professionals recommend that the panels be installed horizontally. This puts the face grain across the studs. Both methods of installation require a ⅛ inch space at all panel edge joints and a ¹⁄₁₆ inch space between panel end joints. The edges run along the long side of the panel; the ends run along the short side. In particularly wet and/or humid conditions, it is sometimes recom-

mended that these gaps be doubled. The local building department can help regarding these spacing needs.

Bracing. Building codes sometimes require that horizontal joints be braced on the inside. This blocking is easy to provide, and is not very expensive. It should be included whether or not the building department requires it.

Building paper. If plywood sheathing is used under plywood finish siding (sometimes called double-wall construction), building paper often is no longer required by building departments or HUD offices. However, it is a cheap way to gain

After the walls have been framed and the sill plate has been secured to the foundation, the exterior must be sheathed. This garage is sheathed in asphalt-coated fiberboard.

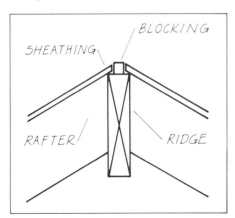

A small board installed on the ridgeboard will take up some of the space created when the sheathing is set on the ridgeboard.

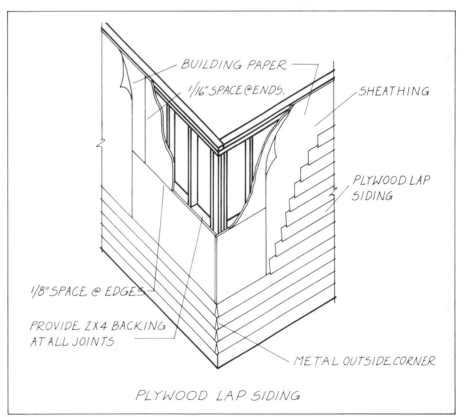

BUILDING PAPER

1/16" SPACE @ ENDS.

SHEATHING

PLYWOOD LAP SIDING

1/8" SPACE @ EDGES

PROVIDE 2X4 BACKING AT ALL JOINTS

METAL OUTSIDE CORNER

PLYWOOD LAP SIDING

2x4 backing must be provided for all nailing edges of sheathing. Sheathing is covered with building paper before plywood lap siding is installed.

additional insulation and protection from the elements, and we highly recommend its use. To install building paper, start at the bottom of the walls. Let the paper extend 6 inches below the bottom of the wall; this protects walls from water run-off. Use a staple gun or roofing nails to secure the paper. Nail it to the studs about 6 inches on center. Overlap ends of the paper by 6 inches.

Nailing. In nailing the panels to the stud wall, use 6d nails for $5/16$ inch and $3/8$ inch thicknesses. Use 8d nails for $1/2$ inch and $5/8$ inch panel thicknesses. Along the ends and edges of the panels, the nails should be spaced 6 inches on center. On intermediate studs, the spacing may be 12 inches on center. Do not line up vertical joints along the same stud in succeeding rows of sheathing. Stagger the paneling to avoid vertical alignment. Cut the panels as required to fit around doors and windows, maintaining the joint conditions described above.

Fiberboard Wall Sheathing

Fiberboard sheathing (asphalt-coated or asphalt-impregnated boards) are available in the same sizes as plywood sheathing and call for similar installation. Use galvanized roofing nails, usually $1\frac{1}{2}$ inches long with $7/16$ inch heads for $1/2$ sheathing and $1\frac{3}{4}$ inches to 2 inches for $25/32$ inch thick. All fiberboard should be nailed $3/8$ inch in from the edges and ends. Typical nail spacing is 3 inches on center at the edges and ends. Provide solid blocking behind all edges and ends. Nail 6 inches on center at the intermediate studs. Follow the individual manufacturer's recommendations for nailing and spacing between boards.

Brick Veneer

The illustration details the use of brick veneer. In this case, brick is what the name implies — a veneer, serving the same purpose as wood or any other siding. The rest of the building is constructed basically the same as before. Note that the soffit is narrower because of the extra thickness of the brick. There is no weight on the brick and it is attached to the frame wall with metal ties at each 5th course, 2 feet on center horizontally. Flashing is required at top and bottom. Weep holes should be provided approximately every 4 feet. Weep holes provide drainage outlets for any moisture that may build up in the 1

Louvers may be installed in siding to permit air circulation and prevent moisture buildup between the siding and the sheathing.

Sheathing may be installed with all edges flush with the rough openings for windows or cut back 1½ inches all around.

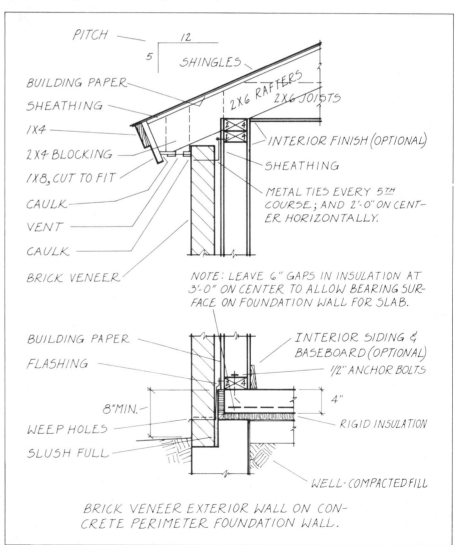

BRICK VENEER EXTERIOR WALL ON CONCRETE PERIMETER FOUNDATION WALL.

Brick veneer may be added to the exterior of a garage following the proper building steps. The brick must be tied to the garage by metal ties nailed to the studs and set into the mortar.

inch space between the brick and frame sheathing.

Windows

There is tremendous variation in window types, sizes, and installation requirements. For this reason, you should select your windows and affirm their rough opening and installation details and show them on your plans before you start building.

In general, your window heads should be the same height as the door heads, but this is not a rule. Install the windows according to the manufacturer's instructions.

A miter box with a backsaw is an invaluable aid for cutting door and window moldings to the correct angles for finish trim.

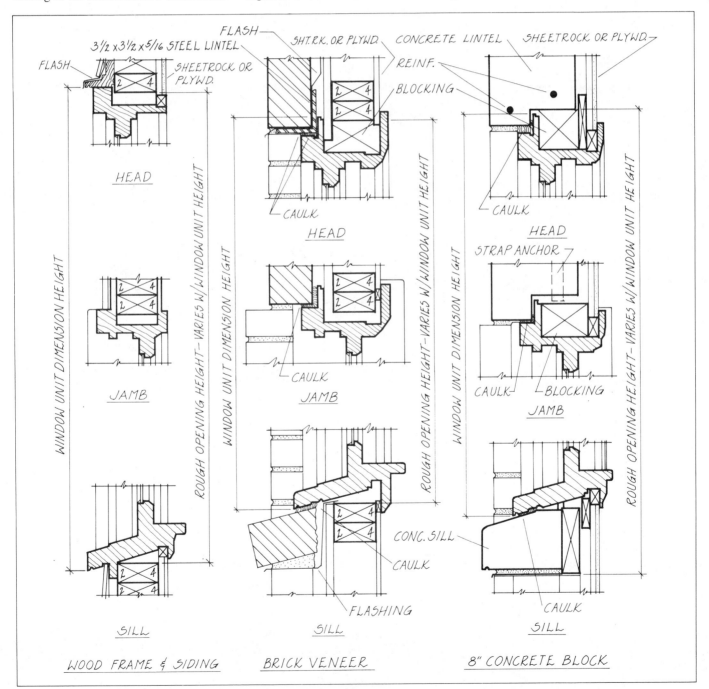

Different types of exterior finish require different types of window framing so units will fit securely and have a reasonable opening recess.

Doors

Shown are details of doors framed for siding, framed for brick veneer, and in concrete block. As in window installation, there are a wide variety of door conditions. Select your doors and note their rough framing and installation details on your plans before you start any work. Refer again to the illustration for rough framing details. It is assumed here that you will buy a prehung door and, as with windows, that you will follow installation dimensions and any special instructions provided by the manufacturer.

Planning the Overhead Garage Door

The overhead garage door, or "sectional upward-acting door", has become standard in many parts of the country. Electrically powered drive components are available for convenience in opening heavy doors, and radio-controlled activators make it possible to open the door without leaving your car. This is a welcome convenience in rainy or snowy weather, and it is a necessity for the handicapped.

This section will discuss: the compo-

nents of the overhead door; what the components do and how; how the components of the overhead door relate to your garage framing; and, what space the components require. This discussion will be general because there are many manufacturers and you should install the door according to the manufacturer's instructions. However, most of the components are similar in function and most of the installation procedures are similar, except for minor construction details.

Overhead doors may be constructed of wood, fiberglass, or metal. Wood is most

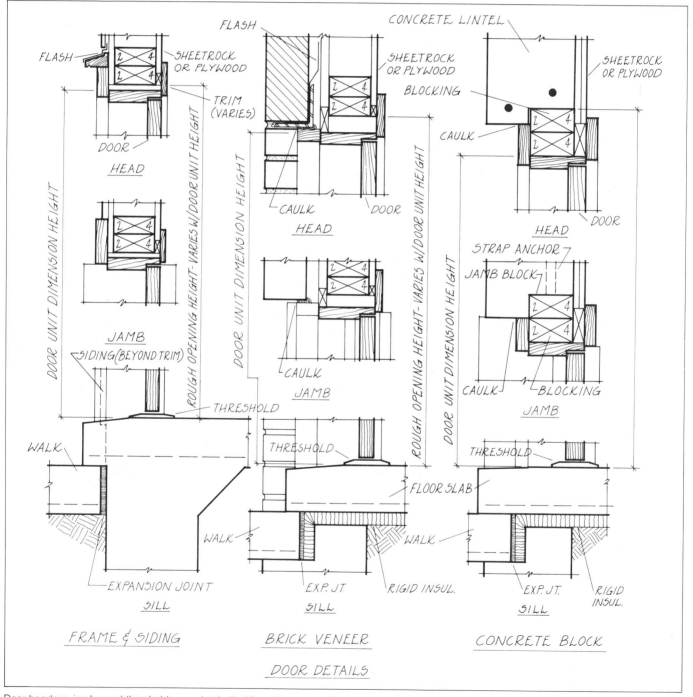

Door headers, jambs and thresholds are also built differently to meet the requirements of different exterior materials and finishes.

favored for residences and will be assumed for the following discussion and installation instructions. Overhead doors are available with or without window units. If you do not use windows elsewhere in the garage, you probably need windows in the door; if you do have windows in the garage, windows in the door are optional.

Door sizes. Garage width depends on the size of your cars and whatever extra equipment, such as washers and dryers, storage or shelves, you wish to include. Car widths, of course, vary much more widely now than ever before. There are so many car models to choose from. But, from a real estate value point of view, it is strongly suggested that you build for full-sized car widths. The suggested minimum inside width for a one-car garage is 11 feet 6 inches, with an inside length of 21 feet 10 inches. For a two-car garage, the suggested minimum width is 18 feet, with an inside length of 21 feet 10 inches. The minimum finished door width for a one-car garage would be 9 feet. The minimum door width for a two-car garage would be 16 feet.

Framing. The overhead door framing is detailed in the accompanying illustration. Select the overhead door before you

do any work, and then coordinate the framing details around the manufacturer's requirements. The framing shown should handle any of the many doors available, but exact door width, heights, and installation requirements are particular to the manufacturer.

Build the framing high enough and the frame opening wide enough to accommodate the particular door, equipment (such as overhead motor and chain drive), and trim. The manufacturer's instructions will give the space needed at the sides and top of the door as well as the space needed for the mortar and chain drive, and will show the suggested trim. The instructions will also show or describe the blocking (wood members such as 2x4s) needed to provide as nailing surfaces for the door hardware.

Timing of door installation. You may install the door before finishing the interior or if it is convenient, particularly if the weather is bad or if you want to secure the garage for materials storage. However, you also may wait until later to install it.

Connecting the wiring. Tie the motor circuit in with the light circuit (assuming you want a motor-operated door). Conduit approved by the local electrical code should be used for the electrical line from the motor to the switch (you will need a

switch in addition to the radio control opener; the switches are similar to light switches). The conduit can be surface-

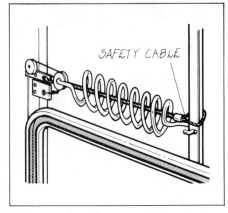

Safety cables prevent extension springs from propelling themselves dangerously if a break occurs. Use two safety cables for a door that has four springs.

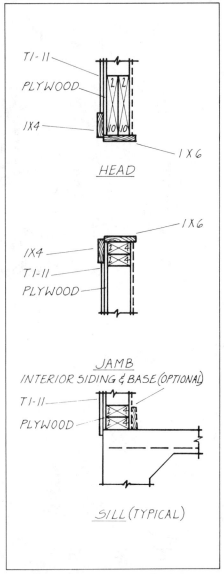

Head and jamb details must be worked out to accommodate the overhead door chosen. The sill probably will be the same for all doors.

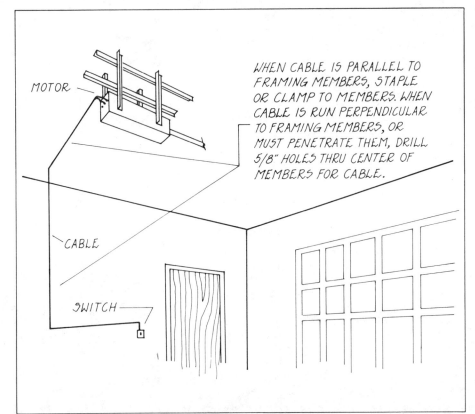

WHEN CABLE IS PARALLEL TO FRAMING MEMBERS, STAPLE OR CLAMP TO MEMBERS. WHEN CABLE IS RUN PERPENDICULAR TO FRAMING MEMBERS, OR MUST PENETRATE THEM, DRILL 5/8" HOLES THRU CENTER OF MEMBERS FOR CABLE.

Run motor switch cable like other electrical cable. If you must penetrate framing, drill hole through center of members; if members are 2x4s, put metal plates at holes to protect cable.

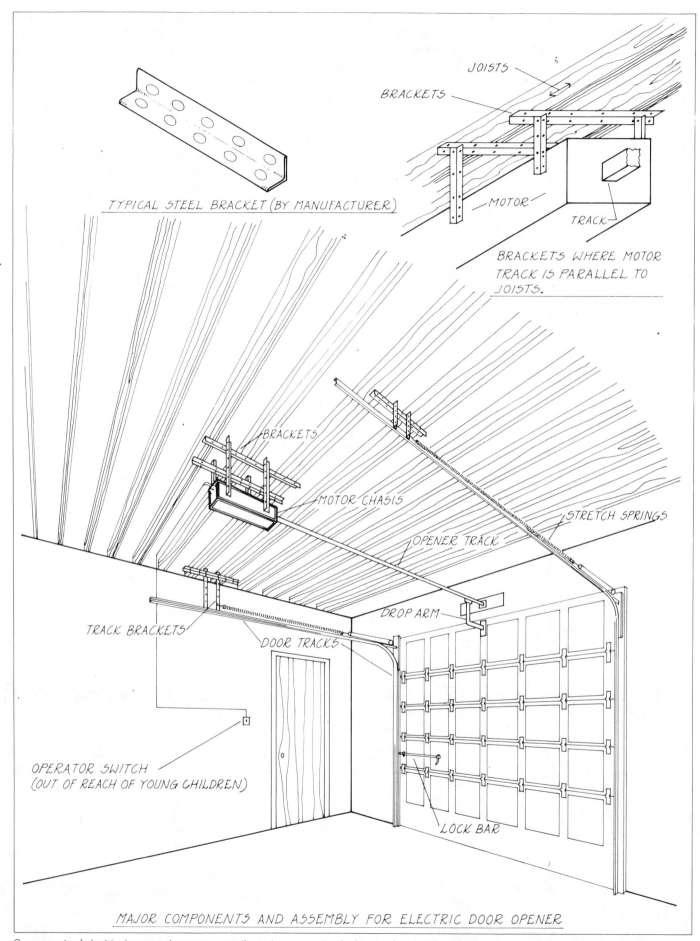

TYPICAL STEEL BRACKET (BY MANUFACTURER)

JOISTS

BRACKETS

MOTOR

TRACK

BRACKETS WHERE MOTOR
TRACK IS PARALLEL TO
JOISTS.

BRACKETS

MOTOR CHASIS

OPENER TRACK

STRETCH SPRINGS

DROP ARM

TRACK BRACKETS

DOOR TRACKS

OPERATOR SWITCH
(OUT OF REACH OF YOUNG CHILDREN)

LOCK BAR

MAJOR COMPONENTS AND ASSEMBLY FOR ELECTRIC DOOR OPENER

Components of electrical garage door opener are the motor, opener track, door tracks, stretch springs, operator switch, and the door itself.

mounted along the bottom of the ceiling joists and down to the switch, if the garage has no interior finish. Or the conduit can be run above the ceiling joists and between the wall studs to the switch, before you finish the garage interior. The switch is located wherever it is convenient to have it — usually in the garage at the entry from the house. If it is used outside, be sure the switch is built to withstand wet weather.

Radio-controlled switches. Radio-controlled units offer convenient operation. The radio-controlled units are usually about the size of small, pocket transistor radios and are often equipped with a clip so they can be attached to the sun visor of your car.

Door construction. The door is constructed in horizontal sections its entire width. These sections are butted together in tongue and groove, rabbetted (overlapped), or similar joints, but the joints are not secured together. Instead, they are secured from behind (inside the garage) with hinges that allow the sections to flex so the door can roll overhead.

The doors move by means of tracks, one at each side (jamb) of the door. The hinges at the door edge fit into the tracks using rollers that mount on the sides of the hinges. The doors are equipped with

springs that are attached to the overhead tracks: these springs act as a counter balance to the door, keeping it from dropping rapidly when it is closed. You can open the door by hand or you can install an opener. The opener consists of an electric motor and a ''drawbar.'' The purpose of the drawbar is to hold a chain that fastens to the top of the door. When the motor is engaged (by switch or radio control), the chain is pulled around the drawbar, hoisting the door. It is possible to use a 1/3 h.p. motor for a single door, but a 1/2 h.p.

motor is suggested for the double door.

The drawbar and motor may be considered a separate operation from installing the door, with one exception: you must provide framing space for the opener as required by the manufacturer (leave space when building the framing or allow the space for a later addition of the opener).

Because the tracks have to be inside so the overhead door can clear the head as it rolls above, overhead doors fit inside the garage, instead of being anchored within the door opening.

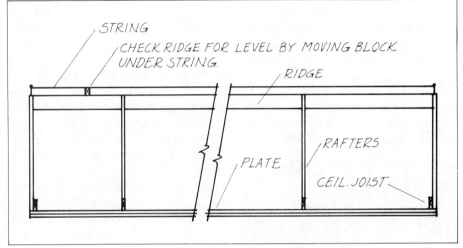

A string and a block of wood will help you level the ridge. Secure the ridge at both ends and at several intermediate points; check for level; add remaining rafters.

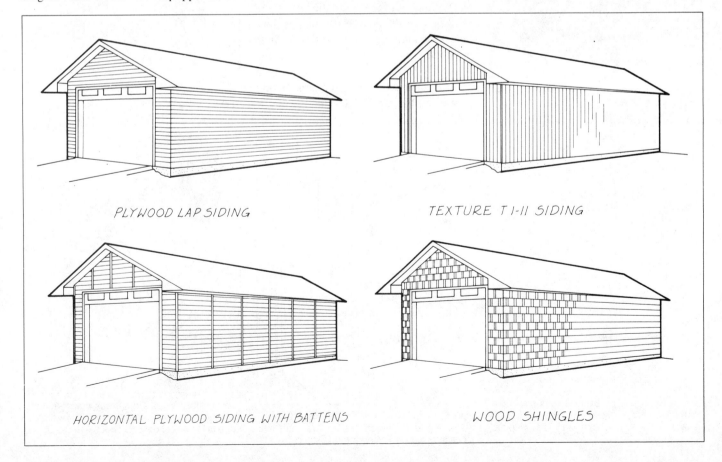

PLYWOOD LAP SIDING

TEXTURE T 1-11 SIDING

HORIZONTAL PLYWOOD SIDING WITH BATTENS

WOOD SHINGLES

SUPPLYING ELECTRICITY TO A DETACHED GARAGE
Bringing the Wiring Outside

This involves connection of the interior wiring to an exterior conduit. You can connect through the foundation wall or through the frame wall.

Electrical materials for underground use. Before bringing the wire from inside the house to outside, you must decide on the type of wire and how the circuits will be installed. Most building codes dictate that all outdoor wiring must be placed in rigid conduit from where it leaves the house to the point at which it disappears underground. It is very important that you check with your local code to determine your specific requirements. Most underground wiring can be UF cable, which is a plastic-sheathed cable designed to be buried directly in the ground. It is available in a three-wire configuration with ground. Wherever the wiring will emerge

In areas of heavy snow, electrical cables can be used around roof perimeter to help melt snow and prevent ice dams.

from the ground, rigid conduit is recommended in combination with type TW wires that have moisture-resistant coverings. When using rigid conduit, there are several types available to you: thin-wall plastic, rigid thin-wall metallic type (EMT), or thick-wall metal type. Plastic is the easiest to work with, although the method of assembly is similar for all three types. They all require a trench of at least a foot deep, in which the conduit is placed.

Adding an LB fitting. If you plan to connect through the foundation wall, junction boxes to which the conduit will be attached must be positioned over an opening on the inside of the foundation wall, so that the conduit LB fitting and nipple extend through the wall into the junction box. Always drill the hole at a point that you know will not interfere with other underground utilities and where you will have easy access from the outside.

Position the LB fitting where you plan to drill and check that the fitting will not overlap with a siding joint (if you have wooden siding; for cinderblock, see below). Drill a ¼-inch test probe to double-check your measurements. Then use a ⅞ inch spade bit to bore through.

Mount the junction box on the interior, over the hole. Then find a nipple that reaches through the wall to the box; place the nipple in the hole to test its position. Screw the nipple to an LB fitting. Adjust the conduit so that it will run from the fitting to the trench. Remove the nipple and LB, connect them to the conduit and then insert the nipple back into the wall.

Now strap the conduit to the outside foundation. Caulk all around the nipple. Inside the house at the junction box, attach the nipple using a star nut and then screw a plastic bushing onto the nut.

How to install a box into cinderblock. Choose a block in the second course down from the siding. Place the box next to the cinderblock and outline its shape with tape. Drill 6 to 8 holes into the central, hollow portion of the block, using a ½ inch masonry bit on a ⅜ inch drill. With the holes completed, use a ball-peen hammer and a cold chisel to knock away any material left between the holes. Then chip out the edges of the box opening until it will hold the box.

Outline box area with tape. Drill holes through block with ½ inches masonry bit on ⅜ inch drill. Tap out material left between holes.

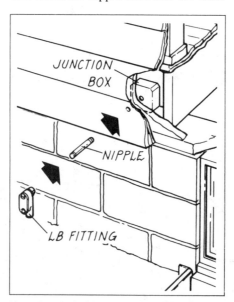

Find hole location by using a reference point accessible from both sides of the wall. The hole must be at least 3 inches from joists, sill plate, and flooring.

Mount box on inside wall over the hold. Choose a nipple that will reach through wall and into junction box; screw nipple to LB fitting.

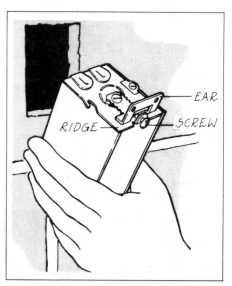

Loosely insert screws into fixture mounting tabs of the box so mortar will not get into screw holes. Edge of the box should be about 1/16 inches out from wall.

If the cinderblock has been stuccoed over so that you cannot find the seams, make a test hole using a star drill. When your test probe finds the hollow center — an area where the drill does not meet any resistance — insert a stick into the hole. Tap around to find each side of the hollow. Now you can follow the steps above

to create a box midway between the sides.

To install, loosely insert screws into the fixture mounting taps (so mortar won't get into the screw holes). Adjust the ears of box so that its edge is about 1/16 inch from the wall. (You will later add the coverplate gasket to form a tight seal all around the ridge.) Slide the box into place and

mortar it in. Use a putty knife; be sure that the gap between the box and the edge of the hole has been completely filled. This protects the unit from wet weather conditions. Once the mortar has dried, you can take the screws out of the mounting tabs.

Thread the wires through the junction box, from the interior to the exterior, through the conduit. The procedure is similar for wire exiting through an eave or through a frame wall.

Exiting wire through an eave. The job will go faster if you have a helper to hold the various components. Position the assembled outdoor box, corner elbow, section of conduit, and nipple, against the soffit board. Keep the conduit next to the house siding and place the box between 2 rows of nails in the soffit. Using the box as a template, mark on the soffit a cable hole and then indicate the holes required for mounting screws. Use a 3/32 inch bit to drill holes for 3/4 inch No. 8 screws; use a 1 1/8 inch spade bit to drill a hole for the cable.

After fishing the cable from an indoor circuit and out through the cable hole, fasten on a two-part connector. Screw the box to the connector. The shape of the connector may make it necessary, for you to enlarge the cable hole with a rasp before you are able to line up the mounting tabs on the box with the screw holes. Mount the box on the soffit. Now fasten the conduit to the wall and the nipple to the soffit board. Bend the conduit as necessary to run it into the trench. If feasible, run the conduit alongside a downspout; it will be visible.

Digging the Trench
Once the wire has exited from the house, you must dig the trench. Always stake out the trench, keeping it as straight as possi-

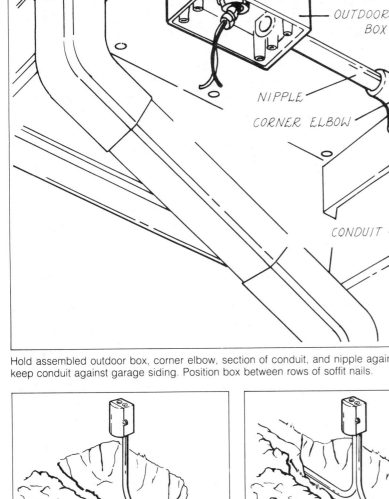

Hold assembled outdoor box, corner elbow, section of conduit, and nipple against soffit board; keep conduit against garage siding. Position box between rows of soffit nails.

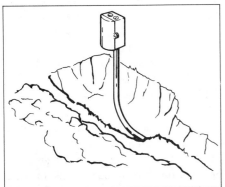

For end-of-run box, dig trench for cinder block 4 inches high. Extend conduit 8 inches above ground; fasten box with threadless connector.

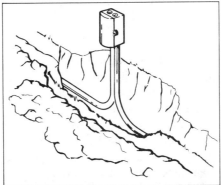

For middle-of-run box, install as for end of run, but use box with 2 conduit openings. Fasten second conduit same as first.

Lower cinder block over the box. Fill in core with gravel. Fish wiring through the conduit and then install receptacle.

ble. If it has many turns or angles, your assembly will be more difficult. If you use plastic conduit, the trench should be 8 inches wide and a minimum of 12 inches deep. If the conduit will go under a sidewalk, dig out both sides to a sufficient depth. Pass a length of conduit under the walk, pushing or tapping it through the space you have dug. You can then connect up the other pieces of conduit. When the conduit surfaces for connection, bring it up inside the cell of a concrete block. This will act as a brace, and as a solid base. Always try to make the wiring connection at least 12 inches above ground level. If the circuit continues, put the conduit back through the block and continue underground. Fill in the block cells with dirt.

RUNNING ELECTRICAL CABLE

Never attempt to do any electrical work while the electrical power is on. Cut off the main power switch before beginning to work. We are assuming here that you will be extending wiring from the house. Evaluate your existing usage to find out if a new circuit is needed. In some cases,

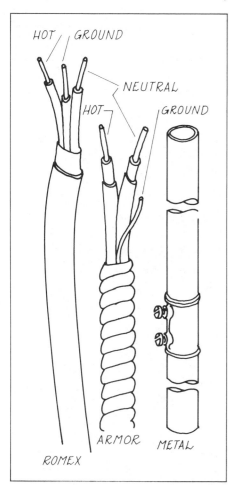

HOT GROUND

NEUTRAL

HOT

GROUND

ARMOR   METAL

ROMEX

Romex is no longer allowed by most codes. New cables are armored and metal conduit.

you may have a circuit available. We suggest that you let the subcontractor handle the actual hookups (unless you have had previous electrical experience). You still will be able to save money by carrying out the repetitive work of stringing cable, cutting openings or mounting boxes.

What Type of Cable Should You Use?

Romex. There are several types of cable, but the one you will be most concerned with is called Romex cable. Romex cable consists of three wires: one wire is the ground wire (green or bare), another is the hot wire (black), and the third is neutral (white). The wires are individually wrapped; the three are then covered with a paper wrapping. Finally they are all sheathed with plastic. The first caution about Romex cable is that it is not accepted by all local codes — your electrical contractor can advise you about the code and how to meet it. If Romex is not acceptable, you may have to use BX cable or run your wiring through conduit, which is discussed below.

Romex cable is popular because it is simple to work with; the flexibility of it allows you to run it easily wherever you need it. The size of the wire is stamped along the outside of the cable, as are designations for use areas. "T" cable adapts well to a variety of temperatures. "TW" is used in damp settings. "NM" cable is for use indoors in dry settings.

Aluminum wiring. We do not recommend using this type of wiring, even if the local code allows it. Aluminum wiring does not have a good track record, and electricity is not something to gamble with.

BX. This cable is enclosed in a flexible metal casing. The black hot and white neutral wires are paper-wrapped; there will also be a green ground wire or a bare ground wire. BX flexes to turn easily around corners. It is good for use in dry indoor locations, especially in areas where wires need protection from nails for later carpentry or decorating projects.

Conduit. In homes with very thin walls, cable is usually enclosed in galvanized steel pipe called thin-walled conduit. In some areas, conduit is required when more than 3 feet of BX cable is exposed in a basement. When using conduit, run insulated single-conductor wires — black, white and green — through the

pipes. Do not try to run plastic or BX cable through a conduit. A conduit can hold a number of cables. It comes in a variety of diameters and in 10-foot lengths. Couplings and joint pieces make it adaptable to most settings.

Anchoring and Supporting BX or Romex

When the cable must go in a direction perpendicular to wall studs, ceiling or floor joists, drill ⅝-inch holes through these members. When you need the cable to run parallel with framing members, clamp it with metal clamps (the clamps are available at electrical supply houses); or, you can use electricians' staples, which are flattened to protect the cable. Tap the staples around the cable lightly, being careful not to puncture the cable or press into the cable. Cables are most often secured with staples because this is the *fastest* way; however, the *best* way is to use clamps.

The ⅝-inch holes in framing members may be drilled with a power drill or with a hand drill (brace and bit). Cables strung through framing members are supported by the members themselves. When clamping or stapling cable parallel to framing, the wire should be supported every 4 feet or less, and not more than one foot away from metal boxes that house convenience outlets or switches.

Precautions when drilling through 2x4s. There is a code precaution required by the National Electrical Code that requires special attention. When you drill through small members, such as 2x4s, you are required to cover the front edge (the edge that faces the finish material) with a metal plate. This is necessary so that you do not hit the wire with the nail when you (or others) nail finish materials over the members. The metal plates are available at electrical supply houses and come with spikes on them so they can be hammered to the studs or other small members. The rule is that the plates should be used wherever the drilled holes for cable are less than 2 inches from the finished surface. Obviously, you do not need to use the metal plates on joists, since — when the holes are drilled in the center — there will be more than 2 inches between the cable and any finished surface in which nailing might occur.

Using furring strips for perpendicular alignment. If you are unable to drill framing members when you are stringing cable perpendicular to the members (such as in the attic, where insulation may get in the way), you can first nail a furring strip (typically a 1x3) perpendicular to the members and then attach the cable with clamps or staples. However, these furring strips interfere with surfacing materials such as sheetrock or paneling. In such cases, your only alternative is to reroute the cable where it will not interfere.

How to Use Conduit

As mentioned earlier, you may be required by the code to use conduit. The code will also specify which kind of conduit you need to use, typically electrometallic tubing (EMT), or Type AC armored cable. Both kinds of conduit are strung in about the same manner as BX or Romex. Run it through the framing members if the direction of the wiring is perpendicular to the framing; hang it with clamps or staples

if parallel. The clamps or staples should be no less than 4½ feet apart. Space a support no more than one foot from all boxes. Have the electrical subcontractor install a run of conduit to show you how it fits to the boxes.

Another way to run conduit perpendicular to framing is to notch the framing enough so that the conduit will be flush with the face of the framing. Then cover the conduit and notch with a metal plate, as described for BX and Romex.

Bending conduit. It would be best to have the contractor show you how to work conduit where a corner must be turned, because bending conduit requires the use of a hickey conduit bender. The hickey

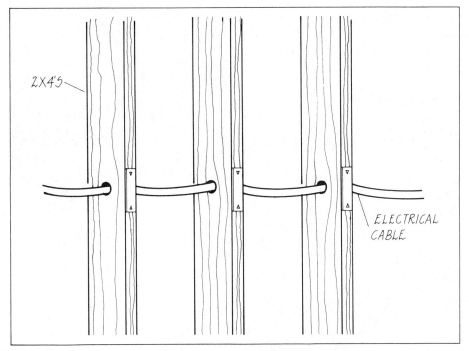

If you must run electrical cable, through framing members, drill ⅝ inch holes for the cable through the center of the members. If the members are 2x4s, protect the cable with metal plates.

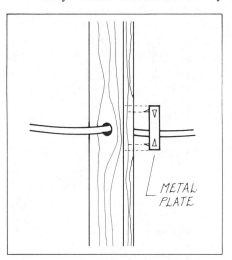

Metal plates protect cable path in framing. Use these plates even if not required by code.

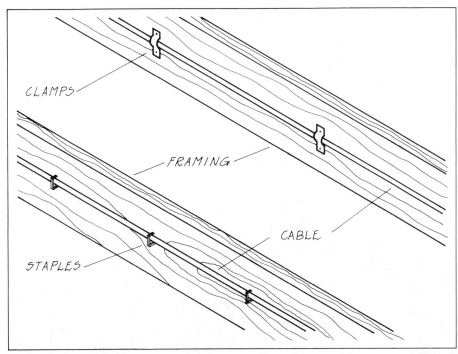

Cable run parallel to framing may be stapled or clamped to members. If you use staples, tap them lightly over the cable or they may damage the plastic skin. Clamps are a better method.

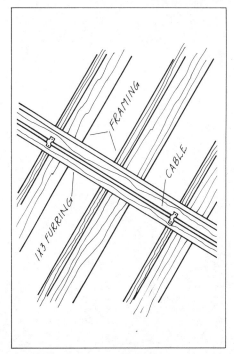

Cable may be laid over 1x3 furring strips in attics or where space is not a problem.

conduit bender is a simple tool shaped roughly like a "T", except the top of the T is curved and has a clamp attachment. The leg of the T (handle) is about 30 inches long. The procedure is a fairly simple one:

(1) attach the conduit through the clamp attachment;

(2) put the conduit on the ground or floor;

(3) with your foot on the conduit, push the handle down, bending the conduit.

Stringing the Wiring Through the Conduit

The next job is to get the wiring through the conduit. Make sure your wiring conforms to the local codes, and that they are color-coded in the standard colors: green or bare for ground wire, black, and white (and red for four-wire circuits). Always use a ground wire. Ask the electrical subcontractor to check your wire before you run it through the conduits. For short runs (several feet), you can simply push the wire through.

"Fishing" the wire. For larger runs you will have to "fish" the wire. Fishing refers to using some wire stiff enough to push through the conduit by itself. Then you hook the more limber circuit wires to the fish wire and pull the circuit wires to the box. Watch the electrical subcontractor "fish" one run of conduit; you can then do the remainder of the work.

The "fishing technique" is often used when moving circuits around, adding to

them, or extending existing circuitry to new construction. There is no magic to the fishing technique, just common sense and patience. In general, extending electrical service from an existing house to some new space, like a converted garage, is a physically simple matter. To get through old walls, all you have to do is drill the holes to string the cables or conduit and wiring. But you are well-advised to do the work under the supervision of an electrical subcontractor. We suggest that you let the electrical subcontractor make the final hookups. (In many areas, this is what the codes require.) Always have the system inspected by the appropriate officials.

Mounting the Boxes

Your electrical plan should pinpoint the locations of all the metal boxes for outlets switches. Then you can run the cable conduit to them.

The boxes are mounted either by nailing them directly to the framing (they come with holes in them for that purpose) or

A special bracket must be used on some junction boxes. It screws on after wiring.

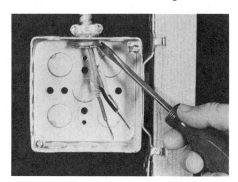

When you have run BX cable to a junction box, secure with the two part cable connector.

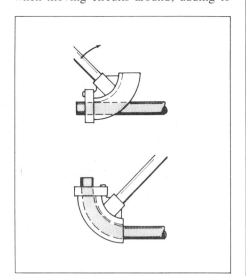

A tubing bender, commonly called a "hickey," shapes and bends thinwall tubing. The hickey comes as curved portion and you provide a length of pipe for a handle. If nonmetallic sheathed cable can be used, don't use thinwall tubing (electrical metallic tubing-EMT).

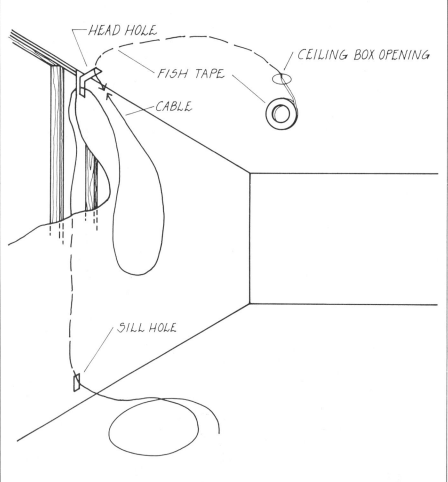

To "fish" wire through walls, cut holes above sill and ceiling. Run tape down from above to sill hole, connect cable, and pull it up. Repeat process from fixture box in the ceiling.

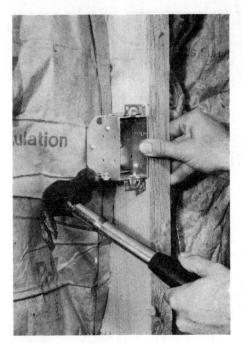

If the box is small enough, a junction box may be nailed securely to a stud.

by attaching them with metal framing devices. The metal devices may be part of the box itself or they may clamp to the box. The metal devices give some latitude in the placement of the box. For example, you may desire to have a light switch closer to the door jamb than the normal positioning of the wood framing would allow. The metal framing device then would permit you to move the box closer to the jamb than would be possible with the existing framing. All electrical supply houses carry these framing devices. If you have had no experience with electrical work, you will benefit by having the electrical subcontractor show you how to mount the boxes — or have him mount the boxes so you can string the cable to them.

ROOFING THE GARAGE
Installing Plywood Roof Sheathing

Both roof sheathing and wall sheathing must be exterior grade plywood. Install roof sheathing as you would wall sheathing. Check the building code for thickness requirements. Place the sheathing flush with the edges of the rafters. This means the sheathing will butt the 1x8 fascia board, and the fascia board will be installed flush with the top of the sheathing (see illustration). Run sheathing to the top of the roof, both sides, to reach just past each side of the top of the 2x8 ridge member. This will leave a small space between the roof sheathing sheets that meet at the ridge — a little over an inch. Cut a 1x2 to fill the space flush with the sheathing edges.

The plywood sheets can be installed as 4x8 foot panels, but they must be staggered so that the joints are at least one rafter apart. Start with half or third panels, alternating with full ones. The grain of the exposed plies should run horizontally across the roof. Use 8d hot-dipped galvanized nails every six inches at the ridge, valleys and rakes, and every 12 inches along the rafters. Leave ⅛ inch between panels to allow for expansion.

Alternative material: Spaced slat sheathing under wood shingles. For roofs on which wood shingles will be applied, open sheathing is suggested. This means that gaps of 1½ to 2 inches are left between sheathing boards. This allows better ventilation and drying of the wood shingles from below.

Roofing Felt Underlayment

Even if your building codes permit roofing felt to be omitted if sheathing is used, we recommend it because it is a relatively cheap way to buy extra insulation and weather protection.

Start at the eaves and lay No. 15 felt, letting the succeeding pieces overlap by about a foot. Nail the felt with roofing nails or staple it. Use only enough nails or staples to secure the felt until shingles are laid. Lay one layer over the ridge; overlap felt ends by about 6 inches. Where the felt overlaps, put on a coat of roofing cement from the edge up to about 6 inches. Position end laps in succeeding courses at least 6 feet from any end laps in preceding courses. At hip and ridges, place the felt so it covers the hips and ridges from both sides and laps by 6 inches. If the roof meets a vertical surface, extend the felt up the surface by 3 or 4 inches.

Valleys. First lay all No. 15 felt horizontally over the decking, letting it lap the valley about a foot in each direction. Secure it with roofing nails. Then lay an 18-inch strip of roll roofing vertically down the valley, face down. Center the felt over the joint. Insert just enough roofing nails to hold it in place, after you have coated a 3-inch band (under the edges) with asphalt cement. Next, lay a 36-inch strip of roll roofing face up, centered vertically down the valley. Secure it with roofing nails, after coating the underside with a 1-foot band of asphalt cement at the edges. Now install the shingles. Typically, leave about 6 inches between the shingles at the top of valley, narrowing by ⅛ inch per foot toward the eave. An alternative, growing in popularity, is to let the shingles overlap several inches at the valley. Then trim them so they butt neatly.

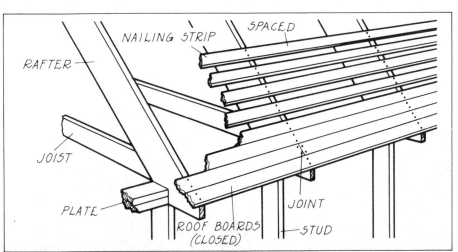

Roof boards under wood roofing may be spaced tightly together (at bottom), but many original wood roofs are nailed to spaced nailing strips, or "slat sheathing," (upper).

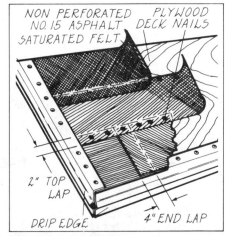

Place the first strip of underlayment at the eaves and overlap with the next strip by 2 inches. Seams overlap by 4 inches.

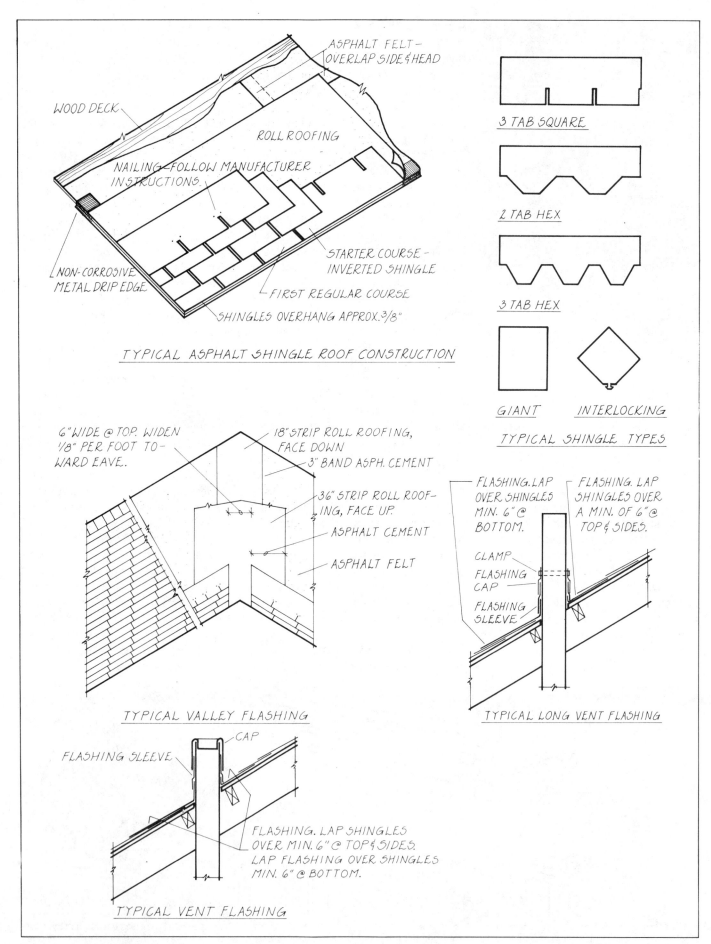

ASPHALT FELT—
OVERLAP SIDE & HEAD

WOOD DECK

ROLL ROOFING

NAILING—FOLLOW MANUFACTURER
INSTRUCTIONS.

STARTER COURSE—
INVERTED SHINGLE

FIRST REGULAR COURSE

NON-CORROSIVE
METAL DRIP EDGE

SHINGLES OVERHANG APPROX. 3/8"

TYPICAL ASPHALT SHINGLE ROOF CONSTRUCTION

3 TAB SQUARE

2 TAB HEX

3 TAB HEX

GIANT   INTERLOCKING

TYPICAL SHINGLE TYPES

6" WIDE @ TOP. WIDEN
1/8" PER FOOT TO-
WARD EAVE.

18" STRIP ROLL ROOFING,
FACE DOWN

3" BAND ASPH. CEMENT

36" STRIP ROLL ROOF-
ING, FACE UP.

ASPHALT CEMENT

ASPHALT FELT

TYPICAL VALLEY FLASHING

FLASHING. LAP
OVER SHINGLES
MIN. 6" @
BOTTOM.

FLASHING. LAP
SHINGLES OVER
A MIN. OF 6" @
TOP & SIDES.

CLAMP

FLASHING
CAP

FLASHING
SLEEVE

TYPICAL LONG VENT FLASHING

CAP

FLASHING SLEEVE

FLASHING. LAP SHINGLES
OVER MIN. 6" @ TOP & SIDES.
LAP FLASHING OVER SHINGLES
MIN. 6" @ BOTTOM.

TYPICAL VENT FLASHING

The amount of shingle to be cut off at the edge of each course will depend upon the pattern (4, 5, or 6-inch, most commonly) you have chosen

Drawing in Chalklines

When reroofing over old shingles, the existing material serves as a guide for the new shingles. For new construction, however, chalklines provide the guidelines that ensure correct application of the shingles.

Horizontal chalkline, parallel to eaves. Measure and mark off the necessary distance on the roof; do this in the middle and at each end. Place one nail on the marks at each end. Stretch the chalkline between the nails and use it to check the alignment of the mark in the middle. Resnap the line from the middle nail to check the positions again.

Vertical chalklines. These not only are important for alignment of cutouts from the eaves to the ridge, but also for alignment of the shingles at the sides of a dormer. This keeps shingles and cutouts even, so they meet above the corner without gaps or overlaps. For long runs, snap the vertical chalkline so it falls in the center of the run. Then you can apply shingles to the right of the line and to the left. Double check the horizontal chalklines for the shingles that approach the ridge; keep the lines for the upper courses parallel to the ridge.

The Soffit

Any appropriate grade of exterior plywood can be used for the soffit. The soffit is cut to fit between the 1x8 fascia board and the siding. Nail the soffit to the flat edge of the rafters and the 2x4 blocking as shown in the illustration. You can buy ready-made soffit vents or you can install a continuous vent. Soffit vents are needed to provide ventilation and prevent condensation. The number of vents and the size of the vents you need depends on the size of your garage or house addition and the way you have it insulated. The building department can tell you how many vents you need and what size they need to be, or you can simply build a continuous vent like the one shown to assure enough ventilation.

Shingling Materials

Asphalt shingles. This is the most commonly used shingle. It consists of an asphalt-saturated base with a coating of weatherproofing asphalt, covered with a surface of colored ceramic granules that protects the asphalt from the sun. Asphalt shingles are currently produced as long,

three-tab units. The shingles have a sealant strip which, located out of sight on the shingle, cements the shingles to bond to the surface below when the heat of the sun acts on the adhesive. This seal keeps the shingles in place during heavy winds.

Fiberglass shingles. The fiberglass shingle has gained in popularity in the last decade. The fiberglass shingle is essentially the same as the asphalt shingle; however, fiberglass replaces the organic felt base of the asphalt shingle. Fiberglass shingles are typically guaranteed for twenty years versus a fifteen year guarantee for the organic base asphalt shingles. The two types of shingles cost about the same.

There are other advantages to the fiberglass shingle. The fiberglass mat used is stronger than the organic felt. It is less bulky but at the same time contains more waterproofing elements than shingles made with organic felt. Therefore, they absorb less moisture (a desirable feature for a sloped roof). Because they absorb less moisture, they do not expand and contract as much with temperature changes; this expansion and contraction wears out the shingles. They are lighter than asphalt shingles, making them easier to handle and install.

Fire-resistance. Fiberglass shingles offer slightly more fire-resistance than asphalt shingles. For both shingle types, however, check the fire rating of the specific shingle you are considering.

Wood shingles and shakes. Wood shingles and shakes are costly, but are very attractive. You probably would choose these for a garage only to match existing shingles on your house. This is especially true if the garage is attached.

Related Materials

Gutters and downspouts. If you intend to use gutters and downspouts, check their installation instructions before you start laying the shingles. It may be necessary to attach the gutter brackets to the rafters before placing shingles. Gutters and downspouts protect the structure's foundation. Too much water around the foundation is a typical cause of foundation problems.

Drip edges. A noncorrosive metal or vinyl drip edge is optional, but it will help protect the eaves from rotting. Roll roofing strips often are also applied along the eaves to protect the roof at exposed edges. Local weather conditions determine how important the metal drip and roll roofing are. We suggest their use because they add to the roof's longevity at little extra cost.

Laying the Shingles

It is best to install shingles during the warm months, in periods without high winds or any rain.

Exposure. The amount of shingle exposed to the elements is called the "exposure" and consists of the height of the shingle minus the distance that is overlapped by the course above. This overlap length is called the distance "laid to the weather."

Patterns. Shingles can be laid in 4, 5, or 6-inch alignment patterns. This means that either 4, 5, or 6 inches is cut off the length of the end shingle of the first course. The succeeding courses each have an additional multiple of the 4, 5, or 6 inches removed. This means that for a 4-inch pattern the first course has 4 inches cut off, the second course has 8 inches cut

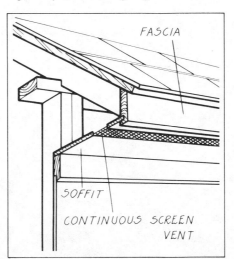 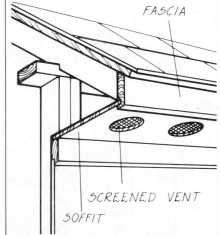

A closed soffit should have ventilation, a continuous strip or screened vent holes. The latter gives a more finished look.

off, the third course has 12 inches removed, and so on. By the ninth course there are only 4 inches left, and the whole sequence repeats starting with the tenth course. This same process is used for the 5 and 6-inch patterns, except that for the 6-inch pattern the sequence repeats every seventh course. For the 5-inch pattern, the sequence begins anew with the eighth course, because there would be only 1 inch left of the first shingle if 35 inches were removed. The full-length shingle begins courses 15, 22, and so on.

The starter strip. An economical starter strip can be made by cutting off the tabs of regular field shingles, and placing a row of inverted shingles along the edge. It is simpler, however, to buy a starter strip of 9-inch, 12-inch (or even wider) roll roofing of the same color. Whichever you use, nail it to the eaves so it projects ¼ to ⅜ inch over the eaves. Use 1½-inch to 2-inch roofing nails every 12 inches in the roll roofing, or four per shingle as in regular nailing. Avoid placing nails where they will be exposed by cutouts of the first course.

To use shingles as a starter strip, cut off three inches from the rake end of the first shingle. If using roll roofing, put a quarter-sized dab of roofing cement under the tabs of the next course of regular shingles. This is not required when using cut-off shingles, because the self-sealing strip is left intact.

Laying the first course. The first course of shingles is begun with a full shingle laid directly on top of the starter strip and lined up with the edges at rake and eave for nailing. Hot-dipped galvanized nails are essential. If possible, use roofing nails, which have flatter, oversized heads. Nails need to be long enough to go through the shingles and then penetrate the roof deck by ¾ inch.

For asphalt shingles, over a bare deck, you will need about 2½ pounds of 1¼ inch (or 3d) long roofing nails for each square of asphalt 16- and 18-inch shingles, and a few pounds of one-inch nails for the underlayment. For 24-inch shingles, use slightly longer (½ inch or 4d) nails. Use four nails per shingle. Place the nails above the cutouts, but avoid locating them where they will be exposed by the cutouts of the course above.

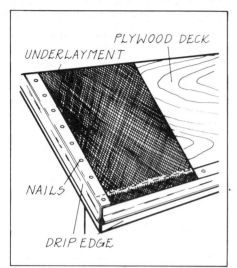

Metal or vinyl drip edges should be applied to the eaves before putting down the underlayment over the bare deck.

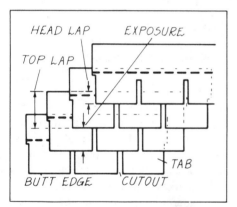

Whether the shingles are three-tab, two-tab, or have no tabs, the course above laps the course below at the top of the cutouts.

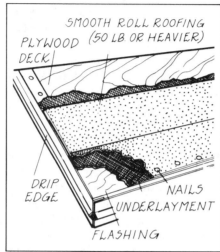

Eave flashing overhangs the drip edge and runs back on the roof to at least 12 inches inside the interior wall line.

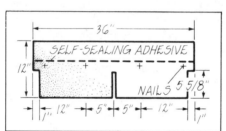

Four nails are always used. The center nails are directly above the cutouts for three tabs, or 11 inches from the outside nails.

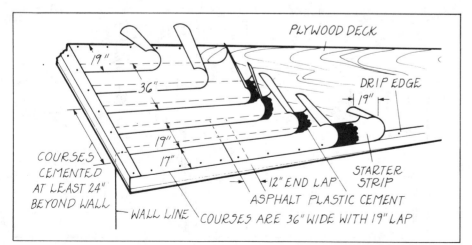

Underlayment for strip shingles on a low slope must overlap at least 19 inches to inhibit water backup under the shingles. A low slope drains slowly.

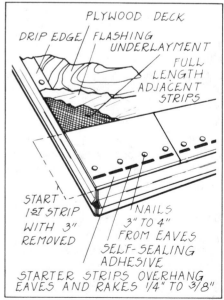

To use self-sealing shingles as a starter course, cut off the tabs and install with the cut edge at the eave line as shown.

Laying the remaining courses. Most roofers prefer to work in pyramid style, working over and up toward the ridge. To do this, lay two or three shingles of the first course, then lay one or two shingles in the second and third courses. Add another shingle to the first course (which is on top of the starter course) and another shingle to the second and third courses, and so forth. Proceed in that manner, following the chalklines.

Flashing. If your garage or house addition has heating and/or plumbing, you will have roof vents that will have to be flashed. Flashing sleeves may be of synthetic materials or they may be metal. The method of installation shown is typical, but always follow the particular product instructions to insure your material's guarantee.

Guarantees. Roofing building materials are expensive and the purchase of them should include a guarantee of their performance for your protection. The manufacturer, to protect himself, will often include his installation instructions somewhere on the product or as a handout. Be sure you get these instructions and fol-

low them to insure that your guarantee is in effect.

Installing Plywood Siding

Plywood panel siding. Plywood panel siding may be installed horizontally or vertically. One sample installation is shown. There should be a 1/16-inch space between all panel edges and ends. If plywood sheathing of 1/2 inch (or thicker) is used, the siding joints do not have to occur at the studs. If no sheathing is used, the siding joints must be backed by studs.

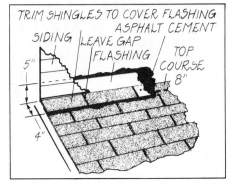

Flashing here fits under siding and over shingles, covered by glued-on cut shingles.

Asphalt roofing cement is used to adhere loose shingles, to seal flashing and fill small holes.

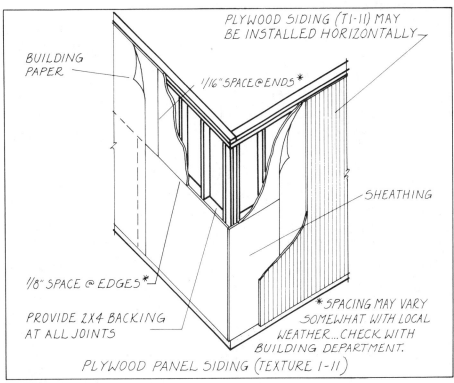

Plywood siding usually runs vertically and is applied over sheathing covered with building paper. Check all building regulations before applying siding.

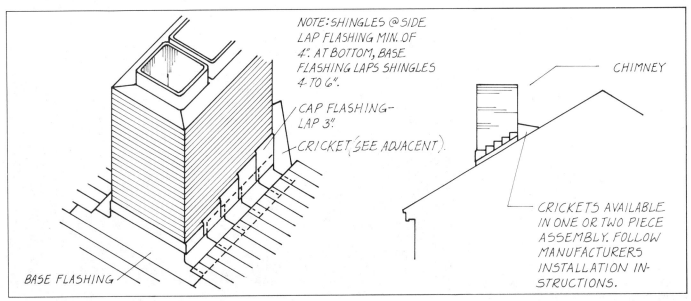

Stepped flashings cover the space between framing and a chimney. Base flashing fits under shingles, and cap flashing overlaps the shingles.

Siding Joints

The 3 common joint methods are the vertical batten, the vertical shiplap, and horizontal joint (flashed). These are shown below, and a typical corner joint for plywood paneling. Vertical joints should be caulked. If joints are shiplapped or battened, caulking may be omitted. Nailing instructions recommended by the manufacturer will differ, but should be provided by each retailer. The inside corner detail shown will work for panel siding as well as for lap siding.

Lap siding. Lap siding does what the name implies: it "laps" itself similar to the way roofing shingles lap. Plywood paneling, on the other hand, is all in the same plane. Exterior plywood lap siding requires blocking behind the end joints. The retailer will often be able to provide you with this blocking, or "wedges", in precut form. Where the joints and wedges occur, the plywood edges should be treated with a water-repellant product and the vertical joint should be caulked. Nails should be spaced 4 inches on center at vertical joints. As with plywood panel siding, the joints do not have to occur at studs if used with wood sheathing a minimum of ½ inch thick. The siding headlap must be at least ¾ inch. Unless you are a really good carpenter, metal outside corners are the easiest and the neatest way to handle corners. These corner pieces are available at building materials supply stores. Detailing for an inside corner with lap siding is shown.

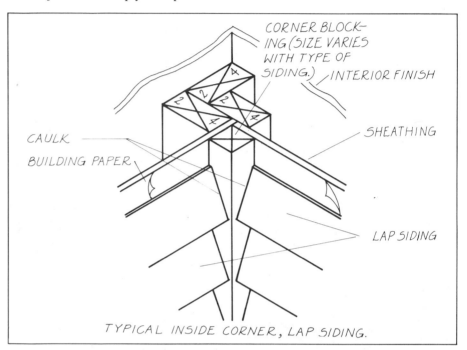

The most common siding joints are the vertical batten joint, the vertical shiplap joint, and the horizontal joint.

A corner block is needed in an inside corner when applying lap siding to provide a neatly finished corner. All edges should be caulked to provide a weatherproof seal.

Standard clapboard, lap siding is used for both traditional homes and for very modern homes such as this ranch style home where the mass of the garage balances the mass of the house.

8

Finishing the Interior

INSULATION FOR WINTER HEATING

	Minimum	Maximum
Zone 1	—	R-19
Zone 2	R-11	R-38
Zone 3	R-11	R-49
Zone 4	R-19	R-57
Zone 5	R-19	R-66

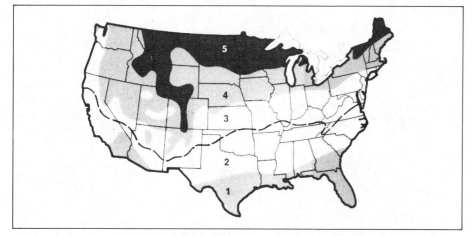

There are various types of weatherstripping and thermal threshold materials that may be used in a garage to seal out as much cold as possible and maintain a consistent interior temperature.

ADDING INSULATION

Insulation is simple and easy to install, when you know what you need. Insulation requirements vary greatly in different parts of the country. At one time, when energy was more readily available and was cheap, insulation was not given much thought. There are many older homes, nicely renovated, that still have no insulation in the walls or the crawl spaces under the house. It is now cheaper to buy insulation than to buy fuel — gas, oil, natural gas, or electricity. The point is to keep the initial cost of insulation as low as possible and pay off that initial cost as quickly as possible with immediate energy savings. So the proper type of insulation, and the right amount, applied in a manner that considers moisture control and ventilation is important to you. It will pay you to consult your building department, HUD, or the utility company for their recommendations for your locality and specific building needs.

R-Values of Materials

Generally speaking, every building material — whether it is the outside siding material, board or plywood sheathing, building paper, even the air space between brick veneer and the frame wall — resists heat flow. Synthetic insulations are just more efficient. Among the available insulation materials, there are performance differences. The scale by which to measure an insulation is its "R-value". The higher the R-value, the better the material resists heat flow. So the first step is to determine what R-value you need for your area, for the space you are building and the use you plan for it. The R-values are different for the walls, ceiling, and floor. The highest R-values are needed in the ceiling, then the walls or floor, depending on the area of the country. In some northern areas the frost line is so deep that the floors need more insulation than the walls.

The typical forms of residential insulation are batt or roll insulation and loose insulation. Generally, batts are used in the walls and under the floors; loose insulation above ceiling, but there are variations.

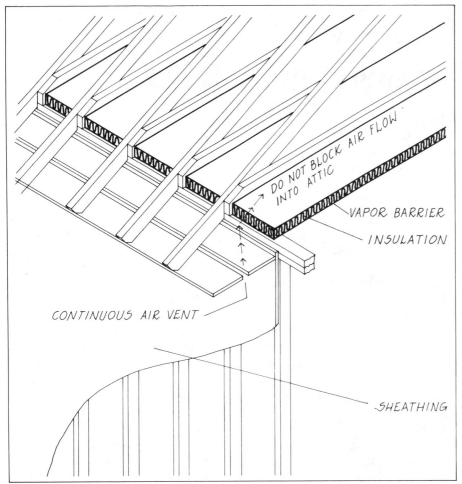

The attic insulation should come over the wall plate, but should not block the flow of air from the soffit vent. Circulation is a must to prevent condensation in enclosed spaces such as attics.

Vapor Barriers

The vapor barrier must be placed on the warm side of the wall, to prevent the warm, moist air of living or working spaces from condensing on contact with the cold wall, ceiling, or floor surface. Typical vapor barriers are made of waxed paper, polyethylene, and copper or aluminum foil. Vapor barriers are readily available at building supply houses. Most batt insulation is available with a vapor barrier foil attached to one side.

Insulating Floors and Ceilings

Insulating unfinished ceilings. Where there is no finished ceiling, batt insulation may be pushed between the joist spaces and secured to the bottom of the joists (batt insulation may be nailed or stapled). Batt insulation in 16- and 24-inch widths is available with R-values to 38 (for the coldest regions). If the insulation you are using does not come with a vapor barrier, staple a vapor barrier to the studs.

When installing the batts, fasten them under joist side, nailing through the flaps provided. Run the insulation over the plates at the exterior walls but take care not to block the eave vents, since ventilation is a necessary component in insulation of a house or garage. Take care not to

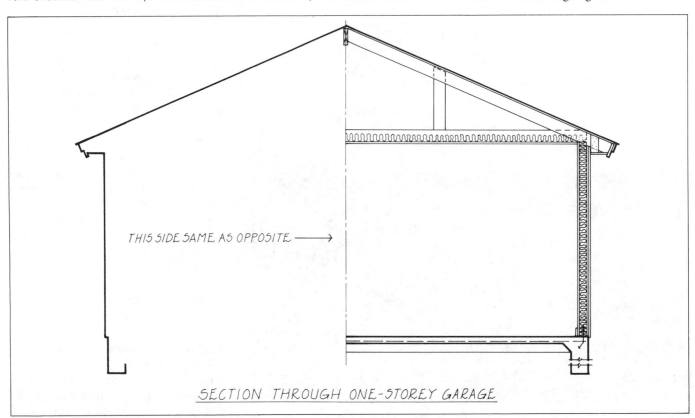

Both the walls and the ceiling of a garage should be insulated. Because heat rises, more insulation is needed on the ceiling than in the walls.

compress the batt insulation; this lowers its R-value.

Insulating finished ceilings. If sheetrock is to be used on the ceiling, secure the batt insulation flaps between the joists to give the sheetrock a tight fit (see illustration). If a vapor barrier does not come as part of the insulation, it will be necessary to add it. Cover the exposed faces of the joists (or studs) with the vapor barrier. Run the insulation over obstructions such as electrical boxes or light fixtures. However, if you have recessed light fixtures, insulation must be kept away from them (typically 3 inches away).

Insulating unfloored attics above spaces that have a ceiling. Here you may use batt or loose insulation; install it with the vapor barrier face down, toward the warm space below. If you use unfaced batts (no vapor barrier), attach a vapor barrier, such as polyethylene, between the ceiling surface and the ceiling joists. If you are adding to insulation already in place, use unfaced insulation laid right over the existing insulation.

Insulating around obstacles. All insulation should go under wiring unless it compresses the insulation to do so. Start at the eaves with the insulation and work toward the center. It may be necessary to add light blocking at the eaves against which to butt the insulation without covering the eave vents. Be sure to fill around chimneys and other framed openings — unfaced insulation is best here. Insulate around openings such as pull-down stairs or scuttle holes. Glue the insulation in place around such movable accesses, for convenience in opening them.

Insulating floored attics. Assuming you do not intend to use the attic for storage, you may lay faced batts, insulation blankets, or vapor barriers plus loose insulation, directly on the floor. If you use loose insulation, you may want to use a contractor to blow it in, or you can buy it in bags and distribute it yourself. If you do it yourself, wear a mask. Be sure that this type of insulation has been pretreated to prevent fires.

Insulating floors above unheated areas, basements or crawl spaces. These can be insulated with faced or unfaced batt insulation. If unfaced, install a vapor barrier between the floor and the insulation. If faced, install the insulation with its attached vapor barrier toward the warm side. Lap the insulation over the sill plate

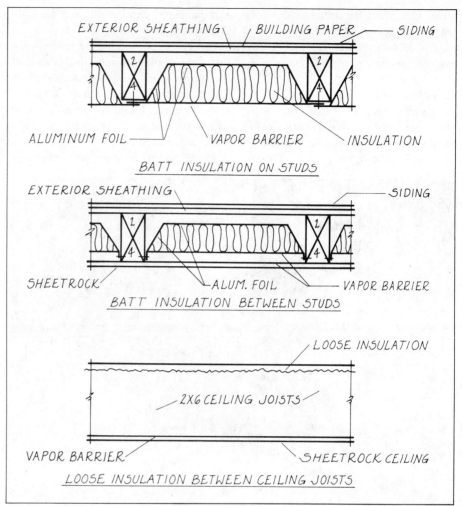

Install insulation with the vapor barrier toward the heated area. If the walls are not finished, install as shown at top. If you finish walls, attach vapor barrier to inside face of studs.

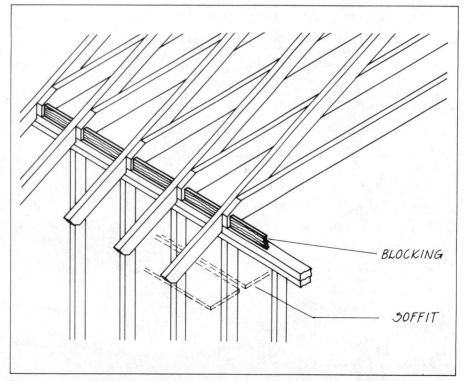

Blocking helps prevent attic insulation from spilling over the plate and onto the soffit. Blocking is especially useful if loose insulation is used.

at the sides. Once the insulation has been installed, stretch chicken wire tightly and nail it to the bottom of the floor joists. This holds the insulation in place.

Insulating Walls

As a general note, do not leave faced insulation uncovered in any area where fire is a possibility; the facings are flammable. Cover insulation in such areas with suitable paneling; check with your building department.

Particular care should be taken when installing insulation in walls because of the narrow spaces and the many openings and obstructions: doors, windows, electrical service, etc. Faced insulation is easiest to use because of the nailing flaps provided at the edges.

If you are using a sheetrock surface, you want a tight fit to the studs, so you should attach the batt insulation flaps between the studs.

The vapor barrier side of the insulation must always face the room. Secure barrier flaps to insides of studs. The flaps should be tight to the studs, with no gaps from which vapor can escape. If the vapor barrier is torn anywhere, tape it to repair it. Securing insulation between the studs leaves the stud faces bare; you may need to cover them also with a vapor barrier, depending on the type of construction and the locality; check with the building department.

Insulating around openings and obstructions. Cover all doors and windows and other obstructions. Then cut the openings out with a sharp knife, making sure the insulation around the obstructions is snug. Fill small gaps around obstructions with scrap insulation and cover these pieces with a vapor barrier. Check that the insulation fits snugly against the studs, sill, and plates that contain it.

If the wall material is not sheetrock, the insulation may be attached to the face of the studs with nails or staples. Lap the flaps and keep them smooth to provide a smooth surface nailing. Unfaced installation follows the same procedures as above. Be sure the unfaced batts are snug

Wear gloves when working with fiberglass insulation. Use a utility knife to cut lengths to fit from long rolls. Guide cut with a straightedge, in this case a piece of board.

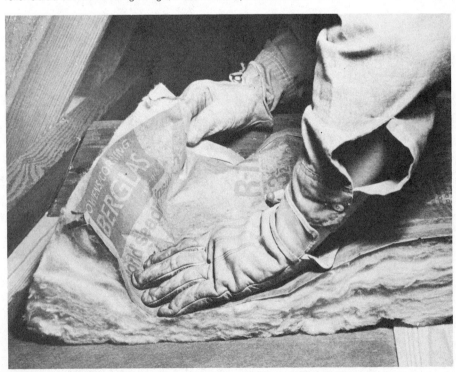

Install with vapor barrier to the warm side. Fit against wall and ceiling plate.

Attach flange of the vapor barrier to the studs. Use a staple gun.

between the studs and at the top and bottom. A polyethylene vapor barrier (4 to 6 mil is recommended) is easily installed. Secure it over all insulation and over obstructions and cut it out as you did the insulation.

Sheetrock plus pre-attached vapor barrier. It should be noted that sheetrock can be bought with a vapor barrier attached to the back. Compare the cost against the polyethylene to determine whether it is worth the labor saving.

Vapor barrier added to old house. One way to add the vapor barrier to an existing wall is to use a vapor barrier paint on the interior wall surfaces. This is not always effective, and sometimes results in mildew in the house. Some people simply concentrate on insulating the attic and floor and leave the walls alone. This may be the best you can do.

The exterior walls of old houses are especially difficult to insulate. Some people make the mistake of assuming that the difficulty is simply getting the insulation into the wall cavity. So they drill holes in the wall plates or find some other hole to pour granular insulation down into the cavity and feel a sense of well-being about solving their energy problem. Several months later they may have problems, because the uninsulated wall cavities were part of the original ventilation "system". So the problem is not getting the insulation into the walls, it is instead: what can you do about a vapor barrier when the interior surface has already been installed without one? There is no simple answer and no entirely effective one.

Ventilation
Many old houses were built without insulation in the wall cavities. Thus, there may be no soffit vents and maybe no gable vents either. When insulating an existing garage, care must be taken to insure adequate ventilation. Ventilation allows the exchange of air, reducing the possibility of condensation. You must have these three elements to avoid problems: insulation, a vapor barrier, and ventilation.

A rule-of-thumb when using gable vents is: 1 square foot of ventilation area for each 300 square feet of ceiling area (when a ceiling vapor barrier is used); or, 1 square foot of free vent area for each 150 square feet of ceiling area when no vapor barrier is used.

FINISHING INTERIOR WALLS AND CEILINGS
Using sheetrock on walls
Sheetrock, also called "dry wall" or "gypsumboard", is perhaps the most common residential interior wall material in use today. The material looks like hardened plaster sandwiched between thick paper. Sheetrock is typically 4 feet wide and comes in lengths of 4 to 16 feet. The most common size for residential use is 4x8 foot sheets. The typical thickness is ½ inch, but it can be bought in other sizes — ⅜ inch, ⅝ inch, and 1 inch.

Sheetrock can be installed horizontally or vertically. Horizontal application requires additional blocking between the studs to provide firm backing for the joints. Horizontal application of recess-edge boards is recommended for the

walls to keep seams easy to reach.

Fastening sheetrock. Nail sheetrock with 5d, 13½ gauge, 1⅝ inch flathead nails, at 6 to 8 inches on center on the walls. The nails should be a minimum of ⅜ inch from the edge of the material. We recommend that these broad-headed nails be cadmium-coated.

Drive the nails flush with the sheetrock. Then give them another hit so that there is a slight depression but not enough to break the sheetrock. You can guard against nails popping out by driving a second nail at each nailing, about an inch and a half away.

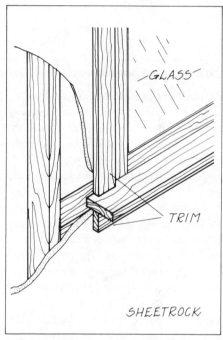
Sheetrock butts against the window blocking underneath the trim. Study the window manufacturers' literature before you install wall finish materials.

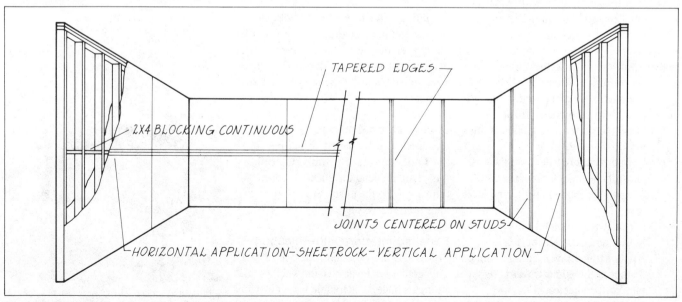
Sheetrock installs vertically on walls; on ceilings, it installs with its length perpendicular to framing. It must have solid backing at edges.

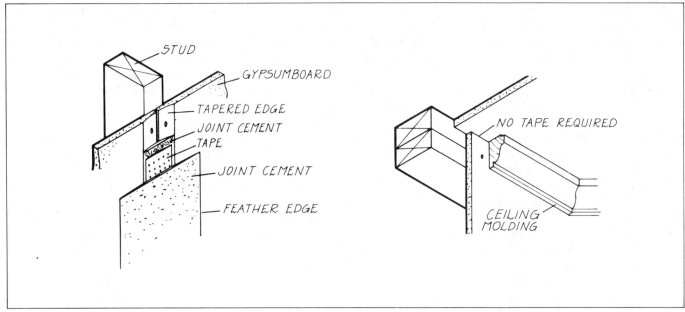

Use a standard cement-tape-cement joint finish to walls. Cover ceiling/wall joints with molding. Lath may cover wall joints in a garage.

Sheetrock around openings. Butt the sheetrock against framing or blocking around doors and windows, as shown. Electrical panels, conduits, and electrical boxes should already be in place. Cut appropriately sized holes to fit around these services.

Taping the joints. You will note that the long edges of the sheets are depressed. When the sheets are butted together, a shallow valley appears. This valley offers the means of finishing the joints smoothly. Paper tape and gypsum joint filler compound are used to fill the valleys. The paper tape, approximately 2 inches wide, has feathered edges and perforations through which the filler passes. Several coats of filler are used.

(1) Mix the joint filler with water according to the manufacturer's instructions and allow it to stand awhile — about half an hour.

(2) Apply the filler to the valley with a trowel or a spatula. Use enough to thoroughly coat the valley but not enough to completely fill it.

(3) Press the paper tape smoothly into the first layer of filler.

(4) Lay a little more filler over the tape, but still not enough to fill the valley.

(5) Smooth the joint carefully and let it dry.

(6) When it is completely dry, sand it lightly and dust off the joint.

(7) Apply a wider layer letting it thin or feather at the edges toward the surface of the sheetrock.

(8) Let this coat dry and sand and dust it off, as before.

(9) Apply the last coat, bringing the joint flush with the surface of the sheetrock.

(10) When the flush joint is dry, sand it smooth and dust it.

Finish all the valleys in this manner. Use the joint compound to fill the short sides, which have square edges instead of the depressed edges of the longer sides.

Taping interior corners. For interior corners, fold a strip of paper tape into the corner right angle. Smooth it over the filler and finish in the manner described above. There will be valleys at the corners formed by the tapered or depressed long edges of the sheetrock, so the finishing is very similar to the finishing of horizontal joints.

Taping exterior corners. For external corners, set the paper tape over the corner on a layer of filler. Place a metal angle over the paper, using filler to hold it on. Then finish out the corner as for a horizontal joint.

Sheetrock on Ceilings
Sheetrock can be nailed to ceiling joists and finished just as for walls. On ceilings it is recommended the sheets be placed at right angles to the joists. Space nails 5 to 7 inches on the ceiling.

Paneling Interiors with Plywood
Plywood is an excellent interior surface. The grades and various thicknesses and strengths make it adaptable for almost any use, from garage work areas to finished

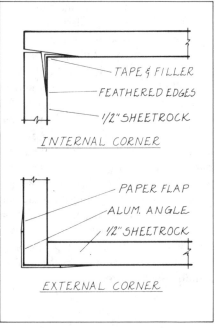

Finish inside corners with tape and cement. Protect outside, butted corners with an aluminum angle, paper tape, and seal with cement.

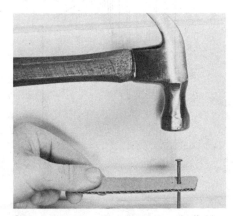

Corrugated strip over nail acts as a buffer between hammer and the nailing surface.

rooms. Interior panels are available in inverted batten patterns (with variously spaced grooves), T1-11, saw kerf (the panels are scored with a saw, simulating joints), and other patterns to meet almost any appearance and function requirement. Plain panels can also be found. Some "plain" panels come with alternating grains that look like closely joined wood boards — this makes it possible to hide the joints. Joints may be square or shiplapped.

Fastening the panels. The panels should be nailed with 4 or 6d casing or finishing nails, providing a minimum of ¾ inch penetration in the studs. Nail 8 inches on center.

Finishing the panels. Plywood interior panels may be left unfinished, or they may be stained with almost any stain or stain wax, varnish, lacquer, paint, or polyurethane finish. Penetrating stains or sealers — clear or pigmented — usually are recommended.

Installing baseboard and molding trim. After the paneling is installed, install the baseboard and molding at the floor and ceiling. There is a wide range of sizes and styles for trim. Vinyl trims are also available; these can be glued in place, if you prefer.

The trim is installed after the interior wall finish material is on the studs and after any floor covering is in place. If there is a gap between the bottom of the sheetrock or paneling and the floor, fill the gap with blocking to make the interior wall surface flush all the way to the floor. Nail the trim to the studs with light finish nails (select the nails for the particular trim when you buy it; the supplier can recommend the right nails).

You need a nail punch with which to recess the trim nails. The punch looks something like a chisel, except that the end is round to let you drive the nail beneath the surface of the wood. Then fill the holes with plastic wood or a similar finishing compound.

Corner cuts. At the corners you will have to cut the trim at a 45-degree angle. For this, you need a mitre box. You can buy cheap wooden mitre boxes, but the adjustable metal ones are better (but more expensive — consider renting a metal one). When you cut the adjoining corner pieces of trim at 45 degrees, you have turned a 90-degree corner. The trim will butt at the corners.

Professional help. All the above concerns wood trim. Vinyl trim is easier to install. Wood trim requires some skill to install — or much painstaking work and patience. Builders often use "trim men" who do nothing but install trim very quickly and neatly; if you decide to hire that part of the work out, call a builder and ask for a recommendation for a trim carpenter.

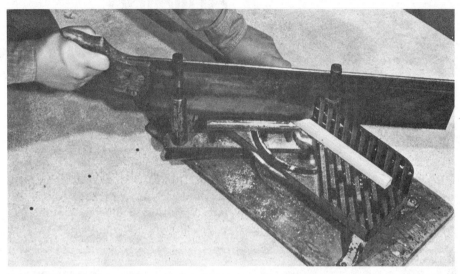

Use a mitre box to cut molding and other boards to proper angle for a neat and attractive corner joint. An adjustable mitre box allows more precise cuts for unusual angles.

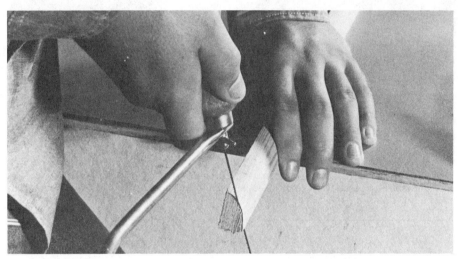

To cut molding to fit over adjacent curved surfaces, use a coping saw. This saw uses interchangeable, fine, flexible blades to allow controlled, curved cuts.

The curved cut, if properly done, will fit like this. For a finer finish, sand edges and use filler before final finishing. Practice on a piece of scrap.

9

Building
a Two-Story Garage

Because a two-story garage most often involves living space in the room above an attached garage, we will cover not only the construction, but also utility requirements. The following instructions are for a detached garage. Variations for an attached two-story will be given at the end of the chapter.

The space above the garage can provide a useful storage or living area. A two-story garage may be in better proportion to the house.

A double garage built into a duplex provides ample parking space and living space above, even on a narrow city lot.

EXCAVATION PREPARATION
Coordination of Responsibilities

Plumbing. Before any excavation work is done, you should have your plumber and electrician under contract. You will need them to coordinate the plumbing and electrical work with the excavation and concrete work in order to plan and place all lines. If they are active during this phase of the work, there should be no complaint later, when the trenches or rough plumbing are done, nor when you bring them back to install the interior fixtures or to hook up the wiring.

The plumber may know an excavator who will, in addition to digging the footing trenches and excavating for the slab, dig the sewer and other plumbing trenches. Even if such an excavator cannot be found, and you must find another person to dig the plumbing lines, have the plumber present during this phase of the operation. He should ascertain that the trenches are where they need to be. Try to get the plumber who will install the interior fixtures to also find all the subcontractors that you need to get you to that stage of construction. That way, he will be encouraged to coordinate the steps beforehand, not ignore them, while waiting for "his work". If, as your own general contractor, you decide to keep the responsibility for coordination with the subcontractors, arrange the job stages so that your subcontractors also are responsible for coordinating with each other.

It will probably be best to install the sewer line from the street at the time of excavation and foundation work. Again, if additional persons are employed to bring the sewer and other lines to the house, have the plumber who will do the inside work present. Have him direct the locations of the sewer and other lines.

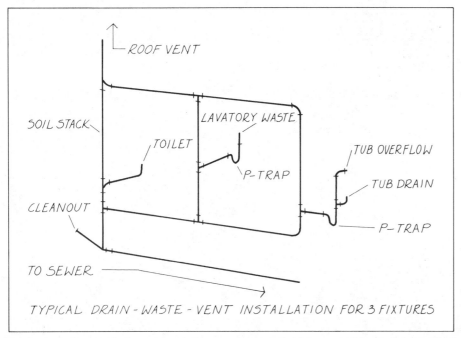

TYPICAL DRAIN-WASTE-VENT INSTALLATION FOR 3 FIXTURES

A full set of adequate drain-waste-vent pipes must be supplied for any plumbing installation. Vent pipe should rise above adjacent structures so gases and odors will not be a nuisance.

This will help assure correct placement for the rough plumbing. When the rough plumbing is in, you can say good-bye to your plumber for a while, until the framing is in. You may want him to come out when the slab is poured for a final check on the rough plumbing.

The plumbing diagram. The diagram the plumber provides, or accepts, should show the exact location of drainage stack locations, tub-and-shower recesses, lavatory bowls, kitchen sinks, and so forth. When you are doing the framing yourself, keep the diagram handy to avoid placing studs and other framing members where they will have to be removed later, when the plumbing is installed.

Similarities to One-Story Garage Construction
Reread the excavation sections for the one-story garage. The layout techniques and some of the construction procedures for the two-story garage will be the same or similar to those for the one-story garage. A little more attention is required in building the two-story garage because of the extra weight involved and the addition of mechanical, plumbing and electrical equipment.

Differences from the One-Story Garage
Floating slabs (also called ''monolithic slabs'' or ''turn-down slabs'' or ''one-piece slabs'') are not recommended for two-story garages. The accompanying illustration shows the foundation in plan and a typical section through the foundation. The depth of footings varies widely according to weather conditions across the

country — from as little as one foot in some southern areas to more than 5 feet deep in some northern areas. Footing drains may be required. These consist of tiles laid around the foundation perimeter in a bed of gravel.

Planning Considerations
Drainage. The ground adjacent to any foundation wall — one or two story — should always slope away to drain. This is particularly important in areas of frost action. In addition to good drainage, the soil under the foundation may have to be gravel or sand to aid drainage and further combat frost heave. Always consult the local codes.

Moisture protection. Under the floor slab, the vapor barrier may be polyethylene or roofing felt. If the felt is used, lap it 6 inches at the edges. The roofing felt used as a vapor barrier typically is 35 lb. weight.

Construction details and notes. Before you begin laying out the foundation, study your building plans carefully. The plans in this book are intended as a guide and should not be taken as working drawings applicable for all parts of the country. In designing foundations, it will pay you to consult a professional and/or the building department for all but the simplest conditions. In our example, the foundation wall is one inch wider all around than the comparable dimension on the floor plan. This extra space allows the exterior sheathing to rest on the foundation wall, flush with the face of the foundation wall. The exterior siding then extends below the top of the foundation wall. Note the termite shield over the top of the foundation wall. You must study your plans in this manner, planning each stage of the work carefully within the work time you have. Doing the plans yourself, or being heavily involved in their creation, will give you a head start in the actual work of construction.

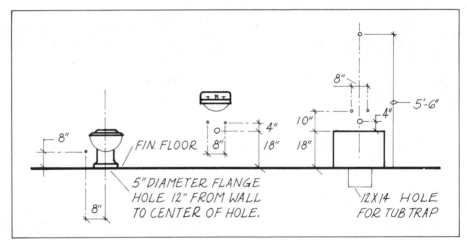

Although it is possible to install plumbing with minor variances from these standards, the placement of openings for pipes and drains shown here are best for easy hookup of fixtures.

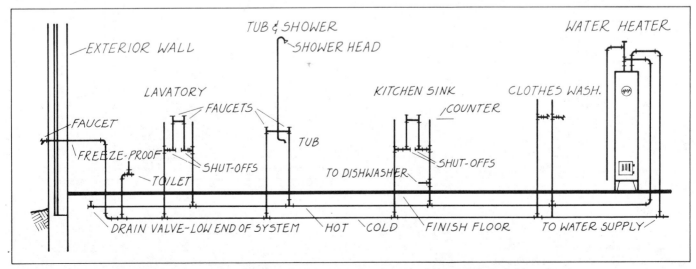

This is a layout of a hot and cold water system. In any garage living area the pipes should be well protected from freezing.

EXCAVATION, FOOTINGS, FOUNDATION WALLS

Lay out and excavate for the foundation in the manner discussed for the one-story garage. As mentioned, however, the one-piece, turn-down slab is not recommended for two-story structures. For two-story construction, separate concrete footings, foundation walls, and slabs are needed.

Type of Forms Needed

For two-story construction, it is advisable to use concrete foundation walls. You will need forms to pour the footings and the foundation. When using separate forms for slab and footing, you will need inside forms for foundation walls. The inside forms are created as for outside ones and they may be leveled by laying a spirit level across from the outside form boards.

Soil Suitability

When digging footings and foundation walls, dig down a minimum of 6 inches into firm, undisturbed soil; that is, dig at least 6 inches into bearing soil. In some areas you will strike rock by the time you get the footing to the minimum depth. If

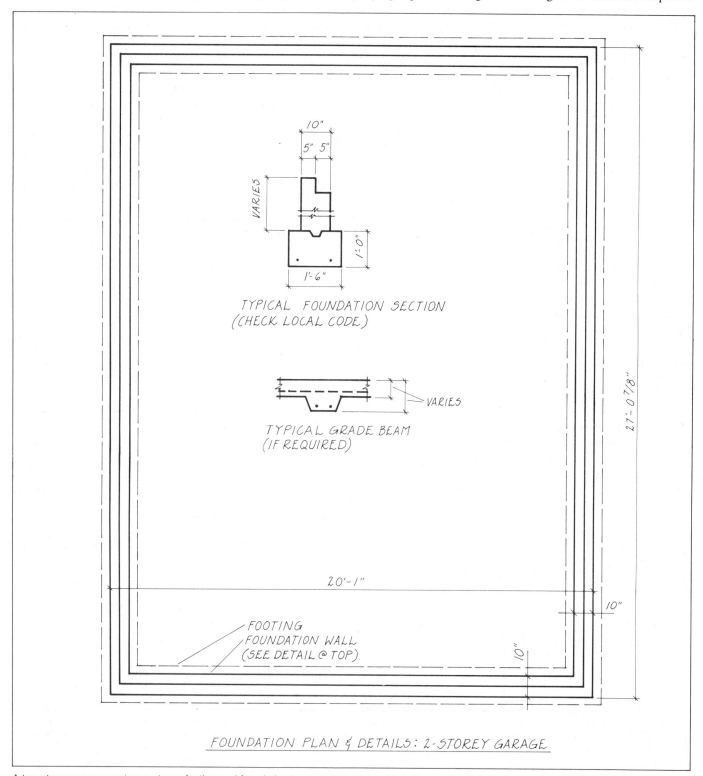

TYPICAL FOUNDATION SECTION
(CHECK LOCAL CODE)

TYPICAL GRADE BEAM
(IF REQUIRED)

FOOTING
FOUNDATION WALL
(SEE DETAIL @ TOP)

FOUNDATION PLAN & DETAILS: 2-STOREY GARAGE

A two-story garage requires a strong footing and foundation to carry the weight of the structure and distribute the load to the ground. The footing is poured with a notch along the top so that the foundation, when poured, will be linked to the footing.

you have doubts about the suitability of the soil for your project, get expert advice and/or a soil test. Whenever possible, avoid building on fill. But if you must build on fill, get a professional to advise you on what kind of fill you need and how to install it. Codes are fairly strict about compacted fill requirements.

Pouring the Footings

Place reinforcing steel bars in the footing forms before you pour the footings. If the separate footings are deep, take care to pour the concrete straight down and from a height no greater than four feet. Otherwise the gravel tends to settle, weakening the mixture. If the pour height is greater than four feet, use a chute or tube to shorten the fall. Move along as you place the concrete, laying it down in fairly thin layers; avoid mounding. Pour from the corners, working toward the center of the form.

Forming a "key". Place a wooden member in the top of the footing; this later will be taken out to form the "key" shown. The key helps bind the foundation wall to the footing.

Pouring the Foundation

Provide for any mechanical, plumbing, or electrical openings in the foundation walls. Then pour the walls. (Although you will provide the balcony and stair foundations at this time also, for simplicity of presentation, they are discussed in Chapter 11. Please refer to this chapter for details.)

It may be necessary to use a vibrator to get the concrete uniformly down into deep foundation wall forms. If so, there are two types you can rent: the external ones that vibrate the forms and internal vibrators that are immersed in the concrete. The purpose is to vibrate the concrete snugly around the steel and evenly within the forms. Do not over-vibrate. If you do, the gravel mix will settle down and weaken the concrete. Do not pour concrete in weather below 40° F. unless you have a means of bringing the temperature in the acceptable range.

Placing Sill Anchor Bolts

Put the sill anchor bolts in place before the foundation wall is set. Sill bolts are typically ½ inch in diameter. Embed them at least 6 inches into the foundation wall. Place a 2-inch washer or similar large nut on the end of the bolt to hold it firmly in place within the wall. Allow enough length above the foundation wall for the bolt to clear the sill plate and still leave enough length to put the washer and nut on it. Maximum spacing for sill anchor bolts is usually 8 feet on center with at least two bolts for each sill piece. Earthquake design in the Southwest and West requires the bolts to be closer, typically 6 feet on center. There should be one end bolt no more than a foot from each corner end.

If earthquake design is not required, steel studs may be substituted for sill anchor bolts. The studs are driven into set concrete with a power tool available at rental stores. Maximum spacing for the studs should not exceed 4 feet on center and there should be at least two studs per sill piece. Steel studs also should be placed close to the ends, with one stud never more than 1 foot from each end.

Installing Termite Shields

When the sill anchors are in place, you can install the termite shield. As the name implies, the termite shield protects against termite infestation. The shields may be galvanized steel, aluminum, copper, or other materials acceptable to the local codes.

The shields are installed continuously over the top of the foundation wall. They are brought away from the wall so that they will be embedded 2 inches into the slab when the slab is poured.

Laying the shield. As you lay the shield, the joints must be locked or soldered. Spot-soldering will not work because the gaps would make the shield ineffective. Similarly, where the shield is interrupted by the sill anchor bolts (again, if you used anchor bolts), the penetration should be sealed. Use pitch or other sealants recommended by the building department.

Rigid Insulation at Slab Perimeter

The rigid insulation shown is 1-inch rigid perimeter insulation. Because there is considerable heat loss from the edges of the slabs, the rigid insulation is necessary. It covers the top of the foundation wall that is in contact with the interior floor, and extends below grade a minimum of 6 inches.

Backfilling

Once the footings and foundation walls are in place and cured, the backfill must be carefully compacted against the walls. Before you put any soil that was removed during excavation back against the foundation wall, be sure that it is free of any organic material such as tree roots, vegetation, or any other foreign matter that would break down later and leave loose fill.

Backfilling is a good job to give to a subcontractor with a bulldozer or a buck-

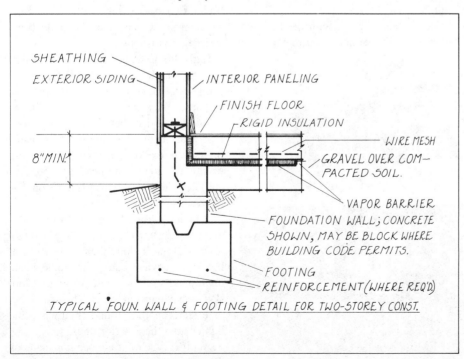

SHEATHING
EXTERIOR SIDING
INTERIOR PANELING
FINISH FLOOR
RIGID INSULATION
8" MIN.
WIRE MESH
GRAVEL OVER COM-
PACTED SOIL.
VAPOR BARRIER
FOUNDATION WALL; CONCRETE SHOWN, MAY BE BLOCK WHERE BUILDING CODE PERMITS.
FOOTING
REINFORCEMENT (WHERE REQ'D)
TYPICAL FOUN. WALL & FOOTING DETAIL FOR TWO-STOREY CONST.

This section drawing shows the footing, foundation, garage floor and base plate for the two story garage. Note the anchor bolt set into the foundation to hold the base plate of the framing.

et-equipped tractor. He can compact the fill quickly, remove the excess soil, or spread it where you want it. But do not let him get too close to the foundation wall; the weight of the dozer may cause the wall to crack. If you have a basement, the foundation wall may need additional support if the backfill against it is over seven feet high. The backfill should be brought up several inches above the top of the wall to allow for settling.

Soil Fill Underneath the Slab

The areas within the foundation walls should also be filled with soil free of organic or other foreign matter. Under the slab, the maximum depth of soil fill, under ordinary circumstances, should be eight inches. The fill should be placed in layers 4 to 6 inches deep.

The above compaction is for slabs that will be directly supported by the fill. For slabs supported at the edge by the foundation walls and between the walls with piers or postholes or other supports, the compaction of the interior fill can be relaxed somewhat. The soil fill, in this case, may be as deep as 3 feet. However, it may be more convenient to you to prepare the soil to accept the load of the slab than to build the center supports such as piers and postholes, or the like.

Soil Treatment

Treat the soil after the filling and compaction have been completed. Soil treatment (or "soil poisoning") like the metal shield, is a safeguard against termites.

Chemicals. The chemicals used — typically aldrin, benzene hexachloride, chlordane, dieldrin, DDT, lindane, or trichlorobenzene — are dangerous.

Many local areas restrict the types of chemicals that may be used. Soil treatment requires the services of a professional. The chemicals must be mixed at the proper concentrations and applied with caution by someone who has had experience. In cases where the owner provides his own water system, care must be taken not to endanger the water supply. However, as the owner/contractor, you need to know something about the kind of job to expect from the subcontractor who is poisoning your soil for you.

Placement. In basement or crawl space areas, the chemical is applied along foundation walls, and around piers. It is applied under porch and other slabs on grade. The chemical is applied within the voids of masonry foundation wall and piers.

For slabs on grade, the entire surface under the slab is treated with the chemical. Also, the area under all porches and entry slabs should be treated.

Timing. Do not allow the treatment to be made too soon after a heavy rain when the soil is wet. Care must be taken to see that the chemical stays in its intended location. Take all necessary precautions to keep people and animals away from contact with the chemical before the slab is poured.

Guarantees. Check with the building department about their requirements for

chemical soil treatment. Then, upon completion of the soil treatment, get a written guarantee from your subcontractor that the chemical has been applied at the right concentrations, and that the application complies fully with all applicable codes. Finally, the subcontractor should provide you with a written guarantee that the soil treated will be unconditionally effective against termite infestation for 5 years from the date of treatment. If there is evidence of infestation before the guarantee is up, the subcontractor is to return and retreat the entire area at no cost to the owner.

Placement of Gravel Fill, Vapor Barrier, Wire Mesh

When the soil treatment is complete, place the gravel fill. The gravel or sand (both washed) on top of the soil fill should not exceed 24 inches. (If the slab is supported at the edge by foundation walls, and between walls by piers, postholes, or other supports, the sand or gravel can be as deep as 6 feet.) Lay the gravel in 4-to-6 inch layers. It may be necessary to exceed the above fills. When this is the case, a soils engineer should be consulted. Then lay the vapor barrier. If felt is used, lap edges by 6 inches. Then place the wire mesh, supporting it on the vapor barrier at a height of about an inch, using small stones or rubble to keep it raised.

Support for Partitions

If your two-story garage will have bearing partitions, you may need a grade beam under the partitions.

Light loads. You may be able to simply thicken the slab under the partition wall when the floor slab is poured. To prepare a thickened area, you would dig an additional 4 inches deep by about one foot wide below the bottom of the usual floor slab excavation. The wire mesh would dip down for the deepened concrete, remaining about an inch from the bottom.

Heavier loads. In addition to the normal wire mesh in the floor slab, you might need steel mesh along the concrete beam. For still heavier loads, the grade beam might have to be separated from the floor slab with expansion joints. This would be, in effect, another foundation wall, but lighter than the exterior ones.

Another type of grade beam is made by digging postholes at about 4 feet on center under the partition walls and down to bear-

This garage/apartment unit is large enough to provide comfortable living space for two units. The design is both functional and attractive, offering a balcony for leisure activities.

ing soil. When the slab is poured the concrete runs into the postholes, forming little "columns" for the partition to rest on.

The two-story garage in this text does not have bearing partitions and does not use grade beams. If bearing partitions are needed due to weight requirements or design, consult your building department, an architect or a plans service. Have an expert design and explain the beams so that you can prepare for them before the slab is poured.

POURING THE SLAB
Building the Forms

There are three likely arrangements for slab forms.

Slab inside the foundation wall. When the slab edges will meet the inside faces of the foundation wall, the walls will serve as forms. Just add an isolation (expansion) joint along the inside face before pouring the concrete.

Slab overlapping foundation walls. A second situation occurs when the slab will extend beyond the inside face of the foundation wall, but not flush to the outside face of the foundation wall. The bearing (overlap) distance must be at least 4 inches. The remainder of the wall thickness takes a masonry filler all around and flush to the outside edge of the foundation wall. The masonry then acts as the form.

Slab flush to outside of foundation wall. In this case, separate forms must be built. A typical situation will use 2x10s, 6 inches of which fasten to the outside of the foundation wall and 4 inches project above the top of the wall.

Placing and Finishing the Concrete

The floor slab is poured to be at least 4 inches thick, and greater where the design loads require it. After placing the slab, screed the surface with a 2x6 while the concrete is still plastic. Then finish it as needed. A smooth, dense surface created with a trowel after floating (see Chapter 6) is best if you want to paint the surface or if you intend to tile the floor. A broom finish is good for a nonslip surface. Before the concrete becomes too hard, provide control and isolation joints. Control joints should be cut every 6 to 10 feet; isolation joints, for expansion and contraction, are needed at adjoining materials. Let the slab cure at least 7 days. Now you are "out of the ground" and ready to erect the two-story garage.

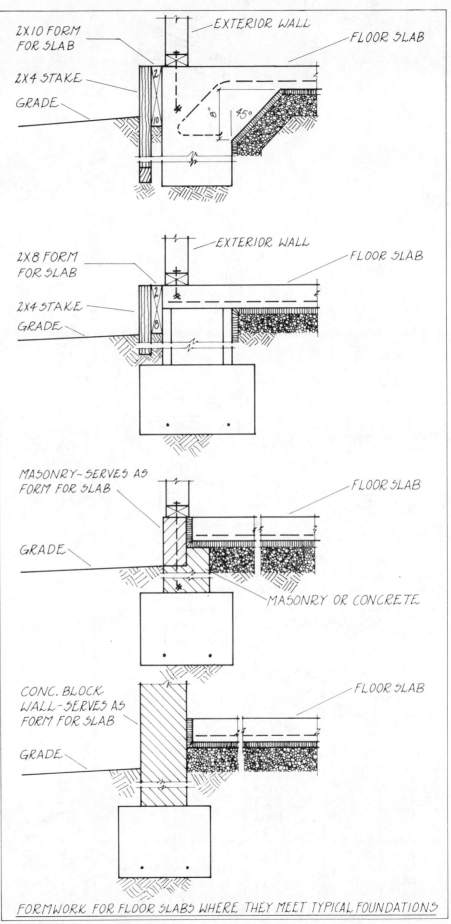

FORMWORK FOR FLOOR SLABS WHERE THEY MEET TYPICAL FOUNDATIONS

If your floor slab will be one piece with an edge stiffener (and no foundation) or overlap the foundation, you will have to build separate forms to hold the concrete when it is poured.

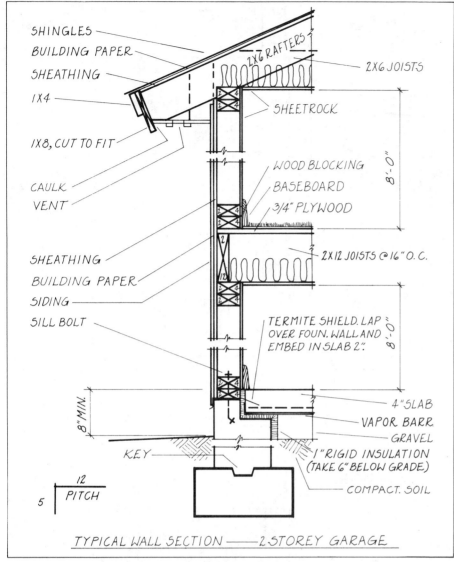

SHINGLES
BUILDING PAPER
SHEATHING
1X4
1X8, CUT TO FIT
CAULK
VENT
2X2 RAFTERS
2X6 JOISTS
SHEETROCK
8'-0"
WOOD BLOCKING
BASEBOARD
3/4" PLYWOOD
2X12 JOISTS @ 16" O.C.
SHEATHING
BUILDING PAPER
SIDING
SILL BOLT
TERMITE SHIELD. LAP OVER FOUN. WALL AND EMBED IN SLAB 2".
8'-0"
8" MIN.
4" SLAB
VAPOR BARR.
GRAVEL
KEY
1" RIGID INSULATION (TAKE 6" BELOW GRADE)
COMPACT. SOIL
12
5
PITCH
TYPICAL WALL SECTION — 2-STOREY GARAGE

This wall section shows the typical, standard construction for a two-story garage and shows construction materials and structural requirements for a well-built, stand-alone unit.

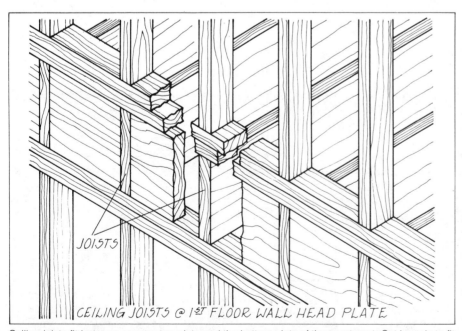

JOISTS
CEILING JOISTS @ 1ST FLOOR WALL HEAD PLATE

Ceiling joists fit between garage top plate and the bottom plate of the apartment. Cut boards to fit space between first-floor top plate and second-floor bottom plate and joists.

ERECTING THE FRAMING

Study the plumbing, heating and cooling, and electrical plans and diagrams before you start framing. Keep them handy as you frame, providing space for ductwork. Lay out and assemble the wall framing in the same manner discussed for the one-story garage. Remember that ductwork takes up more space than either plumbing or electrical work, so it must be planned for first. The mechanical plan will show you where the horizontal and vertical duct runs are. In the case of the two-story garage, the mechanical planning should be very simple. The plans usually will call for an extension from your existing furnace and should be based on the manufacturer's requirements for that unit. The horizontal ducts can be run across or between the ceiling joists. Round ducts are simple and are typically used for residential construction. See Chapter 14 for instructions on extending heating ducts.

The ductwork from the furnace will require coordination with the framing planning.

First-floor Joists

The real framing difference between the one and two-story garage begins with the floor joists for the first floor. You need 2x12 ceiling joists at 16 inches on center. You could span the distance with 2x8s, but a springy, creaky floor is not desirable. Install the 2x12s as shown, providing a continuous 2x12 header around the wall plate. Next, install the flooring, in this case ¾-inch exterior plywood. The plywood should be installed according to the manufacturer's instructions, paying particular attention to the required spacing between the edges and ends similarly to the requirements noted earlier for wall sheathing and siding. Stagger the plywood joints.

Ceiling Joists, Rafters, Eaves

The second floor ceiling joists, the rafters, and the eaves are constructed as for the one-story garage. Again, you have the same choice of trusses or rafters for the roof. The remainder of the two-story garage is finished in the same manner as the one story.

VARIATION: ATTACHED TWO-STORY

The advantages are obvious: there is one less wall to build, and you can extend existing utilities through the adjoining wall.

Electrical Responsibilities

For an attached structure, you will simply be extending the wiring from the house through the adjoining wall. (See Chapters 7 and 14.) In these cases, you would rarely require a new service panel. It is suggested, however, that you have an electrician set up a separate circuit.

Other Utilities

Heating, cooling and plumbing can be extended through the adjoining wall. The steps involved are the same as those given in Chapter 14.

Matching Interior Wall Finishes

When you attach a two-story garage to the house and use the second floor for living space, your one exterior wall of the existing house will now become one of the interior walls of the second-floor room. If the house exterior is brick, stone or redwood, you may choose to leave this wall as an accent wall. Or you can paint existing brick, or stucco any wood or masonry.

Attaching Furring Strips to Wood or Aluminum Siding

You may wish to finish this wall to match the other walls of the room. The easiest way to do this is to fur out (add furring

Although it is always easier to nail furring strips to wood-frame wall studs, the strips can be attached to masonry walls using masonry nails or specialized fasteners.

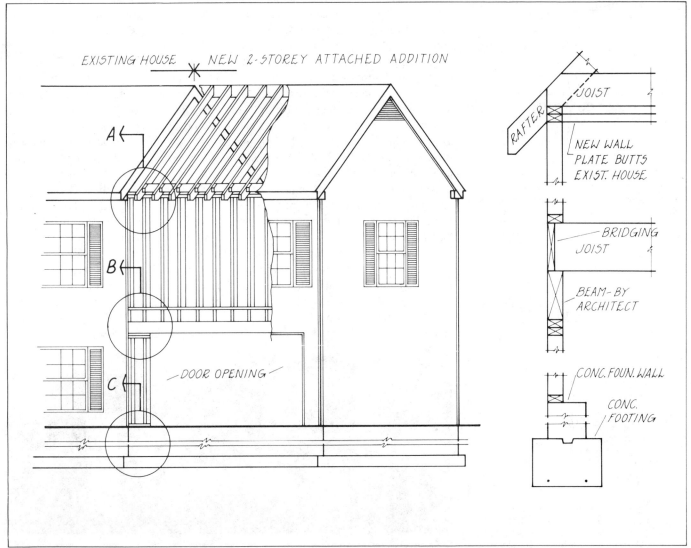

EXISTING HOUSE   NEW 2-STOREY ATTACHED ADDITION

A

B

C

DOOR OPENING

RAFTER   JOIST

NEW WALL PLATE BUTTS EXIST. HOUSE

BRIDGING JOIST

BEAM-BY ARCHITECT

CONC. FOUN. WALL

CONC. FOOTING

Attach the new structure so it carries its own weight, rather than "hanging" it on the building. Consultation with an architect is a must!

strips) to the wall so you can attach the new finish material to the strips.

When furring out, attach 1x2s or 2x4s, flat side down, to the old surface. Fasten them to the studs, which will be 16 inches o.c. in most cases. For wood or aluminum siding, use 10d nails or screws (screws are better) to attach the strips to the wall. Then nail the wallboard or paneling to the strips.

Attaching Furring Strips to Masonry

When attaching furring strips to masonry provide a nailing backing for wood paneling, sheetrock, or other materials you might want to use to cover brick, the material with which you cover the brick will influence the arrangement of the furring.

Read the material manufacturers' installation requirements. For instance, if

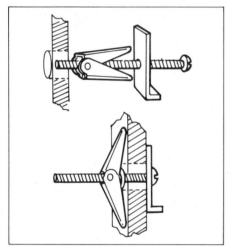

To use a toggle bolt, slip the screw through the item, slip on the "wings" and push the collapsed wings through the hole in the wall. Inside the wall the wings will pop open.

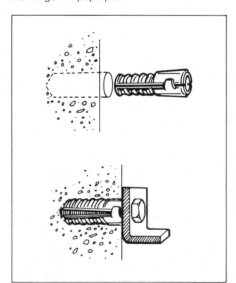

An expansion sleeve is inserted into a hole drilled in masonry. Then the screw is passed through the item and turned. The sleeve expands, locking the fastener in place.

you are installing sheetrock over a brick wall, you would try to duplicate the stud spacing of a wood frame wall (since sheetrock is normally placed over wood frame walls). Furring would be wood members secured to the brick walls at 16 inches on center for the full height of the brick wall. You could use 2x4s, secured with the wide side against the brick. Remember to provide backing for the horizontal joints (if any). The 2x4s can be secured with toggle bolts, or with lead shields and anchors. Furring for most paneling can be handled similarly.

Using toggle bolts. If you use toggle bolts, 1/8-inch diameter bolts should be adequate. The length of the bolts will be the sum of the width of the brick and the narrow side of the 2x4s they have to penetrate — about seven inches long. To be safe, drill through a mortar joint with a drill bit the same size as the mortar joint (usually 1/2 to 3/8 inch) and use a coat hanger to measure the exact width of the brick. Add 1 3/8 inches for the 2x4, and another inch to give you room to work with the bolt.

The toggle bolts should go through the center of the furring members. When you have the bolt holes through the mortar joints (use a power or manual drill), place the furring members next to the holes and mark the hole locations on the furring members with a pencil. Drill the same size holes in the furring members that you drilled through the mortar joints. Try to get a toggle bolt close to the ends of each furring member, but not closer than one inch from the end.

Hold the drilled 2x4 furring members against the drilled brick joints and push a toggle bolt through about the middle of the member, but do not tighten it. Then push another toggle bolt through near the top and another one near the bottom to hold

the member while you install the intermediate bolts. Do not tighten any of the bolts until they are all loosely in place.

The bolts have collapsible nuts, similar in appearance to wing nuts. These collapsible nuts make it possible to screw on the nuts (close to the ends of the bolts) and then to push the whole assembly through the furring members and brick at the same time. Once inside, the nuts pop open to their full size. When all the bolts are in place, tighten them with a screwdriver.

Lead shields and anchors. If you use lead shields and anchors, their spacing is the same as for the toggle bolts above. The difference is that lead shields and anchors do not penetrate all the way through the brick mortar joints; 1 1/2 inches into the mortar joint should be enough. Instead, drill holes in the mortar; then insert the lead shields (which are lead cylinders). Fit the anchor (which in this case is a wood screw) through the furring member and screw it into the lead shield. As the screw is turned into the lead shield cylinder, the lead is forced against the walls of the hole.

HOW TO CUT AN ACCESS DOOR

When building an attached two-story, where the second floor will serve as additional living space, you will have to create a doorway. The location of your door is partly a matter of choice, but it must be located where it will not cause any structural problems.

The ideal place for the door is at the end of an upstairs hallway. However, few homes these days are constructed with long, upstairs hallways. The next best location would be in a relatively unused guest room. If neither of these locations is possible, condider shifting room assignments so that the person whose bedroom contains the access door to the deck is unlikely to be disturbed.

Creating an attached garage with a living area above can make the addition an integral part of the building and eliminate any sense of being "tacked on."

Making the Interior Wall Cut

Using an existing window location. If there is a window in the adjoining wall, try to use this as the location for the door.

First, locate the studs in the adjoining wall. These should be every sixteen inches on center, but you may find that they are closer together or farther apart. When you have found the studs, you will be able to tell if the window is framed against supporting studs or extra studs. If it seems to be framed between regularly spaced studs, then the framing space will probably be wide enough for a practical door. Remove the window by prying off the interior facing and molding and by lifting off the window sill. Then remove any nails or screws that hold the frame in place.

Cutting where there is no window. If the attached garage is on a side of your house that has no window, you will have to cut an entirely new opening through the wall. To do this, locate the studs, determine the desired location of the door and cut away the plaster or wallboard. Locate the door so it will be between studs so that you will have to cut out only one stud.

Remove the wallboard or plaster from the center of the stud on one side of the door location to the center of the stud on the other. Measure up the height of the door rough opening, plus the allowance

for the threshold, and mark the center stud. Add to this the thickness of the doubled header that must be installed. Since exterior walls are load carrying, prop the ceiling before removing the stud.

Cutting the Exterior Surface

Remove the plaster and lath or gypsum wallboard below the window. Cut it away so that it is even with the wallboard that was under the sides of the window frame. You can now see the depth of the exterior siding. Use a circular saw set to the thickness of the siding to cut through that material. Remove the siding and any insulation below the window to the centerline of the framing studs on either side of the opening.

Cutting a brick exterior. This is not an easy process, and may require hiring a professional. To cut through brick you will need to first determine the location on the outside wall, then bore the holes using a masonry bit. Use a brick hammer and masonry chisel to remove the bricks between the lines. In most cases this means you will have to remove the bricks a little farther out than necessary, remortaring some bricks back in place later.

Framing the Door

Framing the door at old window location. If you have removed a window that has filled the space between studs, there should be a rough opening approximately 30 inches (32 inches from stud center to stud center.) There should also be a doubled header across the top of the opening with a cripple (partial) stud above the header. If the window opening is high

enough to accommodate a door, you will only have to remove the framing below the opening, add new side trimmer studs, install a new threshold so the door will be above the finished level of the deck, slip the proper-sized door in place, shim to level and plumb, and secure the door.

When not using an old window. If your window was too narrow to accommodate a usable door, you will have to adjust the spacing of the studs, adding studs as required to provide necessary wall support and to provide the proper frame width for the door.

If you have had to cut through a solid wall, you will have to cut through the center stud and remove part of it. The amount that you remove will be the length of the rough opening height, the height of the finished threshold, plus the thickness of two 2x4s used as the doubled header. Measure this carefully, checking the manufacturer's information and the actual thickness of the lumber you are using. Toenail the header boards to the side studs and into the cripple stud.

Installing the door. When the framing is complete, slip the new door into place. Check for level and plumb and shim as needed before permanently mounting. Follow manufacturer's mounting instructions. Finish the inside and outside with facings to match the inside and outside trim.

Add a drip cap flashing over the door trim. This may be either preformed flashing or a section of sheet metal that you bend yourself. The top fits under the siding; the bottom fits on and over the top of the door framing.

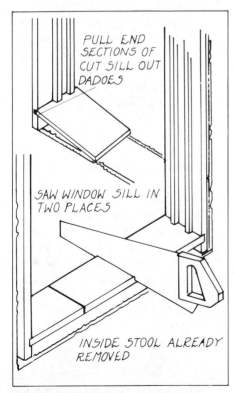

To remove window, first cut twice across stool (inside sill) and remove section. Pull out side pieces, which are in dadoes.

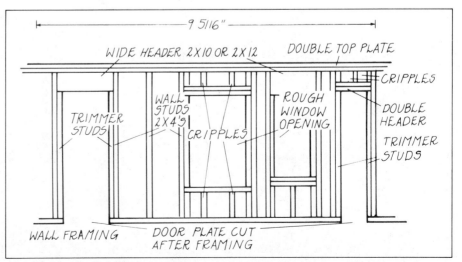

Window rough opening and door opening have double header at top, single at bottom, with filler (trimmer) studs at sides for double side studs. Cripples at top and bottom of opening are short support studs. If a wide window is installed the header can be of doubled 2x10s or 2x12s.

10

Constructing a Carport

The open carport in the text is simply an attached garage without the side walls. The construction sequence is the same as if you were building the double garage in this text, and almost all the construction techniques are the same.

LAYOUT AND PLANNING
Slab and Foundation Work

First, locate the carport on the ground. Since the carport is attached, your reference points are all extended from the house. This means you need not go through the rather elaborate procedure described for the double garage. For the slab layout, you can follow the instructions for expanding a one-car to a two-car garage.

For slab excavation, study the slab excavation for the double garage. As with the double garage, you may be able to use a one-piece slab and foundation, depending on the climate in your locality and on local codes. With either kind of foundation, you must dig footing trenches and use forms. These procedures are covered in Chapters 6 and 9.

The structure should be independent of the house, but it will touch the house. The carport roof will touch the house gable; you will need to flash where they meet.

Place the slab and foundation per the double garage instructions. Use a ½-inch isolation joint where the new slab meets the house foundation wall.

Supporting the Columns

As when you lay the slab for any structure, plan the installation of sill bolts to be placed in the concrete while it is still stiff enough to keep the bolts from falling over, but not so stiff you cannot get the bolts in. For the carport, you will need only the sill bolts required to accommodate the columns that support the roof and ceiling joists. Study Chapter 11; the section on the balcony shows the column layout for a two-story garage balcony with metal sill anchorage for the columns. This method raises the columns a bit, and keeps them out of water, which prolongs the life of the columns. Your carport column anchorage should work similarly. Note the foundation supports (piers) under the columns. The piers for the carport are built right into the foundation wall. This is simple to accomplish, since you dig the piers at the same time you dig the footing trenches.

It will be necessary to install expansion joint material (½ inch) around the piers to separate them from the slab. This prevents cracks in the slab due to the concentrated loads at the columns.

Even if you do not use a professional for anything else, consider hiring an architect, plans service, builder, or civil engineer to plan your foundation for you in order to comply with local codes and to avoid structural problems.

FRAMING AND FINISHING
Installing the Columns

Four-inch pipe columns, or 4-inch-square steel columns (both hollow) make good carport columns. However, check the sizes with a professional before you buy and install them. You also may want to check into decorative metal columns. All these columns are available at metal supply houses and builder supply houses.

Temporarily brace the columns on the slab as discussed for the balcony for the two-story garage (Chapter 11). Remove the bracer when you have installed the beams at the front and back, per the fol-

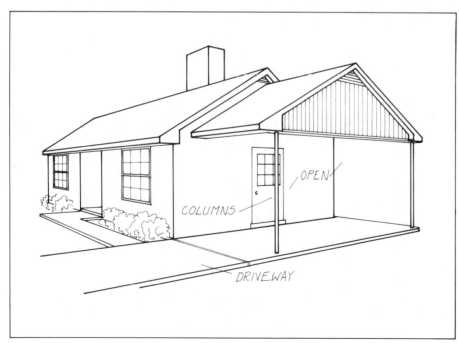

The open carport provides sun and rain protection for automobiles in mild climates where security is not a concern. The needed beams at the front and rear of this carport are supported by 4″ (square or round) pipe columns.

lowing discussion of construction.

In the text example of the carport, it is assumed that the ceiling joists run from the front of the house (and carport) toward the back. So you will need supporting beams at the front and back of the carport.

The ceiling joists, rafters, roofing, and so forth, are installed as for the two-car garage.

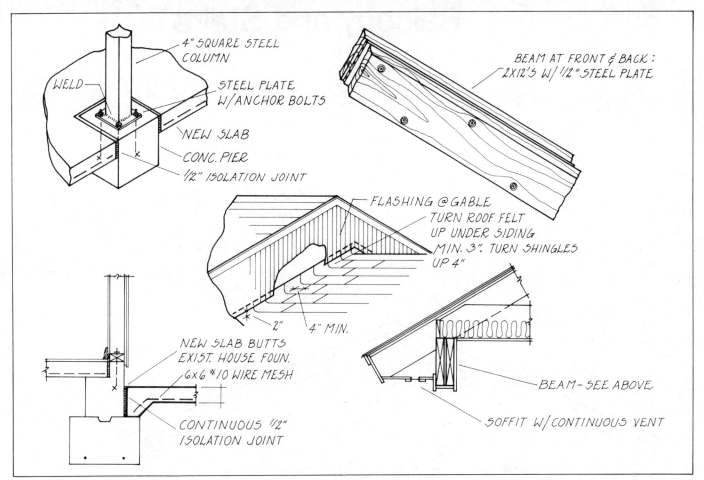

There are five elements that deserve special attention when attaching a carport to an existing house. If the carport is open, and you use columns set on piers, be sure to use isolation material around the piers. The beams needed at front and rear can be built with 2x12's and steel plate. Where the carport butts the existing gable, flash under the siding. Since there will be no wall plate, the soffit must be built around the dimensions of the beams. Where the new slab butts the existing house, use isolation material. Remember, these solutions shown are typical; you may need architectural consultation for your particular situation.

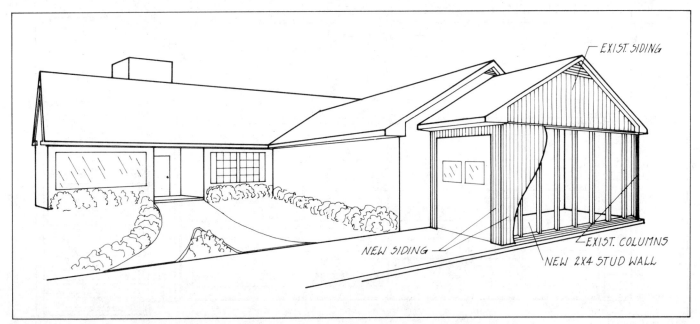

If you already have an open carport and you want to enclose it, you can do so very simply. Use normal stud wall construction to fill in between the columns. Remember to obtain your door before you do any framing on the front wall; plan your framing around the door dimensions.

11
Balcony and Stairs

In this chapter we offer two projects: a deck built on a flat-roofed garage and a post-and-beam balcony for a room built over a double garage.

THE BASIC BALCONY STRUCTURE
This balcony is a post-and-beam structure. It consists of two parallel rows of wooden 4x4 posts, supporting double 2x12 beams.

The ends of the beams are faced with additional 2x12s. The decking surface is laid with a one-inch space between the 2x6s. Use 1x4s as spacers. Nail the 2x6s into

SIDING (HORIZONTAL)   SIDING (VERTICAL)

FRONT ELEVATION

Stairways from the second story are essential to the usefulness and safety (in case of fire) of a two-story garage addition.

position with 10d galvanized nails.

The structure is supported by 12 inch x 12 inch (or 12 inches in diameter) concrete piers sunk at least 12 inches underground. The piers should always go beneath the frost line, if possible, or conform to local practices to offset frost heave. The piers should extend above grade by 4 inches. The grade should be set such that the top of the piers is one step beneath the finished floor level of the garage — not more than 7 inches, (6¾ inches is preferred). If you set the piers in this manner and decide to build a patio later, you can pour concrete around the piers, after first placing an isolation joint around them. The concrete must be poured so the patio will be at the right level relative to the garage.

A small sun deck, with an access door leading to it, is a feasible project above nearly any attached garage. If the roof is flat, the project is very simple.

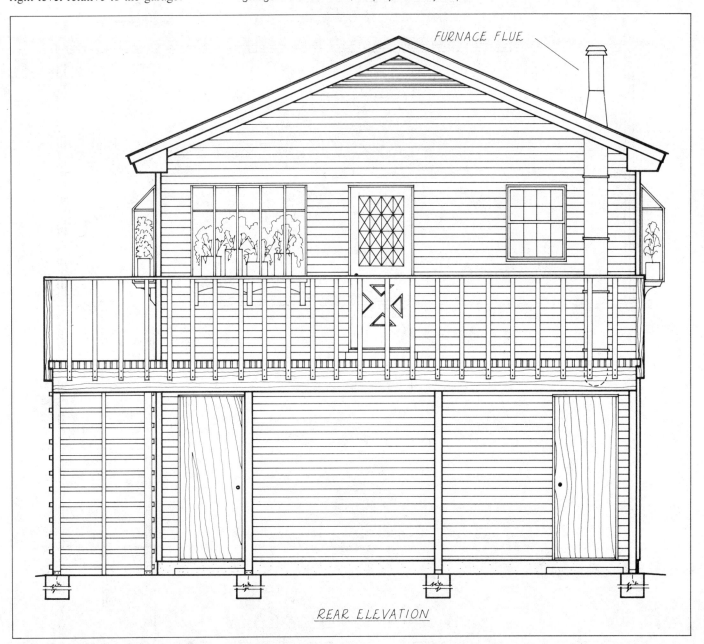

FURNACE FLUE

REAR ELEVATION

The front of this garage faces the driveway, so the balcony was placed at the rear for a backyard view. The area under balcony may be paved.

CONSTRUCTING THE BALCONY
Setting the First Two Corner Posts

Post locations. Stake out the post locations using the layout techniques discussed earlier for slabs. The center lines of the posts should be also the centers of the piers.

Digging and filling postholes. Dig the holes with a spade or clamshell posthole digger, to the depth required by code. Place a layer of gravel and tamp. Then pour the concrete.

Installing the post bases. Before the concrete sets, install adjustable post bases, using stakes and string to set them on the pier base centers. There are many types of post bases available. We recommend that you use an adjustable one, because it makes it easier to line the posts up when the time comes. Select an elevated post base; this keeps the bottom of the post away from moisture, prolonging its life. The post base you select should come with instructions. However, the general rule is to set the steel post base and, when the concrete has cured, hand-tighten it down enough so that it does not move easily.

Positioning posts on the bases. Nail a post cap to the top before you raise the post. You will need a helper to hold the post in place while you nail it to the post anchor. The illustration shows the post anchor before the last leaf has been lifted up. Leave this leaf down, but nail the other holes. Start with a corner next to the house.

Bracing the posts. With the helper holding the post steady, brace the post with two lengths of 2x4s, one on each side of the post. To do this, first trial-measure the 2x4s so that they will be attached about 2 feet down from the top of the post and several feet out at the bottom — 8-foot 2x4s usually will work. At the bottom of the brace you need a 2x4 stake (one for each 2x4) to hold the braces.

Nail one brace to the stake and then, with your helper still at the post (and with a level to check for plumb), adjust the brace so that the post remains plumb. Nail the brace to the post. Do the same thing

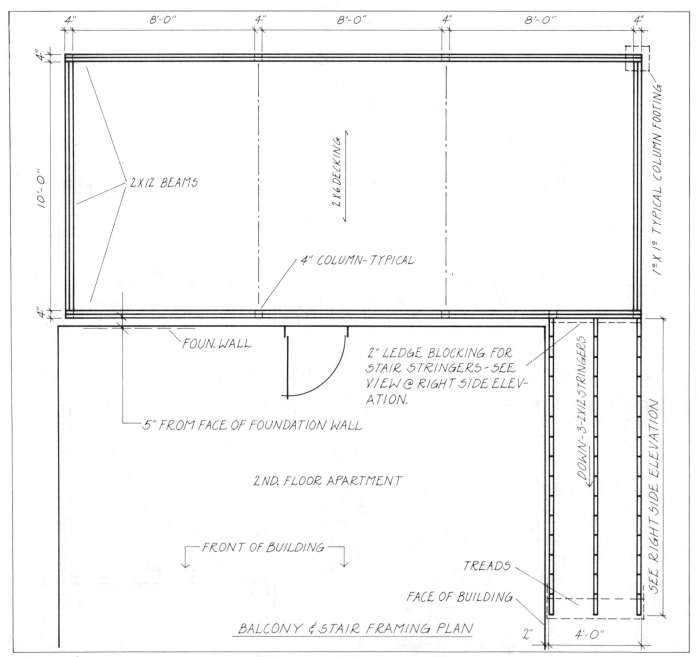

After the footings set and columns are up, set the long beam runs in place; use metal post caps. Secure shorter end beams with joist hangers.

with the other brace to secure the post.

Final adjustments. Now you can tighten down the adjustable post anchor. There is space provided to allow final tightening after the posts are up. Pull up the remaining leaf on the anchor, and nail it.

Setting alignment for intermediate posts. Move to the next corner (on the long side of the balcony next to the house) and set another post, as above. Now tie a string between the posts, flush with the tops. This will help you set the intermediate posts, because the string serves as a guide to keep all the post tops level.

Setting Intermediate Posts

Set the intermediate posts just as you did the first two corner posts. Before you nail them to the post anchors at the piers, check their tops against the string to be sure they are level with the corner posts. If they are too long, cut them to fit. If you have to use shims, shim them up from below, driving the shims between the bottom of the posts and the post anchor. The shims should be of pressure-treated wood. These often are available at building materials stores. Drive them snugly together under the posts to provide a solid, uniform bearing.

As you level each post, nail the post anchor to the posts and brace the post in position, checking for plumb and alignment. Proceed in this manner for all the intermediate posts.

Nailing the First Beam

Once you have the row of posts next to the house in place, install the double 2x12 beams. Nail them to the post caps. The post caps have nail holes; nail through them, using 16d nails. Nail the 2x12s together with 16d nails at 1 foot on center, top and bottom. Stagger the nails at top and bottom so that they do not line up vertically. Check the beams with a level as you work.

Setting Remaining Posts and Beams

Install the last two corner posts, away from the house. When you install the first one (it does not matter which one is first), level it with a corner post next to the house, using string as you did for the first row of posts. Then place the opposite corner post in the same manner.

Install the intermediate posts as you did before. Use joist anchors to install the double 2x12s at the ends.

A handrail, placed around the edge of the garage on a flat-top deck addition, is necessary to insure the safety of the users.

Instructions for building a flat-topped sun deck above the garage, similar to the one shown here, can be found beginning on page 123.

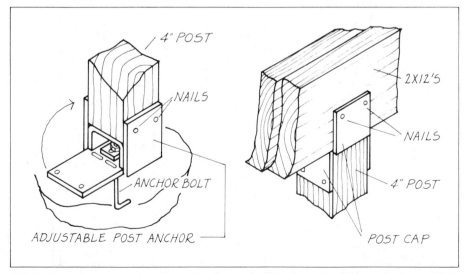

Adjustable post anchors and post caps simplify construction of a post-and-beam structure and help tie the structure together. The post anchors help protect posts against rot.

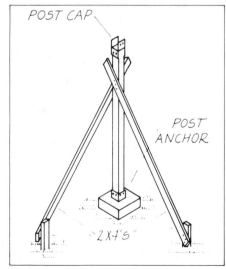

Leave post braces until decking material is laid. Make sure braces are plumb.

Adding the Decking

Lay the 2x6 decking after notching each piece 2 inches from its ends. The notch will fit over the beam and there will be a 2-inch overhang all around. The decking is separated by 1x4 spacers between the regular 2x6 decking material. Toenail the 2x6s with 10d nails, two on each side of the 4-inch part of the decking (2x6s). Nail one 10d nail through the top of each 2x6, into the 2x12 stringers.

Installing the Railing

The handrail and the handrail pickets are 2x4s. The illustration shows the handrail and pickets in elevation. The pickets 2x4s mount to the stringers at the stair and all around the balcony. Fasten the pickets to the stringers with two ½-inch steel bolts, 7 inches long. Use two 10d nails through the handrail and down into each picket, nailing from the top. At the stair, there is a picket centered on each stringer at the tread. Around the balcony, there is a picket every fourth 2x6 decking member.

BUILDING THE STAIRS

The stairs are constructed of three 2x12

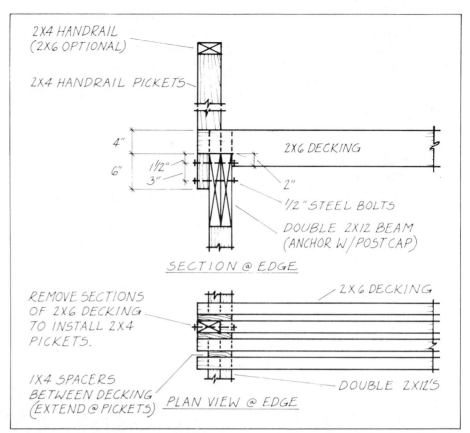

This balcony is simple and easy to build. To avoid later maintenance problems, try to use pressure-treated wood. The wood can be left to weather naturally, or stained or painted.

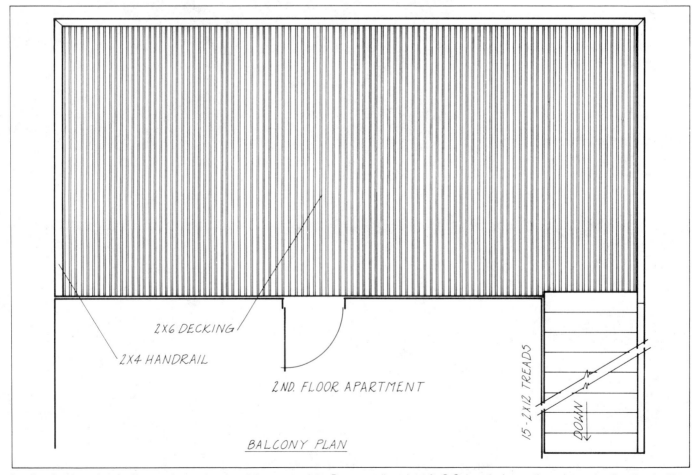

Lay the decking when footings, columns, beams, stair are complete. Draw pencil marks 1 ft. O.C. lengthwise on the columns to align the decking.

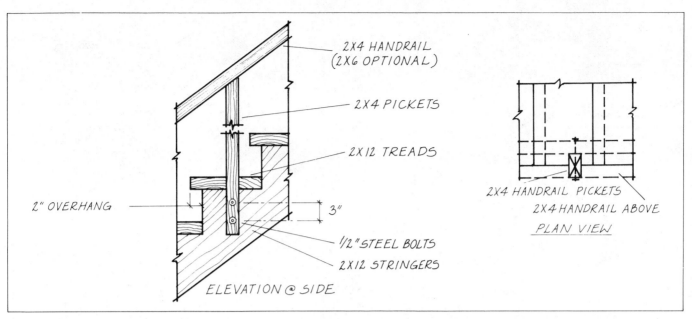

2X4 HANDRAIL
(2X6 OPTIONAL)

2X4 PICKETS

2X12 TREADS

2" OVERHANG

3"

1/2" STEEL BOLTS

2X12 STRINGERS

ELEVATION @ SIDE

2X4 HANDRAIL PICKETS
2X4 HANDRAIL ABOVE
PLAN VIEW

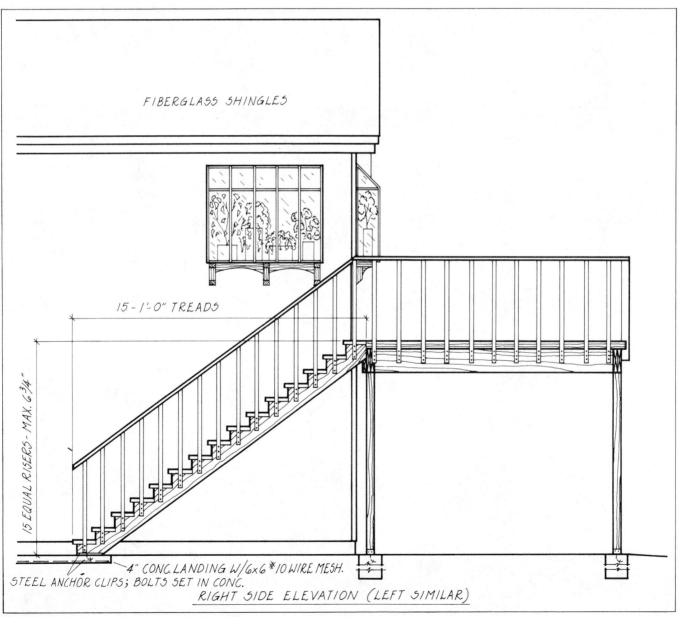

FIBERGLASS SHINGLES

15 - 1'-0" TREADS

15 EQUAL RISERS - MAX. 6 3/4"

4" CONC. LANDING W/6x6 *10 WIRE MESH.
STEEL ANCHOR CLIPS; BOLTS SET IN CONC.
RIGHT SIDE ELEVATION (LEFT SIMILAR)

The stairway is shown on the right side, but the whole second floor plan could be rotated, if that were more desirable.

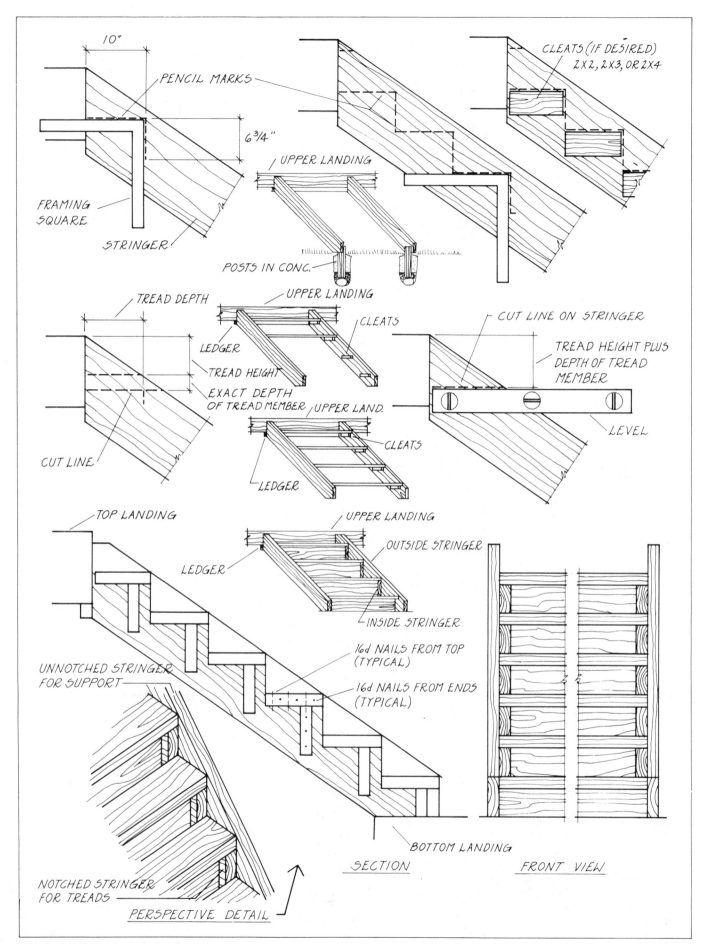

10"

PENCIL MARKS

6 3/4 "

FRAMING SQUARE

STRINGER

UPPER LANDING

POSTS IN CONC.

CLEATS (IF DESIRED)
2X2, 2X3, OR 2X4

TREAD DEPTH

UPPER LANDING

CLEATS

LEDGER

TREAD HEIGHT

EXACT DEPTH
OF TREAD MEMBER

UPPER LAND.

CLEATS

LEDGER

CUT LINE

CUT LINE ON STRINGER

TREAD HEIGHT PLUS
DEPTH OF TREAD
MEMBER

LEVEL

TOP LANDING

UPPER LANDING

OUTSIDE STRINGER

LEDGER

INSIDE STRINGER

16d NAILS FROM TOP
(TYPICAL)

16d NAILS FROM ENDS
(TYPICAL)

UNNOTCHED STRINGER
FOR SUPPORT

NOTCHED STRINGER
FOR TREADS

PERSPECTIVE DETAIL

BOTTOM LANDING

SECTION

FRONT VIEW

Tools for building stairs include a framing square, a carpenters' level, a hand or power saw; and heavy-duty, noncorrosive nails.

stringers with 2x12 treads. The illustration shows the stair in elevation.

Treads and Risers

First, compute the number of risers you need to descend from the second story. The maximum riser height recommended is 6¾ inches. All the risers are equal except for the one next to the ground, which is shorter than the others.

The stair stringers, from outside stringer to outside stringer, are 4 feet wide. Code regulations vary concerning stair width, so check your local code. Use the 2x12s for the stringers. As shown in the elevation, there are 15 equal risers in this example and none of them exceed 6¾ inches in height. The tread notches are 10 inches, so that when the 2x12 tread is nailed down, it overlaps the stringer by 2 inches.

This creates a tread depth of 12 inches. Nail the 2x12 tread down to the stringers with four 10d nails at each stringer.

The Landing, Treads, and Handrail

The landing is a 4-inch concrete slab, reinforced with 6x6 #10 wire mesh, like the floor slab. Before the slab sets, install framing anchors to hold the 2x12 stringers. When the landing concrete has cured, install the stringers. Finally, install the treads and handrail. Fasten the stairway railing in the same manner as the balcony handrail.

BUILDING A DECK ON AN ATTACHED GARAGE
Access to the Roof

For instructions on how to create a doorway that allows you to step out onto the deck, see Chapter 9.

Code Requirements

Before pursuing any building plans for including a deck on the attached garage roof, check with your local building department to find out what code restrictions, if any, govern use of these areas.

Roof Deck Structural Needs

To support the additional expected load, you must use certain dimension sizes of the lumber and spacing of the joists and rafters. Rafters should be 2x6s on 16-inch centers for a porch nine feet or less in width. If the span is greater than nine feet, but less than eleven feet-eight inches, you cannot build a deck unless the rafters are at least 2x8s. If the span is greater than this, the roof structure will have to be even stronger.

The basic construction of a deck becomes a more complicated job when the

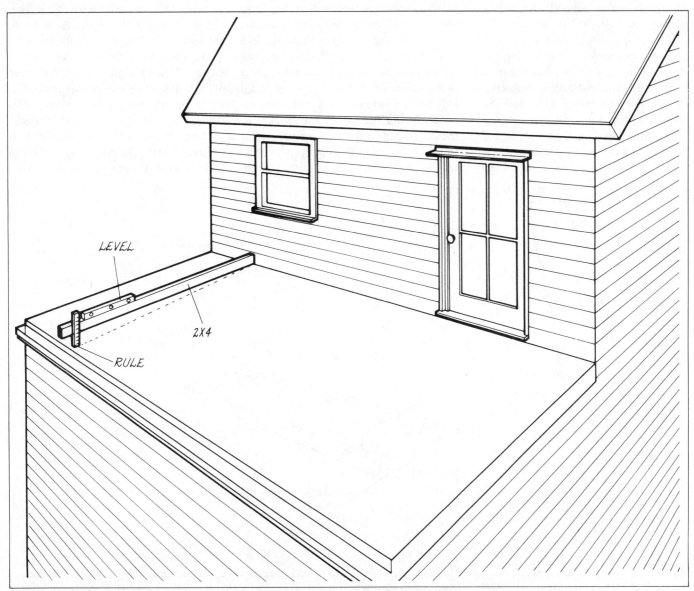

Your roof will have a slope and your deck should be level. Measure slope by lifting a 2x4 to level and noting height.

roof area is extensive because more complicated support framing is required for the deck itself. The garage roof should be built nearly flat so the deck need not strongly compensate for the pitch (slope) of the roof. For any slope greater than ¼ inch per foot, you should compensate for the structure of the base framing, or the deck will have an uncomfortable slant to one side.

Building the Deck

Decks are built with openings between the boards for quick drainage; this means you will have future maintenance of the roofing surface. Therefore, your deck should be constructed so that sections of the deck may be removed easily to let you do maintenance work on the roofing material. The deck sections may be built as a series of modular units, held together by screws through the railing supports. Railing supports are also attached to the house.

If the slope of the roof is only ¼ inch per foot, your deck can follow that slope. However, if the pitch is greater than that slight slope, you will have to compensate for the slope by providing a deck base built of wedge-shaped boards.

Planning the construction. Measure the area that you will be using for your deck. A single-car garage roof will provide approximately 10x20 feet of area. Allow an area 3 inches wide between the outside edges of your deck and the edge of the roof. This way, any rainfall dripping off the railing will fall on the roof and run into your gutter/downspout system rather than dripping directly to the ground. The additional setback will also provide a greater sense of security for those on the second-floor deck.

Modular units. It will be easier and more economical for you to build the deck in sections between 30 and 48 inches wide, but you may choose to build smaller sections if you are working alone. If you choose to build your deck the full size of a 10x20 roof area, you can construct six modular units 9 feet 9 inches long by 39 inches wide (10 feet minus 3 inches; and, 20 feet minus 6 inches divided by 6). You may also build 13 units each 18 inches wide, if you think this will be easier to handle. You may decide to deck only part of the roof to create a 10x12 deck. Note that any modular unit that is over 28 inches wide will require a center support board. Units 28 inches or less in width may be built with only side rail supports.

Measuring the slope. Lay a 2x4 (or thicker board) on the roof, perpendicular to the house wall. The board must be at least as long as the roof is wide. Lay the board widest side down. Place a level on the board and begin lifting the end near the edge until the bubble in the level is centered. Measure the distance from the roof to the level board. If the slope of your roof is ½ inch per foot, this will be approximately 5 inches.

If you are using 2x4s or 2x6s for your decking and you lay the boards flat, the decking thickness will be 1½ inches. If you have set your access door so that the bottom clears the roof surface by 4 inches, you will have to cut the decking support (foundation) boards so that the end nearest the door will be 2 inches thick. The other end will be 7 inches thick to bring the deck to an even level. You will be able to cut this from 2x8 stock 10 feet long.

Marking and cutting the boards. Lay your boards flat and measure off the width of the roof less three inches. Assuming a 10 foot width, this will be 9 feet 9 inches. Cut the boards at this mark. At one end, measure down 2 inches from the top edge; at the other end, measure down seven inches. Draw a straight line across the face of the board between these two marks. Cut along the line using a circular saw or reciprocating saw. You will need 18 boards — three for each of the six modular units.

Constructing the modules. To build a 39-inch-wide unit, lay out three of your

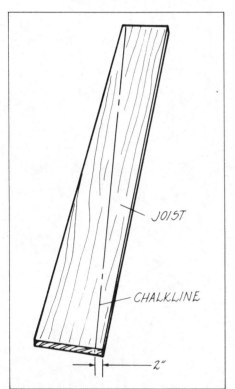

Mark the foundation boards to level and even out the deck. A 2-inch height should allow for door to clear finished deck level.

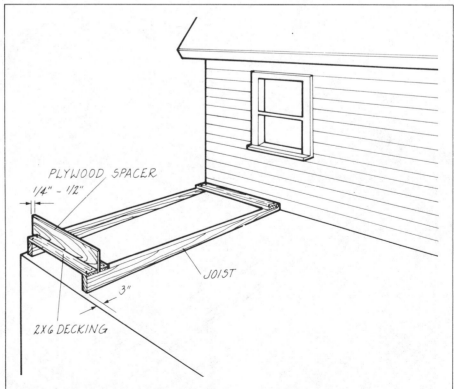

Build deck a unit at a time, attaching first two boards at either end of the foundation boards. Use a spacer to maintain even placement of boards along the run of the unit.

foundation boards so that they are evenly spaced, 39 inches from outside edge to outside edge. The middle board will be located exactly on a 19½ inch center from the outside edges of the side boards. Using 10d galvanized nails, nail one 2x4 or 2x6 piece of decking flush with each end to hold the foundation boards in position. The decking boards should be cut to fit the exact width of the modules. Allow approximately ¼ inch space between boards for drainage. It will take 31 2x4s or 20 2x6s to deck each module with approximately ¼ inch spacing. This will give you ¾ inch of excess space to distribute along the run if you are using 2x4s. You will have 2 inches of excess spacing to distribute over the run if you are using 2x6 boards for the decking.

Lay out the decking boards using a ¼ inch spacer, a piece of ¼ inch plywood will do, then adjust the spacing to absorb the excess and mark the positions of the decking boards on the foundation boards. Nail the decking in place with 10d galvanized nails. Repeat for each modular unit needed. Set units in place.

Adding the railings. Cut 2x4 boards to a length of between 43 and 45 inches, depending on the height you want for your top railing. For a 10x20 foot deck, you will have to cut 15 railing pieces. Two boards are attached to the house at either side of the deck. Use 6-inch lag screws driven through the narrow face of the board into the deck foundation boards. Evenly space railing supports no more than three feet on center. Level and plumb along each side. Attach one board flush with the edge at the corner. Butt this rail support board with the board on the other side of the corner. Attach these boards

with lag screws to each other and to the foundation boards. Install one railing support at each joint between modules so that the modules are held together by lag screws through the foundation boards. Check each railing support board carefully for level and plumb. Always keep the spacing under three feet on center; add more boards as needed. Repeat corner and

side installation for the other side.

Center 2x4 railings on the posts and attach with galvanized wood screws. Connect posts with additional bracing. Check codes for minimum construction standards. All rails, braces and posts attach with screws to enable removal as roof repairs are needed.

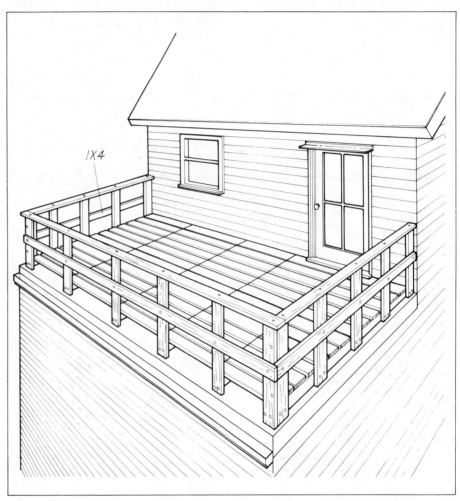

The completed deck is attractive, safe to use, and will add to your recreation area. It can be taken apart for roof maintenance.

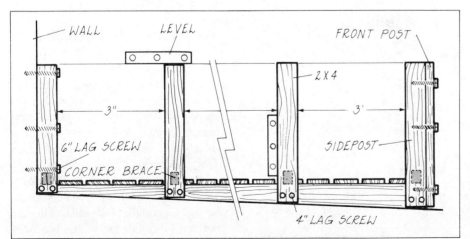

Posts for railings hold deck units together. Attach with lag screws into predrilled pilot holes. Be sure that you maintain level throughout the sections.

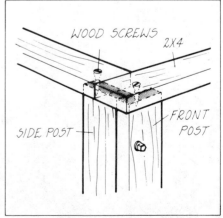

Center 2x4 railing on posts and secure with wood screws. Additional railings can be placed between deck level and top railings.

12
Building
a Concrete Block Garage

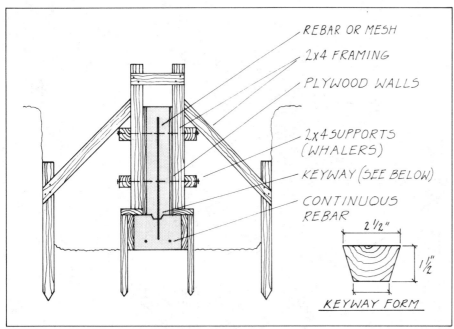

REBAR OR MESH
2x4 FRAMING
PLYWOOD WALLS
2x4 SUPPORTS (WHALERS)
KEYWAY (SEE BELOW)
CONTINUOUS REBAR

2½"
1½"

KEYWAY FORM

A concrete footing and foundation must be poured in a well-constructed form and reinforced with steel rods. A keyway in the footing ties foundation into the footing structure.

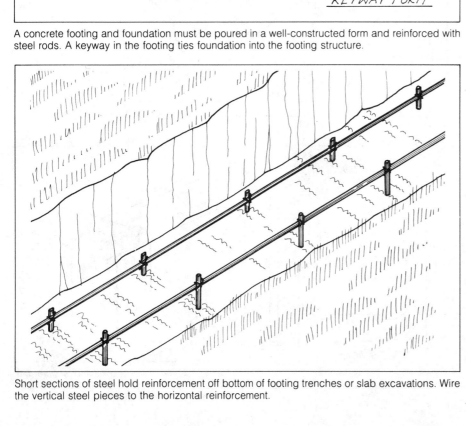

Short sections of steel hold reinforcement off bottom of footing trenches or slab excavations. Wire the vertical steel pieces to the horizontal reinforcement.

FOUNDATION AND FLOOR SLAB
Block Foundation Wall
The garage will be located on the ground and staked out in the same manner as discussed in Chapter 6. However, for a concrete block garage you may want to use a concrete block foundation instead of a concrete one. (The foundation footing for concrete block structures typically is concrete.) For many areas of moderate climate around the country, this is an acceptable foundation. But concrete block is not recommended below ground in areas of extreme cold or where frost heave is a problem. When the foundation wall is concrete block, the top of the footing should be flat.

Concrete Foundation Wall
In very cold areas, use a concrete footing and concrete foundation wall. The accompanying illustration shows the forming setup used for concrete footings and foundation walls. When the footing is poured, a wood member is placed along the center to form a "keyway". When the foundation wall is poured later, it runs into the keyway and holds the foundation wall in place.

   Steel reinforcement. The need for steel reinforcement in foundation components and floor slabs varies with the amount of load (weight) and the way the load is placed on the foundation. For instance, an exterior wall of your house, where the weight at any point along the foundation is the same as at all other points, may not need reinforcement. But if you plan to install a block and tackle in your garage, in order to do repair work on your car, support the block and tackle with "beefed-up" ceiling joists. This produces a "concentrated" load where the load is transferred down to the foundation wall and footing. Concentrated loads require special attention and should be designed by an architect. Some architects routinely place two #4 steel bars continuously around the footing of houses, even though they have no concentrated loads, as an extra safety precaution.

The #4 steel bars are supported in the footing trench with short sections of steel from the #4 bars that you can cut with a hacksaw. The short sections are driven several inches into the ground and extend up enough so that you can wire the horizontal #4s to them. The vertical sections are only for the purpose of supporting the horizontal steel while you pour the concrete. The horizontal steel should be about 1½ inches from the bottom of the footing (and thus, the footing trench). The vertical sections should be spaced every foot or two so the horizontal steel does not sag and does not move when the concrete is poured.

The reinforcement discussed above is for general conditions in residential footings. For any reinforcement beyond simple ''safety'' reinforcement, as above, you should consult with an architect. Foundation walls may need reinforcement and this is another case that needs professional guidance.

Floor Slab

A typical relationship between the floor slab and the foundation wall is shown. The instructions for laying the floor slab for the concrete footing and foundation walls are the same as for laying the one-piece slab and foundation (see Chapter 6).

BUILDING THE WALLS

You can build the example double garage using concrete block. Because there are so many block configurations and sizes available, you should visit some local suppliers — usually lime and cement companies — before you begin the plan, whether you draw it up yourself or instruct a professional.

Block Types and Sizes

The standard concrete blocks you have seen on many residential and commercial projects are typically concrete-colored and ''hollow''. Concrete blocks that have 25 percent or more of the cross-sectional area void are called hollow. The hole sizes vary according to usage requirements. Although you can buy concrete blocks that

are completely solid, they need not be completely solid to be called solid. In addition to the standard concrete-colored blocks, there are other colors, although local availability varies.

Concrete masonry units are usually based on 4- or 8-inch modules. A ⅜-inch mortar joint has become standard by practice. Therefore, the exterior dimensions of masonry units are actually reduced by ⅜-inch to allow for the joints. This allows you to plan the size of your wall dimensions in 4- or 8-inch multiples. However, the nominal sizes (8x8x16, etc.) are also available, so investigate what you are getting. Whether nominal or modular, there are slight inconsistencies in block size, but usually no more than ± ¹⁄₁₆ inch. These inconsistencies are taken up by the joints when you arrange the base course before mortaring.

Wall and ceiling height. Shown is a typical section through a concrete block wall of the example garage. The wall

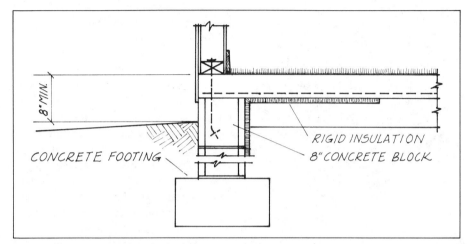

Concrete block can be used for foundation walls only in areas of moderate climate.

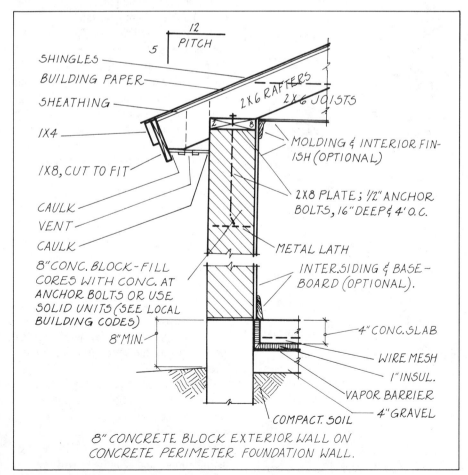

Install sill bolts in the upper block courses to anchor the top plate for rafters.

INTERIOR BLOCK 4X8X16.
CORNERS SAME AS EX. @
BOTTOM.
— 2" SPACE

4X8X16
4X8X16 4X8X8   4X8X12 4X8X16
4X8X16 4X8X12 4X8X8   4X8X16
4X8X16 4X8X12 4X8X8   4X8X16
4X8X16 4X8X16 4X8X12 4X8X16
4X8X12 4X8X8   4X8X16

8X8X16 TYPICAL

At corners, 8x8x16 inch blocks work best, but other block sizes can be substituted.

height will depend on how high you want your ceiling to be. Study the section and you will see that whatever type of ceiling you have will be attached to the ceiling joists. Typical ceilings for garages are sheetrock, plywood, or some type of paneling. These materials can be attached directly to the under side of the joists. So, in considering the *finish height* of your garage ceiling, you must first compute the ceiling height you want and then work backwards from there, taking your materials into consideration — it is just arithmetic. For example, if you want the standard 8-foot ceiling (this is a code minimum in most states), add 8 feet to the ceiling material (for example, ½ inch sheetrock), plus whatever floor material you have, if any. The sum will be the distance between the bottom of the ceiling joist and the top of the concrete floor slab. The ceiling joists rest on a 2x8 plate (which is actually only 1½ inches thick). So, subtract 1½ inches from the sum of the measurements above, and you then have the height distance from the top of the block wall to the top of the concrete floor slab.

But how do you get the top of the block wall to be the right height? You can get the top of the wall where you want it by knowing the block size (height). Then manipulate one course (if necessary) to reach the height you want. For example, if full block courses up from the foundation wall or footing makes the wall 2 inches too high, then you can cut two inches off a course of blocks. This "short course" of blocks can be laid first, where the difference in height of the block will not be disturbing to look at, as it might be if you laid it several feet up. You can cut the block yourself, with a chisel, but this is not recommended. It is much too much work and it is difficult to chisel the blocks as precisely as they need to be. Have the block supplier cut them for you. There are saws for that purpose.

Scaled sketch. Work out a sketch to scale, showing the placement of the blocks. The better you plan your wall before you begin, the easier the work will be when you get into it.

Vertical dimensions are always given in multiples of the full nominal height of the block. An accurately dimensioned sketch, showing the block coursing, corner conditions, top of the walls, and all openings such as doors and windows, will prepare you for the problems you will encounter in

laying the wall. When the concrete block is delivered, store and lay it dry.

Construction details. When you have a choice, plan the wall so that the 4- or 8-inch module is preserved. Whether or not your horizontal dimensions are modular, plan the corners so that you have full 4- or 8-inch units there to avoid ragged conditions. In general, 8-inch block walls offer the easiest corner conditions. Shown are typical corner conditions for 8x8x16-inch block, and one sample corner condition for a 10-inch cavity wall built with double walls of 4-inch-thick blocks.

Mortar

Mortar is an important element of masonry construction. Take care that you have the right mix for the job and that you do not mix more mortar than you can use in about an hour. Any mortar that becomes dried out should not be used again. The mix used depends on the job and the area of the country. But, generally, mortar is a mixture of cement, hydrated lime, sand, and water. It may be hand-mixed if the job is a very small one but, as with concrete, a power mixer is preferable because it gives a more dependable consistency and saves your energy for more important tasks. Power mixers can be rented.

Mortar for stone veneer. Absorbent stone veneer should be moistened before laying; it will pull the water out of the mortar otherwise. Nonabsorbent stone veneer does not have to be moistened. The amount of moisture varies with the stone, as does the way you moisten it. Some stone may need a fine spray from the garden hose and other stone may need soaking. Your stone supplier should be able to tell you how to moisten the stone in which you are interested. When using stone veneer, remember that ordinary portland cement stains most stone. To avoid staining, use nonstaining white portland cement in the mortar. Lime is usually stainless, making portland-cement-lime mortar acceptable. For ordinary usage, mix 1 part masonry cement (this already has lime in it), ASTM Specification C 91 Type II (the American Society for Testing Materials recommendation), with 2¼ or 3 parts masonry sand. Add water to a workable stiffness, so the mortar does not ooze.

Door and Window Openings

Have all your doors and windows on the job before you start the wall. You will need the manufacturer's installation instructions and rough opening dimensions and attachment requirements. Study the accompanying illustration for typical flashing details. Depending on the configuration of the manufactured door, you may or may not have to install flashing before you set the unit in place.

Laying the Block

Tools needed. The key tools you will need include: spirit level, trowel, story pole (see "Building Leads" below), mortar box, string or mason's line, jointers (you should know what kind of joints you will use before you buy or rent the jointers), hammer and mason's chisel, 50-foot metal tape, folding wood rule, 25-inch steel retractable spring rule, hoe and shovel (square) for mortar, line level, handsaw, carpenter's square, stiff-bristle brush (not wire), plumb bob.

The test run. Clean off dirt and debris. Then lay out the first course of block without mortar to establish spacing. Increase or decrease joints as needed to compensate for the slight inconsistencies in block lengths.

First course block placement. Lay the first block on a full bed of mortar. Make sure the block is where you want it on the foundation wall. If it is flush, this will be a simple matter. If the wall must be slightly offset on the foundation wall for some reason, snap a chalkline along the foundation wall to which you can place the wall blocks to help keep them even. "Butter" the ends of the face of the second block and set it next to the first one, assuring good joints. Level the block. Butter and lay several more blocks — three, or the length of your level. Then level them together. Complete the first course in this manner.

Building corner leads. Walls are not built up one complete course at a time. Once the first course has been laid, you will have an outline of the garage. Start the second course at the corner by placing a block overlapping the two butting blocks at the corner of the first course. One end of this block will align with the outside edge of the wall face; the other end of the block will extend halfway over the adjacent block in the first course. This starts the staggered, running bond pattern.

Build up the corner leads several courses above the base course. Check each block for level and plumb, and for

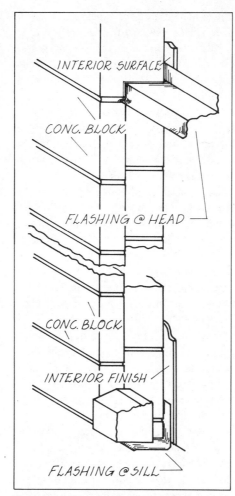

Plan for noncorrosive flashing at the head and sill of doors and windows.

Use smooth-end block at corners; use a mason's hammer and chisel to cut block.

Use jointing tool to smooth mortar for a clean, neat finish to the joints between blocks.

Trowels are the basic tool for applying and smoothing mortar as the blocks are laid.

Stretch a mason's line between blocks to support a line level to check evenness of blocks.

Apply a good bed of mortar to the corner block to provide a seat for the next course.

Remove excess mortar from the face of the joint with the trowel.

alignment in a flat plane at the outside surface. All these checks can be made with a level. Horizontal joint consistency is maintained with a story pole. A simple story pole can be made from a 1x3 wood member, marked at 8-inch intervals. The story pole may be secured against the corner block or used as a frequent check, like the level. More accurate story poles can be obtained at contractor supply houses.

Filling in the courses. The string attached from corner to corner is moved up for each course. Use the string as a guide to guide alignment of the top, outside edge of the blocks. Align the blocks with the string and level them by tapping with the

Butter ends of wall block before laying. Set buttered block into mortar bed laid on top of block courses. Keep mortar out of holes.

trowel handle until the block edges are in line. Then check again with the level.

Keep the work clean as you progress. Do not try to wipe mortar drippings off the wall while they are wet. Let them remain until they are almost dry; then flick them off with a trowel. Bits of mortar will be left; let them dry. Then carefully wipe the mortar off with a piece of concrete block. Remove the rest with a stiff-bristled brush (never use a wire brush).

Doors and windows. Before you lay the block, mark the door and window locations with chalk or crayon on the floor slab. Start building the wall at the corners, working toward the doors and windows. Do not try to do the finished openings until you set the manufactured units in place. Set the doors in place within the wall when you get within a block or so of the edges and when the block is vertically to the door head (top). Then build to the door jambs, securing the door at the jambs, per the packaged instructions. Cut to fit for any odd-length blocks required for a snug, neat meeting at the jambs.

Before you build the wall above the doors, install any flashing or lintels — precast concrete, angle iron, or other. The instructions for window installation resemble those for the doors. Doors and windows, before they are secured to the finished wall, should be braced in place with wood blocking. Use lengths of 2x4s, nailed at the top of the doors or windows and secured with a stake at the ground. Usually, there is no mortar between the

door or window jambs and the wall, but check the manufacturer's requirements.

Lintels. Many sizes of precast reinforced concrete lintels are available where you buy the concrete block. You may also build your own by buying a special U-shaped concrete block (installed open-end up), in which you place reinforcing steel. Mortar is slushed around the steel until the block is full of concrete. When the concrete inside the block cures, the blocks and the steel become one solid, reinforced lintel.

Ends and closure blocks. Use a full-sized block at the end of the wall. Odd dimensions are worked out with a "closure block" placed away from the corner, toward the center. The closure block is cut with a chisel or saw after carefully measuring it to fit the odd space. Finish the edges smoothly before placement.

How to Cut the Blocks

You will have to cut closure blocks, blocks around doors and windows, and blocks in other areas where the block is interrupted or penetrated such as mechanical and plumbing entrances. The best way to cut concrete block is to take it to the supplier and have him saw it exactly where you want the cut. This is especially true for control joints where it is functionally and aesthetically desirable to have a clean, neat, plumb vertical joint. However, where a perfect edge is not important,

Set block firmly so that excess mortar is forced out of joint. Maintain even joint size to keep all courses equal.

Use a spirit level to check each course. Use mason's line as a guide as you fill in courses. The courses must be level and the wall plumb.

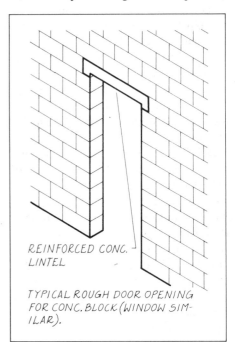

REINFORCED CONC. LINTEL

TYPICAL ROUGH DOOR OPENING FOR CONC. BLOCK (WINDOW SIMILAR).

Reinforced concrete lintel provides stability to door and window openings and supports block courses above the opening.

you should be able to cut a reasonably straight edge yourself:

(1) set the block on its side on a heavy wood scrap (like a 2x12);

(2) draw your cut on the side with a nail and a straightedge (a wood scrap will do), gouging deeply into the block as you draw the line;

(3) place wood blocking underneath the cut, within the cell, to avoid breaking off the block at some point away from the cut;

(4) tap away the excess block until you get fairly close to the line to be cut;

(5) place the chisel on the cut line and tap away from the portion of the block to be used;

(6) if necessary turn the block over and repeat on the other side of the block.

To cut block in half, align cold chisel with the center of block. Mark a scribed line at proper point if a smaller unit is needed.

Strike chisel firmly; the block should crack at centerline. Have extra block for practice cuts. It may take time to learn the skill.

Types of Mortar Joints

Mortar joints are important to the appearance of your wall and to its function. Common joints include: concave, vee, flush, raked, extruded, beaded, weathered, and struck. Each of these joints gives a particular aesthetic effect. Concave joints contribute to a flat wall appearance, where this is desired. Vee joints emphasize shadows. Raked joints create dark shadows; the joints are raked back about a half inch, not more. Beaded joints suggest a formal appearance. Extruded joints give a rustic appearance. All extrusions create shadow lines, but give a different shadow effect from the raked and vee joints. Struck and weathered joints create small shadow lines across the building. Flush joints, of course, offer no shadow at all.

Joint types can be mixed for a desired aesthetic effect. For example, you may choose flush vertical joints and extruded horizontal joints to produce long lines of vertical shadow — or you could try the reverse. Consider carefully what you are trying to achieve by mixing joint types, because mixing them is tedious and time-consuming.

If you are building a garage or room addition with the same masonry material as the house, you will achieve the best effects by matching the joint type and color to those of the house.

Structural effects. All the joints affect the function of the wall. Flush joints are desirable where stucco will be used to finish the block surface, but they will soak up water if exposed. Concave and vee joints drain well. Raked joints look good in dry, sunny climates, but they collect snow and ice in cold areas. Beaded, struck, and extruded joints are not watertight joints.

Color. Mortar color also influences the appearance of your walls. Color mixes are available. Mortar mix is affected by moisture and the moisture must be consistent if the color is to be even. If you are interrupted by rain, you may have to wait until the mortar in the wall dries a little and for the weather conditions to resemble those in effect when you started laying the wall.

Tooling the Mortar Joints

Some of the joints can be made with a trowel, some with an appropriate-sized pipe, and others require special tools. Plexiglass jointers should be used for white or light-colored mortar in order to avoid stains.

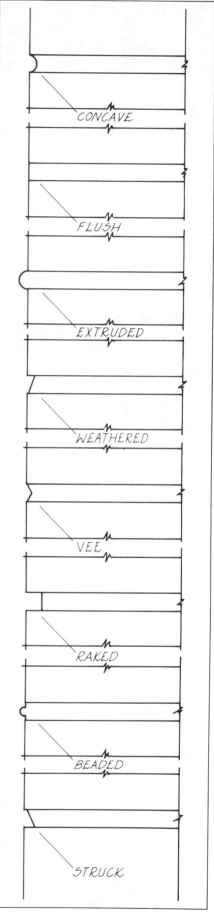

Shown are the eight most common types of mortar joints for concrete block and brick.

Rough finish joints with a trowel to remove excess mortar and to clean mortar from block.

When mortar has set enough to hold a thumbprint, smooth the joints with a jointing tool.

Test the mortar by pressing it with your thumb. If your thumbprint remains and the mortar does not stick to your thumb, the joints are probably ready to be tooled.

There will be joint patching to do, regardless of how carefully you work. It is best to patch when the mortar is still plastic. But if you must patch after the mortar hardens, gouge out the joint about a half-inch, wet it, and patch with fresh mortar.

Adding Control Joints

Control joints help avoid large cracks that occur due to expansion and contraction of the blocks during weather changes. There are many ways to build control joints, but three types are most common: the Michigan type, the tongue and groove, and the premolded rubber insert.

Michigan type. This is built using typical flanged block. You simply fold in a strip of building paper on one side of where the joint is to be, all the way up. The core between the two blocks that make up the joint is filled with mortar. The building paper allows the mortar to bond only to the units the mortar touches. The mortar plug in the core keeps the wall from moving from side to side, but it allows up and down movement and lateral movement. Regular block coursing is used in this method. Where the joint occurs, the block is cut to accommodate it.

Tongue and groove control joint. Special block units are used at these joints.

Premolded control joint. In this joint a rubber insert is placed along a precast vertical joint.

Caulking the joints. All control joints should be caulked. When the mortar in the joint becomes stiff, rake it out about ¾ inch. Coat the sides of the joints with a sealer and grease the back of it with a bond breaker. Caulk will adhere to the sides of the joint without drying out, so it can slide against the back of the joint.

FINISH COLORS AND STYLES
Color in Concrete Blocks

The type of aggregate, cement, and mix ingredients determine the "natural" color of concrete block. You don't have to use the gray ones you are accustomed to seeing. Most block becomes darker with age.

Painting is still the most common means of adding color. This removes the concern about color uniformity (block color varies slightly from lot to lot — try to buy all you need at once and check for color uniformity) and it is a simple way to achieve the desired color scheme and service requirements. It is possible to buy ground-face units that expose the natural color of the aggregate. There also are more and more units becoming available with integral coloration. Some of the standard colors available for integrally colored concrete block are tan, buff, red, brown, pink, and yellow. Green, blue, black, and gray may also be found. You can find mortar colors that match the colors chosen for the block.

Surface Texture

Surface texture of concrete block can be varied by aggregate, mix, wetness of the mix and compaction. Textures are generally classified as open, tight, fine, medium, and coarse. Usage determines which classification is best; stucco, for example,

Control joints allow vertical shifting to prevent cracking. Building paper allows movement.

A brick veneer will help dress up backing walls of concrete block, concrete, or wood, as long as some sort of connecting fastener is used.

clings best to a coarse-textured block. A fine texture is more easily painted.

There are also "prefaced" units available in many colors, patterns, and textures. They may be scored, patterned, or dappled. Ceramic and mineralized glazes are also available. These units may be used uniformly or combined for desired design effects.

Using Stucco

Stucco, or cement plaster, is a mixture of portland cement, masonry cement or plastic cement, sand, and water. Color may be mixed into stucco, and a wide variety of textures is possible. Rough textures tend to hide minor imperfections in the wall.

Stucco is a thin mortar-coat surface applied in three separate coats. The first coat is called the scratch coat, the second layer is called the brown coat and the last layer is the white or finish coat.

New concrete masonry walls provide a good base for stucco. Whether new or existing block, the wall should be free of dirt or any material that might reduce the bonding effect. The wall should be damp, but not wet, before the application of stucco. Sprayers are better than hand methods for dampening the block. If the water is not readily absorbed, or droplets appear even though you are not spraying enough to wet the surface, a bonding agent should be used to prepare the surface (1 part portland cement, 1 to 2 parts sand, and enough water for a heavy, paintlike mixture).

Applying the scratch coat. Make up a mix of 1 part mortar cement and 4 parts sand, and add just enough water to make the mix workable. Use a steel trowel. Starting at the bottom of the wall, trowel on a coat that is about ¼ inch thick. Once you begin, you must complete the wall, otherwise there will be start and stop lines. A piece of cardboard held against window and door frames and at the corners helps create an even start and stop in those areas. As soon as you have covered an area, it should be scored with a scratch tool. This is a homemade shop tool.

Applying the brown coat. Apply the brown or second coat as soon as the scratch coat can hold up to it without cracking while the brown coat is troweled on. If you must wait longer, spray the surface of the first coat with a fine mist of

Broomed stucco surface on concrete block wall seals surface and increases visual impact.

water. Keep the delay between the scratch and the brown coat short; this results in a better bond and cure.

This second coat is mixed and applied in the same manner as the scratch coat. It is allowed to set for about 6 hours, and then is lightly moistened with a fine spray of water. Allow the wall to cure for about 2 to 3 days, moistening it every few hours.

Applying the white coat. For the last coat, moisten the brown coat with a water mist and apply a coat made up of 1 part white cement and 3 parts white stucco sand. This coat should be about ⅛ inch thick and is applied in the same manner as the first two coats. The white stucco coat can be textured in many different ways. If you flip the stucco onto the finished surface, the surface ridges can then be troweled smooth or only slightly leveled down to create a roughened, pocked surface. You can also use the float to create unusual textures. After it has been installed, allow the stucco surface to cure by keeping it damp for a week.

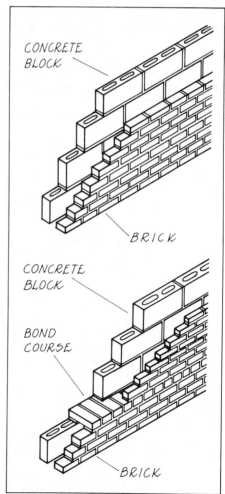

If the brick veneer has no structural attachment, it must be secured to a structural wall with a wire anchor or reinforcement.

STUCCO:
SCRATCH COAT
BROWN COAT
FINISH COAT

MASONRY WALL

SELF-FURRING
WIRE FABRIC LATH.

DRIP SCREED

STUCCO ON MASONRY WALL

Stucco is applied in coats to block wall. Base is applied over wire lath to hold plaster to wall. Two more coats of plaster are applied before the wall surface is complete.

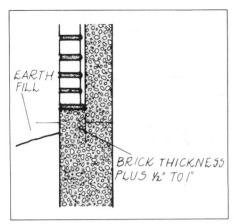

Brick veneer must sit on foundation base that is wide enough to allow for the brick and an air space for best construction practices.

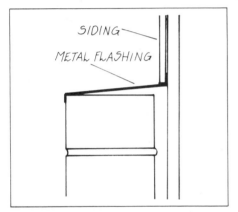

Flashing fits under siding and over brick if veneer comes part way up a wall. Flashing protects walls from water leakage and seepage.

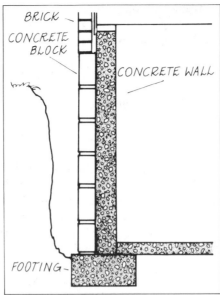

Brick veneer only where it will show. If your construction is poured concrete, veneer foundation with block to support the brick.

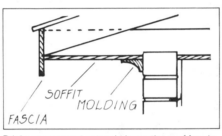

Brick veneer must extend above the roof fascia. Butt joint of soffit and veneer should be covered with a broad molding.

Adding a Brick Veneer

The techniques for laying clay brick and concrete brick are similar to those for concrete block walls. Brick is an effective and handsome veneer over concrete block, or brick may be bonded with concrete block.

Laying the Veneer

Build up corner leads, fill in, and continue the process until the veneer is as high as you desire. Leave a ½ to 1 inch space between the wall and the veneer. This air space serves for ventilation and moisture control. Don't let any mortar drop behind

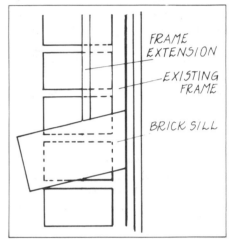

Often the window or door framing is not wide enough to accommodate veneer. If so, attach a frame extension with masonry anchors.

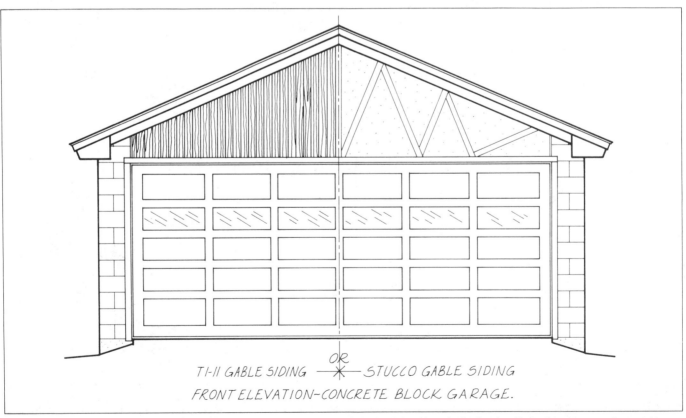

Plain concrete block walls may be combined with a more elaborate gable finish and door for a look of style without the expense of veneering.

the bricks or protrude behind them. Use a piece of wood about the thickness of the air space to scrape away the mortar that squeezes out as you seat the bricks.

Installing a moisture barrier. A moisture barrier installed in the mortar joint between the second and third course of bricks prevents ground moisture from seeping up and saturating the mortar lines. Although the barrier is not required, it is recommended, especially in areas of the country subject to high levels of ground moisture.

The barrier is a sheet of 4 or 6 mil polyethylene cut to the width of the course. Spread a thin layer of mortar on the bricks. Lay the sheet on top of the mortar. The front edge of the sheet should fall slightly back from the front edge of the bricks so that the sheet will not be exposed when the joints are tooled. Lap cut edges by about 4 inches. Then place a layer of mortar over the sheet and seat the next course.

Adding weep holes. Weep holes must be placed in the lower brick courses. The holes provide an exit for any moisture that may accumulate between the two walls. In vertical mortar joints set in special 3/8-inch metal tubes that are long enough to reach from the outside of the veneer to the air space. Space them 2 to 3 feet apart. The metal tubes should angle downwards toward the outside of the wall. Then lay the mortar and the next course.

Using wall ties. To hold the veneer in place (and to keep it from collapsing into the yard), the structure is secured to the wooden frame wall with metal wall ties placed on 3-foot centers in every fourth course. One end of the tie is nailed in place with ring shank nails; the other is laid on the mortar bed. The next mortar application and brick course holds the tie in place. Offset the ties from one course to the next so that they do not align vertically. The ties give the veneer overall support.

Finishing window and door openings. *Window sills.* When you come to a win- dow, you can choose from at least two finishing methods for the sill. The most common treatment is to lay a series of rowlock headers, which will form a brick sill. Set the headers at about a 20 to 30 degree angle to maintain proper drainage. The sill should extend at least one header's width on either side of the window open- ing. The mortar will hold the bricks in position so they won't slide into the yard.

Door and window lintels. Work up the wall space on either side of the window or door until you reach the top of the open- ing. Throw a mortar line over the courses;

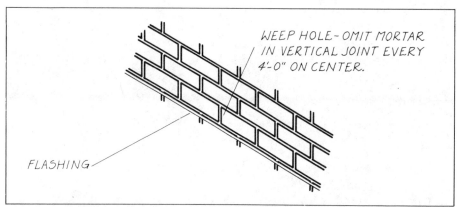

Leave space for weep holes in large expanses of veneer. Place flashing below weep hole to prevent moisture from reentering the masonry and causing damage.

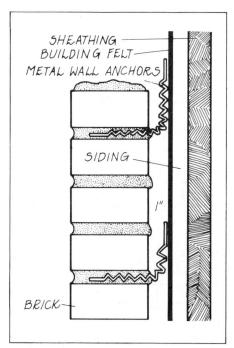

As you lay the bricks, install one end of a metal wall anchor into the mortar bed between courses; nail the other end to the framing.

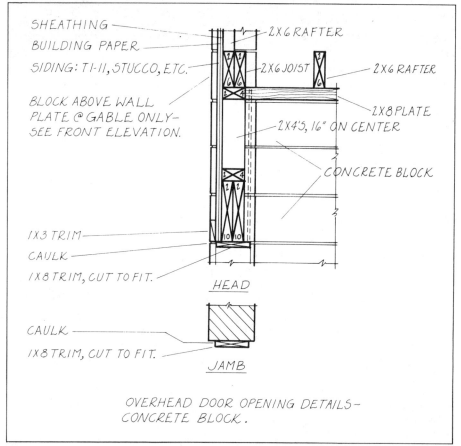

Framing for overhead door must be installed as the block walls are constructed. Caulk joints between wood and block to prevent water or air leaks that could cause damage or discomfort.

then install a piece of angle iron lintel that is long enough to span the opening and extend from 6 to 8 inches beyond either side. Cover the lintel with mortar and lay the course of bricks above the lintel. Then continue working up the wall.

USING STEEL REINFORCEMENT

Plain masonry walls are those without reinforcement. Reinforced walls, in construction terms, usually refer to walls in which the reinforcement is an indispensible part of the wall structure. For residential purposes, the need for reinforcement will often fall somewhere between these two cases.

Continuous horizontal metal ties in masonry joints prevent obvious cracks caused by shrinkage and temperature movement. There will still be cracks, but they will be too small to be easily noticed. Joint reinforcement is placed on the bare block, then covered with mortar. At corners, prefabricated corner and T-type reinforcement are preferred, although corner reinforcement can be job fabricated. Joint reinforcement is especially important at wall openings — windows, doors, vents, and so on.

Concrete wall footings often need continuous steel bars or wire mesh reinforcement. Where a poured concrete or reinforced block foundation wall is required, or in the case of a concrete retaining wall, it is often necessary to use steel dowels turned up from the footing; the foundation wall is poured over the dowels. Where concrete walks are driven over by automobiles or subjected to other heavy loads, wire mesh or steel bars are used.

There are additional special reinforcement requirements for hurricane and earthquake areas.

The variety of designs and individual usage requirements make it impractical to present other than the typical examples of steel reinforcement above. However, most home projects are subject to the pro-

Block provides solid construction for this garage largely below grade. Brick veneer matches the house. Note catch basin in drive to collect water runoff and prevent flooding of garage.

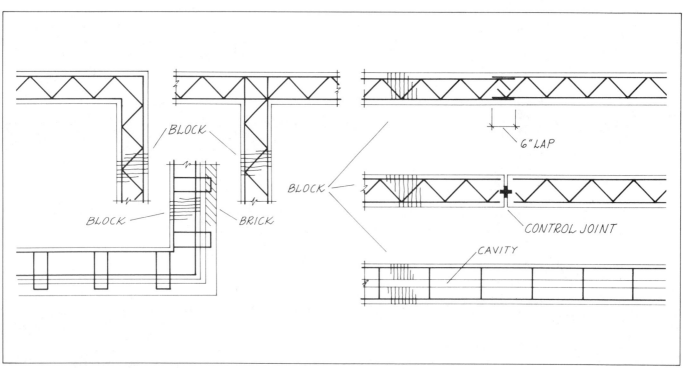

Shown are methods of dealing with masonry corners, laps in reinforcement, control joints, walls with cavities, and walls butting other walls.

visions of local building codes which you can read at the library. Also, local HUD offices provide guidelines for their localities. If you are unable to get the information you need from the city building official or HUD, it will pay you to seek professional design consultation. Guessing on structural data will often result in either a higher cost than the professional consultation would have cost (due to over-designing), or will result in an unsatisfactory wall that leans or cracks.

ATTACHING THE ROOF
Installing a U-Block Lintel
The tops of the concrete block exterior walls require special attention before they can receive the ceiling joists and roof rafters. The second course from the top course should be a ''U-block lintel'' or ''bond beam.'' This is a specially cast block shaped like a trough or flower planter box (window box). These blocks have the same outside dimensions as the other concrete blocks. You would not be able to tell the difference between the U-block and a regular block, once it is laid.

The purpose of the U-block is to hold concrete, and it can do this because of its trough shape. Instead of placing regular block in the second course from the top, lay a U-block lintel and fill it with concrete before you lay the top course. After the top course is in place, trowel the concrete into the top two courses (the U-block and the regular top block course), flush with the top of the blocks. What happens is that the second course down, the U-blocks, stop the concrete from running down into the wall block cells below. This enables you to anchor the 2-inch plate. In this case use 2x8 lumber because 8-inch block is used in the example garage. You could use 6-inch, 8-inch block, 12-inch or even 4-inch block. However, 8-inch block is typical and is the easiest size with which to work.

Placing the Bolts
The anchor bolts (½ inch diameter, 18 inches long) must be long enough to hold the nuts and be threaded on both ends. Space the bolts at least 4 feet on center and in no case more than 8 feet on center. There should be one bolt placed no less than 12 inches from each end; there will always be a minimum of 2 bolts in a plate. When the concrete has dried enough so that the bolts will stay perpendicular when

placed, set the bolts a minimum of 15 inches deep, with the washers or nuts inserted into the concrete-filled cells. Work the bolts around so the concrete is all around the bolts; do not let the concrete set too long or it will not be plastic enough to do this. Let the concrete set fully before you place the 2x8 plate over the bolts.

Adding the Plate
When the concrete has set with the bolts in it, have one person hold the plate lumber up to the wall top from a ladder and mark the locations of the bolts on the lumber. The plate lumber can be handed down to someone on the ground, who can drill the

holes with a power or hand drill (⅝-inch holes for the ½-inch bolts). The plate selected should be about 3½ inches thick (for a doubled plate). It should be approximately the width (not more or significantly less) than the block it sets on.

Install the plate over the bolts and tighten the nuts with an open-end wrench. Use washers between the nuts and the plate. Do not tighten the nuts too much, just enough so that the washer begins to impress itself in the plate (seat itself).

Once you have the plate in and tightened down, the ceiling joists and rafters and other roof components are installed just as for the frame garage.

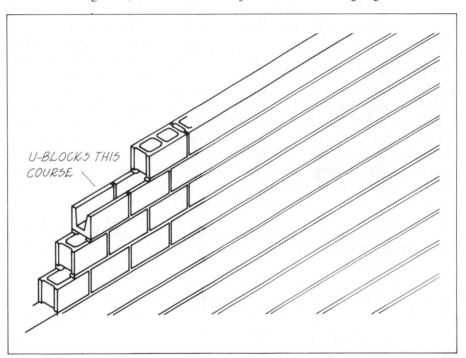

The U-block lintel is a concrete block whose shape resembles a window-box flower planter. When the block is filled with concrete, it can serve as a beam.

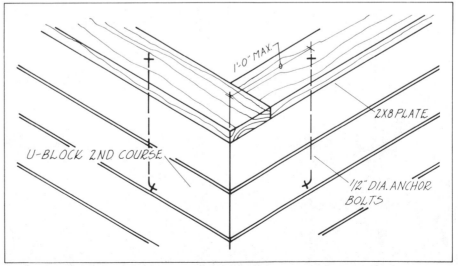

Wall head plate bolts in the concrete block garage should be spaced at least 4 feet on center, but never more than 8 feet on center. With bolts within 12 inches of corners.

13

Expanding a One-Car Garage

You will notice that many of the procedures for an expansion duplicate those involved in construction of a new double-car garage.

EARLY STAGES

The first step is to extend the slab. Stake out the new slab area, which is (for this example) an area off the side of the existing garage about equal to the slab (floor) area on the existing side. Use batter boards and strings. The layout will be simpler than when building from scratch, because you have the existing slab to supply the reference points.

Footings and Foundation

Excavate the area for the new slab, level it, and put in 4 inches of gravel. This garage "addition" can be built with a one-piece floor slab (4 inches thick) and foundation or, if it is an older garage you can duplicate whatever foundation it already has — probably concrete footings with masonry or poured concrete foundation walls. The excavation should be 4 inches down for the gravel, and 4 inches for the slab — a total of 8 inches. The footings, of course, will be deeper, depending on the frost conditions in your area (refer to Chapter 6). Install the form boards.

Extending the old foundation. Before you pour the slab addition, secure ½-inch expansion joint material to the edge of the old slab. At the edge of the old slab, you also will need a foundation for the new slab, because the new slab portion will not be connected to the old slab with mesh reinforcement. The best way to proceed is to dig down beside the old slab, at the side where you intend to pour the new slab, to see what kind of foundation is down there. You can, as mentioned earlier, duplicate the kind of foundation that is there; or, you can build your new slab as a one-piece slab and foundation (you may need to consult an architect for advice about the best way to tie in with an existing foundation, especially since the old foundation may be substandard by present-day building standards).

Laying the subbase and reinforcement. Once the foundation has been excavated, lay the gravel. Position a vapor barrier over the gravel and lay 6x6 #10 wire mesh reinforcement 1 to 1½ inches up from the vapor barrier. Keep it at that height with small stones or brick rubble.

Pouring the concrete. With a helper, pour the concrete; level it with a 2x6 screed. When the concrete has been leveled, you can match the finish of the old garage or change it if you like. The expansion joint will provide a good separation line between the two surfaces. Before the concrete hardens too much, set the sill anchor bolts, as discussed for the new garage.

Driveways. You will have to modify your driveway for the new space you are creating; it can be done now or later. If you are using ready mix, you should ar-

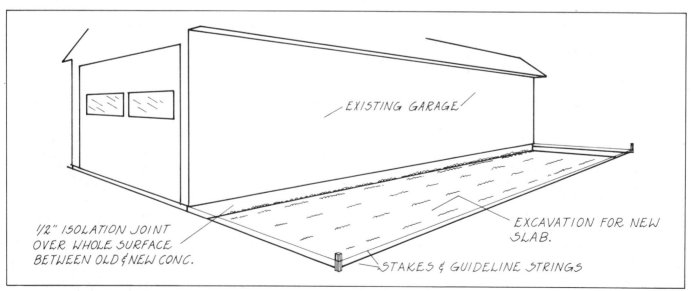

Laying out the slab for an expanded garage is simple because you can use the existing garage for reference points. Use stakes and guideline strings to extend the existing slab as shown.

range for the driveway modification to be handled at the same time you do the slab additions. If you are mixing your own concrete, you can carry out the drive changes whenever it is most convenient to you.

Removing the Old Roof

Remove the roof shingles and felt from the roof and discard them. Take off the sheathing and remove the nails. Take off the rafters, remove the nails, and stack the rafters nearby. A discussion of how the old rafters can be used for the ceiling joists of the added portion will be given later.

FRAMING THE EXPANSION Walls

When you have the old roof off, brace the end walls with 2x4s nailed at the top of the wall (the wall plate) and secured at the ground with 2x4 stakes.

Now you must consider the old side wall. The old side wall supports the existing ceiling joists. So, you can either take out the old (existing) ceiling joists and replace them after you install the new center beam (discussed in the following text), or you can support the old ceiling joists with adjustable scaffolds while leaving the old ceiling joists in place as you remove the old wall. Then you can build the center beam under the old joists and remove the scaffolding when the beam is in position under the old joists. Either of these methods will work but, obviously, you will save time by using scaffolding to avoid removing the old joists.

Taking Out the Old Side Wall

If possible, remove the old side wall with the siding intact (assuming the sheathing and siding are adequate and that you intend to save it). Removing the whole wall, siding and all, may not be feasible because of the weight. One option is to hire a backhoe operator to rig lines to the wall and pull it to where you want it after you disengage it from the end walls. You also might try it by hand, if you could find enough help — probably six or eight people, depending on the weight of your particular wall. Generally speaking, it will be best to remove the siding from the old wall and to then remove the framing intact, as one unit.

Dismantling the old siding. Carefully remove the siding and sheathing with claw hammers and crow bars. Remove any other material from the wall framing. Remove all old nails.

Disconnecting the side wall. Free the side wall from the front and back walls (also called "end walls") and from the concrete slab. The side wall will be nailed to the end walls. Brace the side wall before you disconnect it from the end walls. When the side-wall framing is disconnected, move it close to the edge of the new slab and lay it down so that it can be tilted into place when you are ready. You will need at least two people to help you with this job.

Preparing the side wall. Lay the old framing out and do any patch work or bracing that may be necessary to provide a stable, plumb wall for the addition. See Chapter 7 — the old wall should be

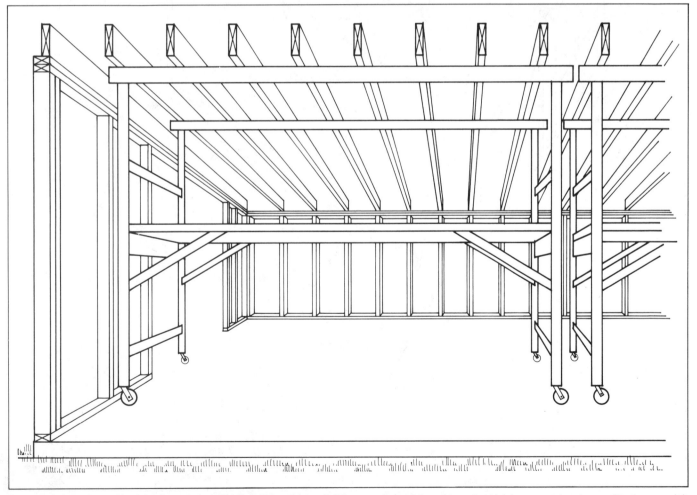

One way to keep the ceiling joists is to use scaffolding. Place the scaffolding near the existing side wall, which is removed and moved to the new slab edge. The scaffolding can remain in place while you build a beam underneath the joists.

Replacing the Side Wall

Extending the front and back walls. Move the sill of the old wall to the edge of the new slab and mark the position of the anchor bolts on the sill plate with chalk, or crayon. When you move the old side wall out, so it can become the side wall of the new addition, you must fill in the front and back walls. That is, you will fill in the additional space created by the extension. This ''filling in'' is simple stud wall construction, 16 inches on center. You will need another door like the one you have (check that a duplicate door is available before you begin the job). If you cannot find a duplicate door, or your old one is in too bad a shape to use, you will have to buy two new doors and reframe the front wall so that it will accommodate the larger door.

Adding sill plate bolts. Drill the holes for the sill plate bolts with a power or manual drill. Drill them slightly larger than is necessary to fit over the bolts so you will have some room to adjust the frame when you tilt it up. If the anchor bolts are ½ inch diameter (typical), then drill the holes about ⅝ inch.

Positioning the frame. Tilt the frame into position and tighten the sill bolt nuts by hand. Do not use a wrench until you are ready to set the bolts permanently. Check the frame for plumb. Check the top plate to be sure it is level. Make any adjustments necessary. When the wall frame is plumb and level, nail it to the extended end walls. The wall plates should overlap, as with the plates for the new garage. Tighten the sill nuts with an open-end wrench so that the washers impress into the wood, but do not tighten too much; you can split the wood or damage the threads of the bolts.

Installing the Center Beam

The center beam can be installed under the old ceiling joists while the old joists are being supported temporarily by scaffolding, or you can tear out the old ceiling joists, install the center beam, and then install both the old ceiling and new joists.

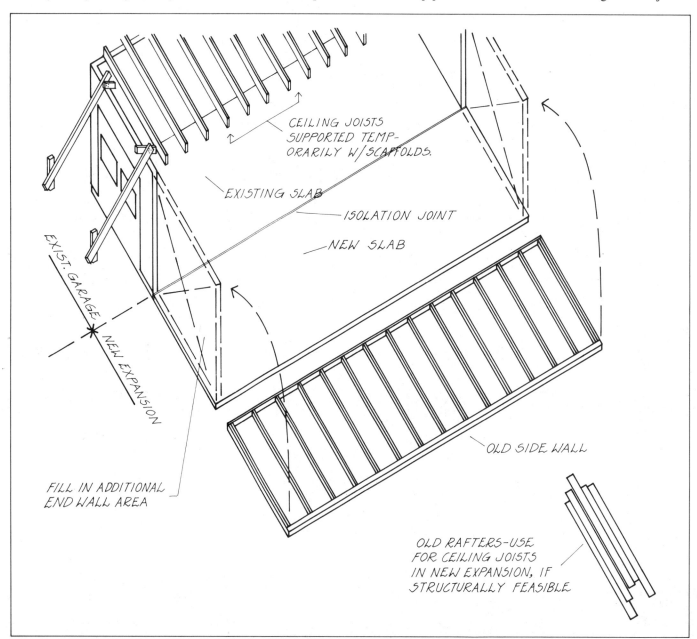

To expand a garage, remove the roof; support ceiling joists with scaffolding; remove the old side wall, fill in; replace sidewall and roof.

The beam will run down the center (length) of the garage; its purpose is to support the ceiling joists. The beam has an economical as well as a physical purpose; and that is to save the old rafters for use as the new ceiling joists. Save the roof rafters and use them for ceiling joists for the new garage addition. You already have the old ceiling joists for the existing section of the garage.

Creating the beam. The beam discussed here is for typical conditions. If you plan to have any weight on the beam itself, or if you plan to floor the ceiling joists and use the attic for storage, you should have the beam designed by an architect. But if you have no load on the beam, and it does not span more than 25 feet, build the beam with two 2x12s and a ½-inch steel plate, 12 inches wide. The steel plate is sandwiched between the two 2x12s. Drill holes in the steel plate to hold

½-inch bolts one foot on center. Stagger the bolt holes — one at the top, the next one at the bottom of the plate (at least 1 inch from the edge), and so forth. Ask the steel supplier to drill the holes for you. The 2x12s should be drilled with holes to match up with the steel plate holes — you can do that. You will need ½-inch bolts and nuts to sandwich the beam together. The bolts need to be long enough to go through two 2x12s plus the ½-inch steel plate — about 4 inches. Provide washers, about an inch or greater in diameter, for both the head of the bolts and the thread end. Put the steel plate between the two 2x12s and tighten the nuts just until the washers impress into the 2x12s.

Placing the beam. The top of the beam should be installed flush with the top of the frame's wall plate. Where the beam meets the end walls, it should be supported with three 2x4s at each end; just add

extra studs to the framing wall. The 2x4s should be butted together at each end under the beam so the beam is resting centered over the three 2x4s. This produces a 4x6 column or post under the beam at each end. Nail the three 2x4s together with 10d nails at 8 inches on center.

For a general idea of what the beam looks like, and how it works, study the new garage framing details and overhead door opening. The comparison is not exact, but the two conditions are similar.

Joists and Rafters

If the old rafters have sagged too much to make good ceiling joists, sell or trade them for whatever you can get. Use framing 2x6s long enough to span the width between the beam and the expanded garage area and to fit the plates properly; that is, fit so that they extend over the plate far enough to gain the eave condition you want.

The garage roof will be framed as in Chapter 7. This is assuming you do not have extraordinary snow loads, in which case you might have to increase the size of your roof rafters, or increase the slope of your roof, or both. If you are in an area of extreme snow, you should consult with your building department or an architect for local practices in dealing with heavy roof loads. As in all the examples in this book, the designs are typical for areas of moderate climate.

The doors for an expanded garage can either be two matching single-width units, so you can keep the old door, or one of double width.

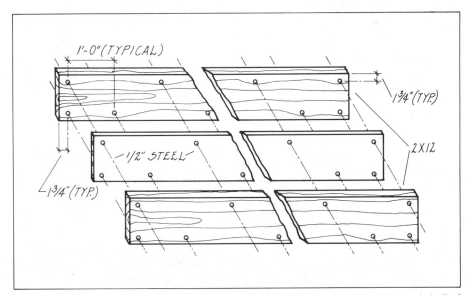

Consult an architect for design of any but the simplest beam. A typical residential beam is built of ½ inch steel plate sandwiched between two 2x12s.

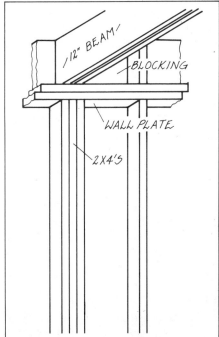

Secure three 2x4s to the wall 2x4s under the beam, with 2x12 blocking on each side.

14

Converting the Garage For Living Space

Rather than filling the location of the old garage door, this homeowner used the openings to create an airy, light-filled room.

The attic of a detached garage was able to serve as extra living space once a large dormer added the necessary light and headroom.

When converting a garage to living quarters, you must keep in mind the basic utility, light and ventilation requirements.

Everyone has seen garages and carports converted to additional bedrooms, dens, and other living spaces. Too often, the former use of the space is unpleasantly apparent. A successful conversion is more easily recognized than analyzed. So, for the moment, let it suffice to say that a successful conversion allows a person to fully enjoy the new space for what it has become, rather than feeling like it is still a place to change the car's oil.

In addition to the obvious finishing considerations, such as matching the exterior finish and trim, you will also have to take into account an existing driveway. An asphalt or concrete driveway leading up to a bedroom certainly is a giveaway. Solutions include first breaking up and digging out the old driveway, and then adding fill, resodding, starting a vegetable garden, adding planters or beds, or any other type of activity area desired.

PLANS AND PLANNING
The plan should accurately describe the existing floor plan, the existing mechanical, electrical, and plumbing plan, and extensions of utilities. The plans should also have sections through for all the areas that involve the addition.

Enclosing a Carport
The addition or conversion should always start with an investigation of the existing structure. Find out what is there. Dig down around the carport slab enough to discover the kind of foundation. Locate and size the existing plumbing, mechanical, and electrical systems. Sketch the existing house services and the existing structure, to scale. Then consult with experts to determine how to tie in with the existing services and to create a plan for each of them.

Enclosing the sides of carports, installing windows in garages, and the general construction work in this section, follow the same principles outlined elsewhere in the book. However, if you will be re-using old windows, old doors, and other equipment, you have the problem of first dismantling the equipment and then planning for its new use.

If you are enclosing a carport, you need to match the wall materials you add to those of the existing construction, both

with the house itself and with any portion of the carport that may be enclosed (some carports, for instance, have low walls, four feet or so, on two sides).

Physical Limitations
At this point, ignore any problems you may see with the mechanical, electrical, and plumbing; consider only the circulation and use of the room. The utilities must serve your plan, not the reverse. How does the garage or carport physically relate to the house? What are the floor level differences? Consideration of these questions will help you arrive at design priorities. The finished plan should successfully blend the circulation of the new space in with the rest of the house. Adjoining garages that are entered from the kitchen door are often suitable for dens or family rooms. It may be more difficult to make bedrooms of them. So it is necessary to consider the conversion in view of the entire house. An adjoining garage might become the den and the old den could become a bedroom.

Existing doors and windows should be thought of as existing equipment that you may or may not be able to use. Do not let the equipment dictate your design. If you can use existing equipment for the design you want, do so. If it does not work in with your plans, try to sell or trade the equipment. It is usually best to keep the floor and ceiling levels of the conversion the same as those of the house. If this is not possible, or if doing so is out of your budget (the rafters can be moved up in order that the floor may be raised, but this is expensive), the transition between levels must be carefully studied.

PLANNING FOR UTILITY EXTENSIONS

Conversions and additions require the modification and/or extension of mechanical, plumbing and electrical services.

Sketches and Work Plans

Your sketches are valuable aids in planning and designing your additional utility requirements. Study your mechanical, plumbing, and electrical sketches to determine any particular problem that may affect room design. For example, assuming you are including a bathroom, can you locate the bathroom conveniently to the existing plumbing lines without seriously compromising your plan? Is there space for a water heater if you need one?

Now is the time to make minor modifications in your room design that enable the most practical use possible of your existing utility arrangement. If you are not knowledgeable enough about the mechanical, plumbing, and electrical services to know the possibilities, you should consult with an architect or general contractor.

Heating and Cooling Requirements

If you have a forced-air heating system and a condenser that utilize the same duct for cooling, you must determine whether or not the system is adequate for tying in to your conversion or additon. The round, flexible ducts are probably most convenient for conversions and additions; one popular arrangement brings the ducts through the attic to the room registers. If you do not have a central heating and cooling system, now is a good time to plan one, if you can fit it into the budget. If not, or if your central system is inadequate, consider gas-fired wall heaters or electric baseboard heating units. You can cool with a window unit or a through-the-wall air conditioner.

A lot of items can be neatly stored without taking up a lot of room, as shown in this shelving-pegboard-hook arrangement.

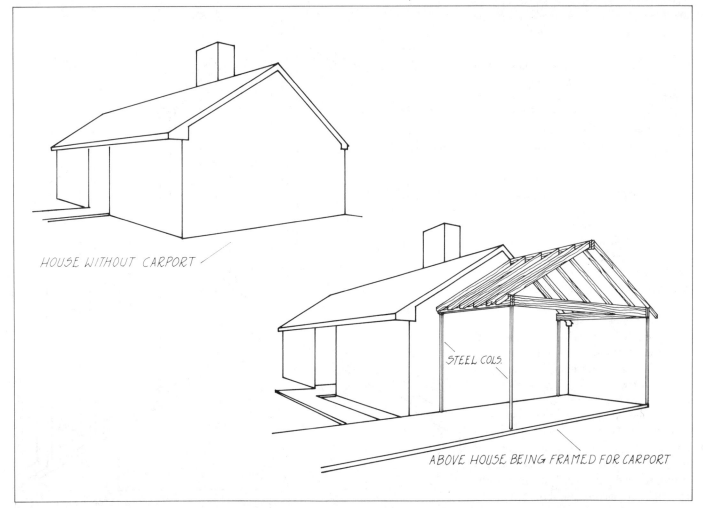

HOUSE WITHOUT CARPORT

STEEL COLS.

ABOVE HOUSE BEING FRAMED FOR CARPORT

When adding on, try to make the new structure self-supporting. However, if you attach the new structure to the house you can use fewer columns.

Plumbing Requirements

The plumbing system is made up of the DWV system (drain-waste-vent), the water supply, and the gas supply.

DWV system. The DWV system is a pipe network(s) that connects fixtures such as toilets, bathtubs, and sinks to a line that runs to the sewer; the vent part of the system is an open line going up through the house roof. The various waste lines have P-traps.

The main line to the sewer is typically run parallel to the house, as this simplifies any house connections by making them 90 degrees. But this practice is not essential if your site plan does not lend itself to the convention. The slope of the main line, (usually 4-inch pipe) is the most important thing; it is typically ¼ inch per foot. Stacks in the house are often 3-inch pipe if copper or plastic, and 4-inch if cast iron. In the DWV system, there are main lines with branches off to the fixtures.

Water supply system. The water supply system resembles the DWV arrangement. There are two parallel pipe runs, one hot water and one cold water. The supply mains will probably be ¾ inch, or whatever the size of the line from the street is.

The water supply usually comes from a single small pipe off the street line. In new construction, timing of placement of this line is important because it is the most convenient, if not the only, source of construction water. For water supply, apply to the appropriate officials.

Provisions to bring the water supply line into the house must be made. It may come in through the foundation wall of the house, in which case a sleeve needs to be provided when the foundation walls are constructed. Again, this points out the need to have your professionals help you plan the work, be responsible for coordinating the work, and stick to construction work schedules. A stop-and-waste valve at the point of entry will allow you to cut the water off and drain the line in freezing periods before the system is in use. Also plan shutoff valves so you can cut water to a fixture without having to shut down the water supply to the rest of the house.

The branch supply lines are usually equipped with tee-type shutoff valves at the fixtures. Above these tee-type valves (except for the toilet lines), there are vertical pipe extensions of about 12 to 16 inches in the wall framing. These pipe extensions are open at the top, providing an air cushion which prevents the loud "water hammer" noise that you may have experienced in older homes when you turn the water off.

Branch lines, single lines to outside faucets, and the water heater line are usually ¾ inch and tubing connections are ⅜ inch. Care must be taken when running any pipes through the house framing members so as not to weaken the structure significantly.

Plumbing rough-in. Cold water lines come up to the fixtures on the right side, with hot on the left, as you face them. It looks simple to dimension the plumbing rough-in locations and it is. But you must know the fixtures you plan to use before you do the dimensioning (or before the plumber does them). Get the manufacturer's rough-in dimensions and special instructions, and plan for those specific items.

Plumbing in new construction is normally installed before the flooring is installed. This means you will have to tie into your existing plumbing if possible, and bring it underground to the garage or

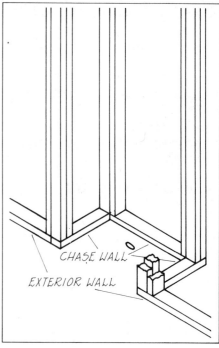

A chase houses and protects plumbing lines that otherwise would be exposed.

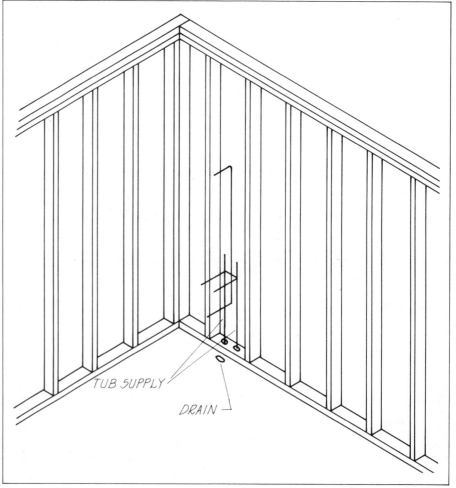

Small holes can in framework be made using a hand or power drill and larger ones by first drilling holes and then cutting out the larger area with a sabretooth saw.

through an adjoining wall of an attached garage. Your bath, shower, or other fixtures, will need to be located at the wall. They should be near the existing plumbing and water lines, if possible. The plumbing probably can be brought up between the wall studs, but if for some reason this is not possible, you can build a plumbing "chase" against the outside wall. A chase is an enclosed space for equipment. The wall cavity between the studs, for example, is the normal plumbing chase. The outside chase can be built to match the existing materials. It is simply an insulated box that encloses the plumbing lines. You have probably seen old houses with plumbing vents running exposed up the back or side of the house; a chase would enclose these pipes, protecting them from the weather and keeping them out of sight. If plumbing waste lines must be brought into the interior of the room, you will have to break out the concrete floor to make way for it.

Determine the locations of all your existing plumbing supply (water) and waste lines and vent stacks. Do a sketch of the plumbing lines, with their sizes (which you can measure), and sketch them freehand on a blueline copy of the floor plan. (Bluelines are literally blue lines on a white background. Blueprints are white lines on a blue background. The "blueprint company" can supply either type.)

Most homeowners are not knowledgeable enough to be able to plan their own plumbing revisions, but with a preliminary sketch, you can talk to a plumbing subcontractor and have him work with you to create a plumbing plan. Then you can decide which jobs you can handle yourself. Two tasks that most homeowners can undertake are extending existing pipes and connecting fixtures. Unless you have had prior experience with copper or steel pipe, use plastic pipe (if codes allow its use). Other work segments of the job you can handle include removal of exterior and interior wall materials in preparation for plumbing line additions, and other preparatory work for plumbing that the plumbing subcontractor would otherwise have to do.

Electrical Needs
Electrical work has little physical impact on building work. If you are adding only a circuit or two, you may be able to tap into an existing panel box. Have an electrician check your electrical plan and advise you. (See Chapter 7 on extension of cables.)

HEATING AND DUCTWORK: DOING THE JOB YOURSELF
Analysis of Current Heating and Cooling System
Planning for the first step in extending heating/cooling systems is to analyze the existing system. Heating/cooling systems are usually sized for the house as it was designed when first built. Therefore, it is not a certainty that your existing system will be able to handle the increased demands placed on it by adding space to heat and cool, without supplementary equipment or without replacing the furnace and condenser with larger units. It is assumed here that you have a forced hot-air furnace that utilizes the same ducts for cooling, with the condenser mounted outside.

The system analysis is best done by a heating/cooling subcontractor. For small jobs like conversions, the subcontractors will often come and look over your existing system at no charge and tell you whether or not the existing system is adequate for your increased space demands. If it is not, he will inform you as to what new equipment must be added. If there is a charge for this consultation, it will be small, and well worth the money. The heating/cooling subcontractor will know the code requirements for the location of condensing units and other equipment, and will know the code requirements for installing new wiring and extending old wiring.

Whether it be in a converted one-story garage, an attached two-story addition, or a two-story attached conversion, extending the ductwork presents the same problems and yields to the same solutions.

Procedures for Extending the Ductwork
You will learn much of what you need to know about installing ductwork by studying your existing ductwork. If you do not have ductwork, or you think the ductwork you have is substandard, go to a subdivision where there is new construction taking place and for a few hours watch how the builders install ductwork. Round ducts, or duct "pipes" are frequently used in residential construction, but you may have rectangular ducts with which you must deal. The round ducts are easiest to work with and may be used for extensions

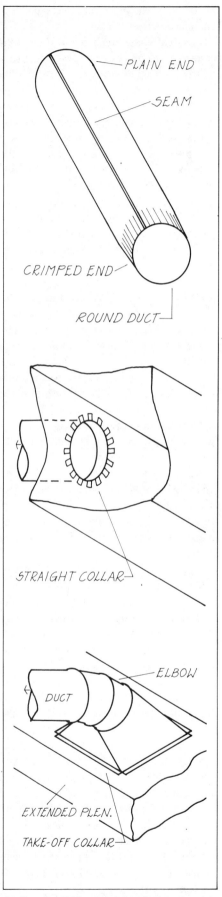

A crimped end of a round duct fits into the plain end, and runs the direction of air flow. Straight and take-off collars bring duct lines off the plenum or extended plenum.

off of both existing round ducts and rectangular ducts.

Physical characteristics of ducts and collars. One end of each round duct section is crimped and one end is plain. The crimped end tapers down several inches so that it fits into the plain ends. Round duct typically is shipped open; that is, the duct has not been fastened together lengthwise. The pipe has a tongue and slot to lock the two pieces together. The fit is obvious when you see the duct. Thread the tongue into the slot. There will be a ''click'' when the two pieces fit properly. Do not hammer the tongue and slot edge together.

The collar, the section of duct that connects a new duct run to the furnace, is best installed by the subcontractor, or by you under the subcontractor's instructions. There are typically two kinds of collars: a straight collar and a take-off collar. The straight collar fits directly to the furnace plenum. A take-off collar is used where there is an extended plenum from the furnace; the take-off collar fits on the top or side of the extended plenum.

Cutting and supporting the ducts. It will be necessary to cut the ducts; usually they can be cut with metal shears. Cut the ducts at the plain ends, not the crimped ends. Ducts may be bought in sections as short as 2 feet, but the typical sections are several times that length. Each length of duct should be supported with at least one metal hanger.

The metal hangers, called ''straps,'' look like metal tape with holes in them. Loop the metal hangers under the duct and bolt the hangers together at the top, nailing through the holes into some structural member of the house such as ceiling joists or floor joists.

In no case should the ducts have less than one hanger every 10 feet. However, this rule does not consider the joints, which are weak spots. Tight joints are important to efficient, quiet operation of the system. So it is recommended that you install a hanger at each joint in addition to the hanger for every ten feet or less along the run of the duct. Most contractors do not do this. But since it is your house and the hangers are cheap — and it does not take much time to take this extra precaution — do it. This will add to the longevity of your system.

Installing the ducts. Pull the insulation away from the existing duct. Locate a joint and take the duct apart there. Install the proper length(s) extension by sliding the crimped end of the pipe into the plain end. Note that the crimped end of the existing duct points away from the furnace. This keeps the forced air from escaping the joint. You will be installing the plain end of your new duct to the crimped end of the existing duct.

Fit the plain end of the duct over the crimped end so that the plain end slides over the crimped end as far as it will go. Save the joint screws you removed when taking the duct apart, and drill holes to accommodate the sheet-metal screws you removed. Secure the joint with the sheet-metal screws and run some duct tape around the joint, covering the joint and the screws.

Insulation. When you finish extending or adding all the ductwork, insulate the ducts and seal joints with a joint vapor barrier on the outside of the insulation (insulation and joint sealers are available at any heating/cooling supply house).

Dampers. Locations of dampers, the metal flaps inside that control the amount of air that flows, should be planned by a professional. You can buy and install prefabricated dampers yourself. They come in 2-foot duct sections, already mounted within the ducts. You simply install the short duct section just as for any other run of duct.

How to Extend Ductwork Through An Adjoining Wall

It is often necessary to extend ductwork through an existing, adjoining wall when a new attached garage is built or an attached garage is converted to living space.

The procedure for extending ductwork through an existing wall is much like the procedure for installing a through-the-wall air conditioner (discussed next in this text). The common problem is to make sure the wall cuts match on each side of the wall; that is, every point on the inside cut should face exactly opposite the same points on the other side of the wall. Always try to plan the duct route between wall studs, so you won't have to cut them. Always turn off the electrical circuit in the wall you are cutting.

How to cut a duct hole through the inside wall. Set a piece of cardboard over the open end of the duct to be extended through the wall and draw its outline on the cardboard. Set the drawing (template) against the wall where you want the duct to go through, and mark through each corner of the template with your pencil, identifying the corners on the wall. You could mark the corners with nails, if that is more convenient. If your wall is insulated, pull the insulation away from the studs before you mark the template corners.

With the markings for the duct corners (or several points around the circumference, if the duct is a pipe) transferred onto the existing wall, connect the dots between the corners (or round out the circle) with your pencil.

On a wall that is covered with sheetrock or plaster, draw the duct on it with the template, as described above. Then score the duct outline with a nail or similar pointed tool and remove the sheetrock or plaster with a chisel, tapping it with a hammer along the scored lines and maintaining a smooth edge.

Cutting wall studs. Studs always are connected at the top of the wall (to the wall plate) and to the bottom of the wall (sill). When you cut through a stud, you substantially weaken the stud and its original function as a wall member. To rectify this

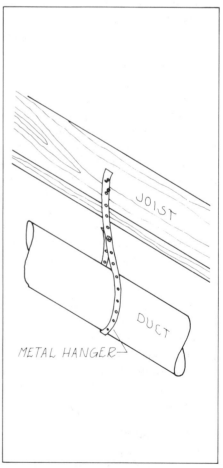

Metal hangers wrap around the duct or plumbing line, are joined together with a bolt, and nailed to the supporting member.

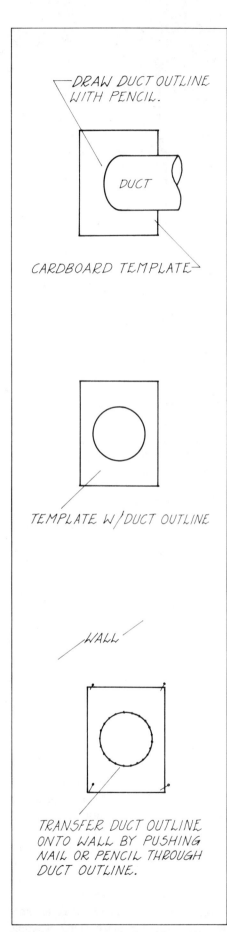

DRAW DUCT OUTLINE WITH PENCIL.

DUCT

CARDBOARD TEMPLATE

TEMPLATE W/DUCT OUTLINE

WALL

TRANSFER DUCT OUTLINE ONTO WALL BY PUSHING NAIL OR PENCIL THROUGH DUCT OUTLINE.

Use a template to cut openings. Secure it to the wall; transfer the duct outline onto the wall. Now you can cut through the wall.

problem you need to add blocking at the top and bottom of the hole and tie it (toe-nail) to the uncut studs on each side of the hole. The cut studs are toenailed to the blocking. Ducts are not heavy; an added horizontal 2x4 at the top and bottom of the hole should be enough.

If you must cut the stud, use a sabre saw, keyhole saw, or rotary power saw. For instructions on cutting through exterior walls of varying materials, see Chapter 9 on "How to Cut An Access Door."

Dust protection. When making a duct opening cut from the outside, you need to cover the inside hole to avoid brick dust or other debris being scattered around the house. Quarter-inch plywood, masonite, or similar materials temporarily nailed over the inside hole with light finish nails will serve the purpose.

Cutting holes for registers and grilles. You may use the same template procedure discussed above to cut holes for supply registers and return grilles.

HOW TO ADD AN AIR CONDITIONER
Window Air Conditioners

Window unit air conditioners are a quick and valid way of cooling some areas. They can, however, interfere with window functions — which are to see out of, to let light in and, on especially nice days, to let in fresh air.

Locations of existing windows deter-

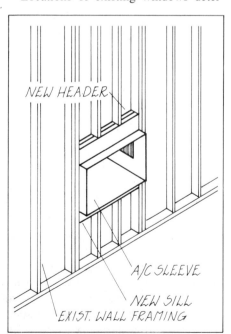

NEW HEADER

A/C SLEEVE

NEW SILL

EXIST. WALL FRAMING

If you cut studs for air conditioning, add support at top and bottom. Supports are 2x6s at the head and 2x4s at the sill, or toenail pieces of 2x4 blocking between studs at head and sill.

mine placement of window units, and this is not always where they will cool best or most efficiently. Add to these negatives the rotting of your window sills, and you may want to consider a through-the-wall installation.

Through-The-Wall Air Conditioners

Finding the right spot. First, decide where you need the air conditioner. Remember that air turns corners very inefficiently. Try to locate the air conditioner where the air flows as freely as possible to the areas you want cooled. Measure the outside of your air conditioner cover or "sleeve" and transfer the dimensions to the outside wall where you want the unit, using a level to keep the hole square. Allow a half inch or so, all around, for insulation; this means it will be necessary to frame flush with the wall opening; 2x4s are recommended.

Remember to always turn off all electricity routed through the area of the wall!

1. Use an electric hand saw with a 7-inch masonry-cutting blade to score the brick. Wear safety goggles for this job.

2. Score about 1 inch deep along the wall-opening outline, using the hand saw.

3. You may prefer to use a larger blade and saw completely through the brick. But the chisel is quite fast. (If you use the chisel, see Step 4.)

4. Start at or near the center of the outline and begin chiseling the brick out with a 1½-inch corrugated masonry chisel. Chisel out the brick as close to the score line as you can. If necessary, finish the roughed-out masonry opening with a 1½-inch flat masonry chisel.

5. Saw out the sheathing and other exterior wall material with a reciprocating saw, using a 6-inch blade. A keyhole saw would work for this part, but be prepared for a lot of exercise.

6. Use a level to project the corners of the brick opening onto the inside wall. Drill through the corner marks to locate the wall opening inside the house.

7. Inside the house, draw the hole opening by "connecting the dots" made by the drill holes. On plaster walls, the outline of the opening should first be tapped all along with the flat chisel, then scraped, using the chisel like

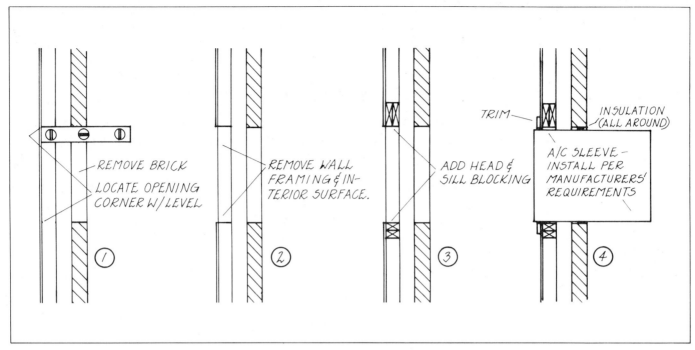

To install a wall unit, remove house siding, locate unit's corners, remove wall framing, add head and sill blocking, and place the a/c sleeve.

a knife to make a path for the reciprocating saw and keep the plaster from cracking. If the wall is sheetrock, the problem is not as great as with plaster — just insert the saw in the drill holes and cut away.

8. Remove all lath and plaster or sheetrock with a reciprocating saw. This assumes that the lath is wood. If the lath is metal, use cutting pliers to snip the metal or a keyhole saw. Be sure you have the correct blade for the best edge. Block off the inside opening when you saw the brick and/or sheathing to avoid dust and debris in the house.

9. Remove the studs flush with the wall opening. Remove any insulation or other obstructions from the opening. It is difficult to get a really smooth edge with plaster or stucco, but unless you badly chew it up, the lip of the sleeve will cover up your inconsistencies.

10. Frame in all around the opening, flush with the edges. Use 2x4s unless the unit is heavy; in that case, use 2x6s.

11. Slide in the air conditioner sleeve and secure it to the frame. Some units are designed to slope about ¼ inch from front to rear. Check the drainage requirements of the particular unit you use. It may be necessary for you to shim the air conditioner at the frame for it to drain properly.

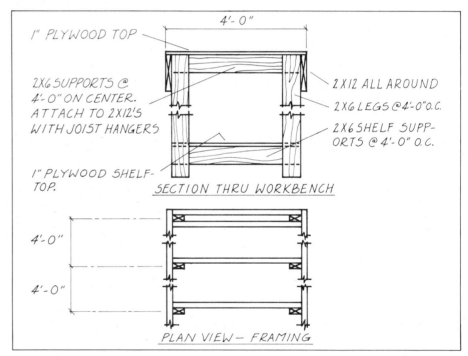

This workbench is strong, simple and fast to build. The shelf underneath is for storage; pegboard against the wall gives easy access to tools.

12. Choose decorative molding and size it according to the way you wish it to fit around the air conditioner. The "hose" type of insulation can be used in additon to the fiberglass insulation typically provided by the air conditioner manufacturer. It is easy to shove into the crevices and it stays tight and waterproof. Caulk all around the sleeve and frame inside with a caulk that accepts paint or stain, whichever you decide to use.

The installation above assumes you are installing the air conditioner in an existing wall of the house. If installing in new construction the job is, of course, much simpler. Just leave a rough-in opening where you want the through-the-wall unit. Then you can brick or put whatever siding around it you choose. The framing of the air conditioner will be the same as other openings described in Chapter 7, a simple 2x4 frame built to the manufacturer's dimensions.

Materials List

1 pc.	24"x49½" Plywood top	24 pcs.	3½"x1"x1" Cleats
1 pc.	4"x49½" Plywood brace	2 pcs.	27"x1"x1" Cleats
1 pc.	20½"x32¼" Plywood leg	1 pc.	27"x14" Pegboard
1 pc.	20½"x31½" Plywood leg	4 Hinges for legs	
12 pcs.	3½"x14½" Shelves	4 Strap hinges	
2 pcs.	49½"x2"x4" Apron	1 Hinge hasp	
2 pcs.	24"x2"x4" Apron	1 Eye bolt	

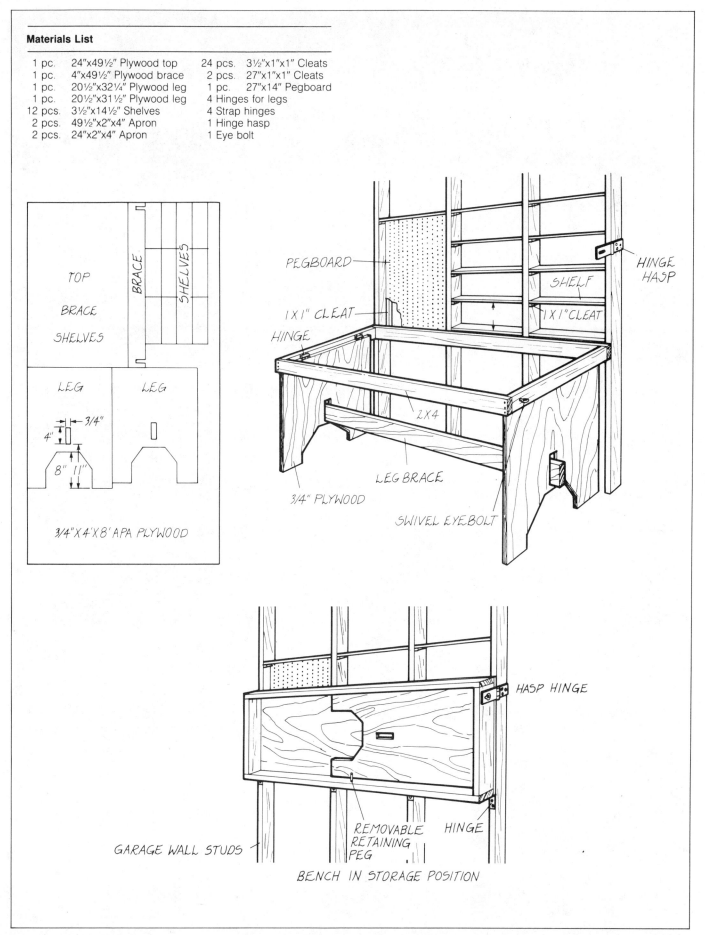

This workbench design was adapted from plans available from the American Plywood Association. Sheets of ¾-inch plywood are suggested.

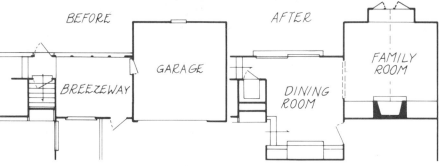

This transformation from attached garage to den was so effective, with its built-in window seat and creative decorating, that the result is hard to recognize as a garage conversion.

15

Adding Driveways

ASPHALT DRIVEWAYS
Types of Asphalt

Hot asphalt. Also called asphalt concrete, it is made by coating crushed rock with hot asphalt cement. It bonds much as concrete does. This is the kind of asphalt you see when the city repaves a street. Paving contractors use special equipment to compact the rock and spray the hot asphalt. It is difficult work, and is not for the amateur. Unless you have some special condition that requires hot asphalt, you probably could not justify the extra cost of using it.

Cold asphalt. This version can be bought in premix form. It is spread out and then tamped or rolled in place. It can easily be worked by a homeowner.

How to Lay Cold Asphalt

Step one: building forms. Prepare the surface to be paved with asphalt, just as you would for concrete. Pay special attention to the form work; it will be permanent because the edges of asphalt crumble unless they have an edging. For the permanent frame, use cross ties, brick on concrete, plain concrete, stone, or nearly any other material, as long as it is substantial enough to hold asphalt in place. Use members at least 2 inches thick and 4 to 6 inches wide. All wood should be preservative-treated. For thicker edges, which are recommended, use higher forms and exca-

vate an extra eight inches at the outside edge to permit a one-foot-wide thickening (2x12s are suggested).

Step two: laying a base. Spread 2 inches of sand uniformly over the area to be paved.

Step three: spreading the asphalt. Spill the mix out in small mounds on the area to be paved. Rake a few mounds level with a garden rake to get used to handling the asphalt. Then dump out some more, but not more than enough to do a few feet of walk at a time. Rake the asphalt to about 4 inches thick. Build the depth up at the center or slope it to the side toward which you want to direct the runoff. Do not let any area become less than 4 inches thick. Thicken the edges to about eight inches, so that there is a one-foot-wide, 8-inch-deep rim around the perimeter.

Step four: leveling the asphalt. You can rent power and manual rollers and tampers to tamp or roll the asphalt. Rolling probably assures a smoother surface, but it still may be necessary to tamp some areas.

Before you begin rolling, brush the roller with water so the asphalt will not stick to it. You can use an old broom with burlap tied over it to spread the water on the roller. Roll the surface until it is smooth and compacted, tamping any high areas. Use an asphalt tamper or make a tamper with a foot-square piece of ¾ inch ply-

wood nailed to the end of a 1x3.

Step five: finishing or adding to the surface. It will take several rollings to reach the tight compaction needed for the driveway. Before the final rolling, you may wish to top the asphalt with sand, gravel, crushed brick or a similar finish. Sprinkle the surfacing material over the rolled asphalt evenly or in a pattern you like, and roll the material flush with the asphalt. This can be very effective because the dark asphalt serves as a backdrop that emphasizes whatever topping you use on it.

Surface characteristics. One major difference between asphalt and concrete is asphalt's flexibility. Asphalt is a very malleable material. This makes the material easy to work with. If the grade changes are

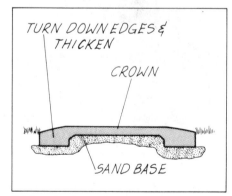

Thickened edges of an asphalt drive, and a crown to aid drainage, contribute to the long life of the wearing surface.

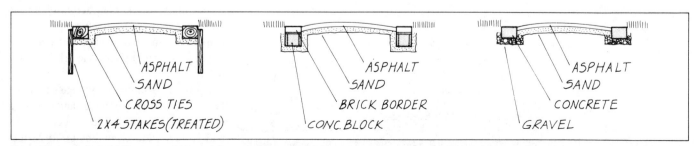

Edges of an asphalt driveway should be reinforced, either with thickened edges or with cross ties, brick, or concrete.

not too steep, the asphalt takes on the contour of the lawn. Any hollows that occur in the laying can easily be leveled later. Also, due to this flexibility, asphalt can be laid thinner than the minimum thicknesses required for concrete.

This thinness and flexibility may sometimes work against you, unless you are very careful about the base preparation. Asphalt will eventually reflect every rip-

Concrete driveways can be dressed up with exposed aggregate and with sections of brick within and around the driveway.

Forms for short, curved sections of concrete are of saw-kerfed ¼-inch plywood that is bent and braced every 6 to 8 inches.

ple on ground you fail to smooth. Therefore, you must be especially careful with the base. If the soil shifts or sags for any reason, the asphalt will follow suit. Mud and moisture will work through the asphalt without a sand base of about 2 inches. In particularly wet areas, it may be necessary to use a deeper sand or tamped gravel base.

Maintenance and protection. Asphalt requires more maintenance than concrete, but the repairs are easier to make. The edges, unless a sturdy retainer is used, are particularly subject to crumbling because asphalt has no structural strength. If a wood edging is used, it should be pressure-treated for below-ground use.

If not well compacted, asphalt will soften enough in hot weather to become dented by sharp objects such as iron chairs, tables, wheelbarrows, and skates.

Oil and gasoline dissolve asphalt. When you build any driveway or parking space, you should leave an open space as ground cover where the oil will drip. You could instead pave that area with brick or concrete or gravel. Or you could paint the area where the car will be with one of the specially manufactured paints for asphalt.

Curing. Asphalt mix contains an agent that must evaporate for the asphalt to cure. This curing will take place within a week or so for walking purposes, but it may take as much as six months for it to cure enough for car-weight loads and complete usage. Therefore, the best time to lay asphalt is just after it gets too cool to sit outside comfortably. By the next spring, it will be almost as hard as concrete.

BUILDING A CONCRETE DRIVEWAY

Pouring a concrete driveway involves basically the same procedures as pouring a slab. However, because of the extra

weight requirements, driveway construction is often well-regulated by local building codes. Make sure you understand all code restrictions before you begin construction. You also must have proper permits. For instance, most municipalities have strict rules governing the steepness, thickness and width of the driveway, as well as the means by which it joins the curbing.

Design Considerations

Most single driveways today are made of a single slab instead of the double-slab ramp drive that has paving only in the areas of the wheels and grass in between. A single slab provides a wider usable surface to serve the wheel base dimensions of more car models. The trend of the times has reinforced the single slab, perhaps partly because a single slab requires less edge forming. Then, too, you do not have to mow the grass between the strips. However, the double slab (also called "double strip") is a functional, economical driveway well suited to the do-it-yourselfer. In fact, many people prefer the grassy strip as a landscape feature. Two-car driveways, on the other hand, must be of full-slab design. (See also Chapter 1.)

Design Specifications

To unite the garage and the street. The edge of the driveway should fall about 1 inch below the garage floor, to prevent water from running into the garage. The drive should slope downward from the garage to the street. If your garage sits downhill from the street, install a drain where the driveway meets the garage. Where the driveway meets the street, raise the edge of the drive just a little above the road to prevent water and debris from flowing from the street into the drive.

Size of the drive. In most instances, the driveway is cast so it is 2 inches above ground level. Slabs for passenger cars are 4 or 5 inches thick; however, a slab that will have truck traffic should be 5 or 6 inches thick. Some contractors make the area near the street 8 inches thick to accommodate the extra weight of trucks that might pull partly up onto the driveway for delivery or collection.

A slab for a single-car garage should be between 8 and 10 feet wide, and one for a double-car garage should be between 15 and 20 feet wide — widths up to 22 feet are common.

DRIVEWAY (SLOPE AWAY)   ½" EXPANSION JOINT   GARAGE FLOOR SLAB

VAPOR BARRIER   VAPOR BARRIER

GRAVEL   GRAVEL

SILL @ OVERHEAD DOOR

Along the edges of the garage slab, where it meets the driveway, install a ½-inch isolation (expansion) joint.

Pitching the driveway. The driveway should also provide a pitch of from ¼ to ½ inch to the foot; this is considered a minimum in most areas. You can give a sideways pitch to the entire drive, but the best plan is to crown the driveway, providing pitch from the center to both sides.

To create the proper pitch from the center to the edges, the slab is poured in two stages. First, the form for the entire drive is built. Then a centered stopboard is inserted lengthwise in the form. It runs from the garage to the street, and must be high enough to create the correct pitch. If your driveway is to be 20 feet wide, the center of the pour must be 5 inches (10x½ inch) higher than the outside edges of the slab. The form boards at the garage and street must correspond to this pitch, and the top edge of the centered stopboard must be 5 inches higher than the side form boards. The center joint between the two sections of the slab will be held together with a butted construction joint.

Build The Driveway Forms

Entryways. For better appearance and easier access, use curved forms to provide curved entryways on both sides where the driveway meets the street. This design is sometimes utilized at the garage entryway as well. (See the section on patio construction for instructions on building curved forms.)

Joining the sections. The two sides of the slab will be held together with No. 4 reinforcing bars that are 36 inches long and are spaced about 40 inches apart. These will be held in place by the stopboard during the first pour. Bore holes in the stopboard. Oil the holes thoroughly, but do not oil the bars themselves. Pass the bars about halfway through the holes.

Base Preparation

Once the area is well excavated and smoothed, tamp it solidly. Unless the soil is extremely hard packed and well drained, lay the base as discussed earlier. Most codes will require 4 inches of gravel or crushed stone plus 2 inches of sand. Tamp the base materials.

Lay reinforcing mesh on rocks, placing it so that it doesn't touch any of the forms. Install isolation joints between the garage and the driveway and between the drive and any existing sidewalks. Asphalt impregnated cane fiber is the most commonly used material.

Making the Pour

The initial pour. When pouring a slab as big as a driveway, start at the garage and work out to the street. If you lay the length of the driveway in sections, install a stopboard at about 10 feet; it will then correspond to the placement of control joints. Place the concrete in this first section only. Tamp and spade as needed, giving special care to edges and tie bars. Screed the concrete off and place it into the adjacent, unpoured section. If you don't screed off, some places will have a lot of extra concrete, which must be moved; other spots won't have enough. You would have to solve these problems by moving the concrete, causing possible separation and weakening of the pour.

Let the slab set up. Cut any control joints as needed, and give the driveway a lightly broomed finish.

The final pour. Once the first half of the slab is finished, remove the stopboard. This will not be easy; it is hard to slip the tie bars back through the holes in the stopboard. Repeat the entire process for the remainder of the driveway, in 10-foot sections as needed to complete the driveway.

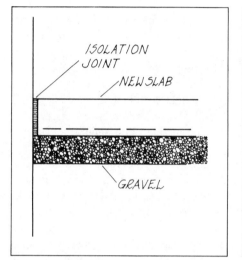

Whenever a new concrete pour meets an old surface of concrete, or any other material, an isolation (expansion) joint must be installed.

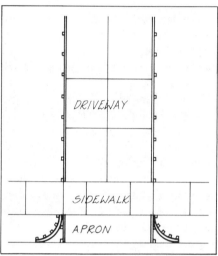

For a new driveway and apron, pour the concrete in sections. First, pour the apron; then pour the two curved sections at the side.

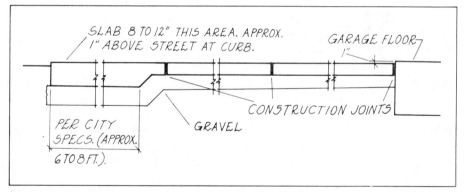

Construction joints are needed for a long drive, which is laid in sections. The sections should be keyed for a slab thicker than 4 inches, but can be butted if 4 inches or less.

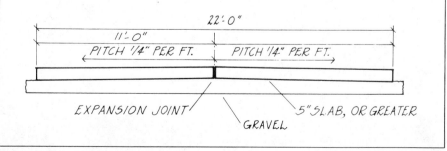

An isolation (expansion) joint should be centered in the driveway if, for drainage, the drive is pitched from the center to the sides.

16

Using Garage Kits

The detached, conventionally built garage in this text is the cheapest way to produce the structure. But it takes the most time to build. If your time is too valuable to spend building a garage from scratch, you may want to consider buying pre-assembled components. Roof trusses and wall frame panels shave some time off the construction schedule, although they add to the cost. But the time savings may be worth the extra money. Your third choice is to buy a completely pre-assembled garage kit and to erect it according to the instructions supplied by the manufacturer. This is the fastest and most expensive do-it-yourself garage. The savings will still be significant when compared to a professionally built garage.

BUYING GUIDE

There are some questions you should have the answers to before you buy *any* kit. First, does the kit meet the code in your area and if not, what must you add and what is the cost of bringing it up to code? Be very careful also concerning the materials specifications. Are the roof shingles and siding up to the quality you want and expect for the price you are paying? If

not, will the manufacturer delete the materials you do not want and give you an appropriate cost reduction in the package? Remember, for example, that there is no advantage in having a manufacturer send roof shingles to you: they are readily available anywhere, where you can see what you are buying. You should not have to pay more for any standard items — sheathing, felt, cement, caulk, nails, doors, electric opening devices, gutters, wiring, and the like, than you would have to pay locally. Buying a kit is something like buying a car. Since the manufacturer may be including locally available materials in his kit, you want to know who manufactures them and what part of the total cost of the package they represent, just as you would expect to know the costs of the air conditioner, the radio, and the other options on your car.

WORK SEQUENCE

You still have to get your foundation down. You can do it yourself, as detailed in the conventional garage section, or you can subcontract it, having the contractor lay the slab to your kit specifications. Before the kit comes, you should be familiar

with its contents and, to the extent possible, have the components unloaded where they will be most convenient to assemble.

Assembly

Following the manufacturer's instructions and keeping in mind the information in the section on conventional garages, the procedure is, generally, as follows.

Wall framing. Set the wall frame panels on the slab, tilt them up, and temporarily secure them with 2x4s nailed to stakes in the ground. Plumb the panel. Proceed tilting up the remaining panels, checking for plumb as you go. The top plate should be overlapped at the corners and nailed securely. The panels are first placed over the slab bolts with the nuts firm but not tight. When all the panels are in place and plumb, tighten the nuts.

Roof trusses. Now you are ready to set the trusses in place. Most trusses for garages will not be notched to fit over the wall plates. Make sure that the overhang is equal on both sides. This can be done by using alignment string, as discussed in the section on roof trusses, or as the manufacturer's instructions suggest. The trusses probably will be designed to fit 2 feet on center, which means that every other truss should be directly over a wall stud. The kit manufacturer will probably supply the gable extension, which looks something like a ladder, and is nailed to the preassembled gable ends.

Finishing interior and exterior. Next comes the sheathing or insulation board, which should come already cut to fit your wall framing and roof, with no additional cutting required. The remaining construction proceeds similarly to the conventional example in this text. All openings should be preframed and ready for the doors, windows, and so forth.

The lumber in a garage package comes precut to your specifications (sample package, Harris Lumber).

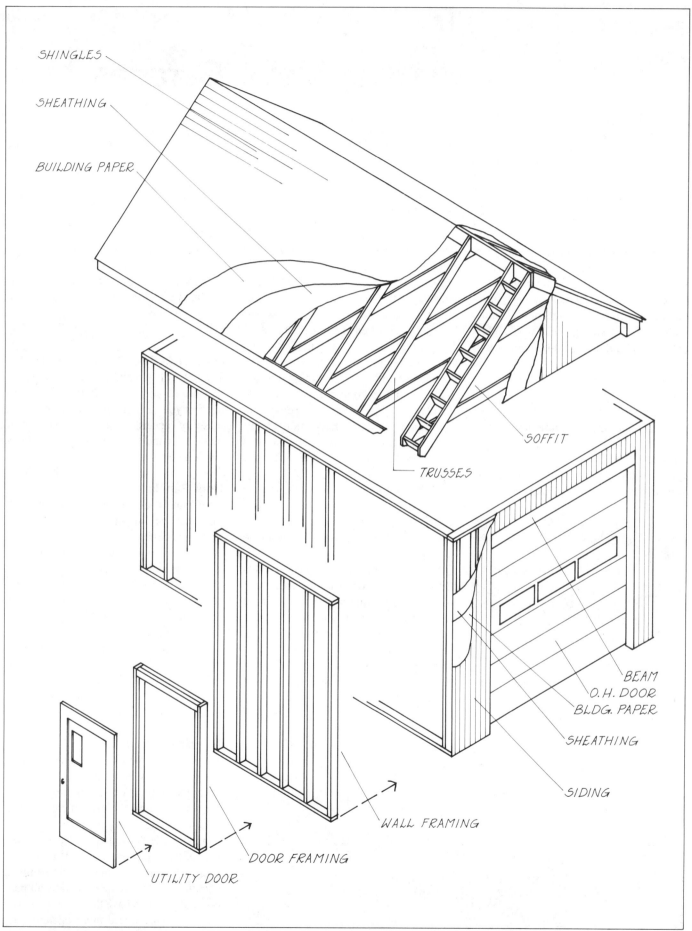

SHINGLES

SHEATHING

BUILDING PAPER

SOFFIT

TRUSSES

BEAM
O.H. DOOR
BLDG. PAPER

SHEATHING

SIDING

WALL FRAMING

DOOR FRAMING

UTILITY DOOR

The major components for a prefabricated garage include: roof trusses, wall panels, and door and window packages.

17
Building Metal Garages

Many of us think of metal buildings as those big, low, plain buildings seen in industrial office parks. Or we might recall those tiny little utilitarian storage structures stuck off in the corners of backyards, looking like a strong wind would blow them away. But the metal-building manufacturers have a range of garage-sized structures you may not be aware of; they can solve many homeowner storage and work area problems. They are easier and faster to build than conventional garages.

ADVANTAGES
Metal buildings offer some definite conveniences over conventional buildings.

A metal roof can attach not only to a metal garage, but also to a garage of other materials.

They are simple, because they have fewer component parts than a comparably sized conventional building. And all their components — the metal structural skeleton, doors, windows, eaves, roof, and skin — are pre-engineered for each building. They are a "package of parts" that you buy and assemble. This means there is less planning and decision-making involved.

Since all the components except the foundation (metal buildings are erected on foundations similar to conventional buildings) are factory built, you can determine early exactly what your building costs will be.

When the foundation is ready, you can assemble the building quickly, sometimes in one day. This quick assembly reduces construction labor; skilled workers are not required.

There are some disadvantages to metal garages. They have a utilitarian appearance that may conflict with the design of your house or with the other houses around you. The selection of colors is far less than you have when you paint your own conventionally built structure. The near-flat look of the gabled roof may be

out of character with your house. The other appearance problems can be dealt with: veneers or siding can soften the building's appearance. However, these are extra costs and must be considered when you make your building decision.

MATERIALS AND COMPONENTS
Typical wall panels are of heavy gauge galvanized steel with factory-applied colors, but you can dress the building up with masonry veneer, if you choose. The buildings take wind loads of about 25 pounds per square foot.

Roof Panels
Roof panels are factory-colored steel or they may be aluminum. It is a virtually maintenance-free roof. The roof is typically designed to take live loads of about 40 pounds per square foot. The roof panels have prepunched holes that allow for expansion and contraction. Buildings with "gabled" roofs slope about 1/4 inch per foot from the peak, just enough for drainage. In appearance, it is almost a flat roof. Shed roof styles are also available. Typical widths are 10, 15, 20, 25, 30, and 35 feet. The building can be as long as you need it to be.

The Basic Structure
The structure itself is ultra-simple. For a garage 20-feet wide by 25-feet long (similar to the conventionally built example in the text), you would have to erect only 4 columns and 2 beams. To support the roof panels and tie the structure together, there would be 4 purlins attached across the beams the length of the structure, plus 2 end purlins. Attach the roof and wall panels, and you then have the basic shell. The doors, windows, and other openings are made to fit the structure you order.

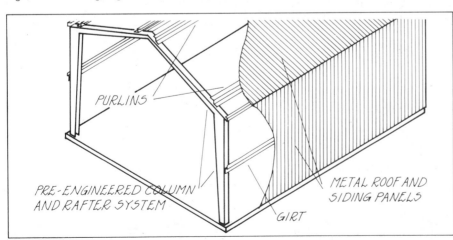

PURLINS

PRE-ENGINEERED COLUMN AND RAFTER SYSTEM

GIRT

METAL ROOF AND SIDING PANELS

The metal panels install over purlins that span the walls and roof of the structure.

INDEX

Agreements/contracts, 21-22
Attached garage, 9, 13-14, 17-18
  addition, 18
  expansion, 17-18
  two-story, 17-18

Balcony, 116-120
  construction, 118-119
  decking, 120
Baseboard, 103
Batter boards, 58, 62
Brick veneer, 80-81, 134-137
Budget, 8
Building paper, 79-80

Cable (electrical), 88-89
  anchoring, 88-89
  BX, 88
  conduit, 88, 89-90
  Romex, 88
Carport, 15, 16, 114-115, 142
  attached, 15
  detached, 16
  enclosing, 142
  open, 16
Climate, 49
Code/inspections, 22, 24, 70, 123
Concrete block, 127, 128, 129-131, 132-133
  color, 132
  control joints, 132
  construction, 128, 129-131
  mortar joints, 126, 131
  texture, 132-133
  types, 127
Concrete block garage, 126-137
Concrete work, 19, 28-29, 44-48, 65, 66, 67, 108, 109, 114, 126, 138-139
  aggregate, 45
  air-entrained, 45
  bolts (sill), 65
  broomed finish, 66
  control joints, 48, 66
  correcting mix, 47
  curing, 67
  delivery (access), 48
  estimating quantities, 44
  finishing, 109
  floating, 65
  isolation joints, 67
  hand mixing, 46
  placing, 65, 109
  proportions chart, 46
  ready mix, 47-48
  reinforcing, 65
  silt test, 46
  slab, 108, 109, 114, 138
  subcontractors, 29
  testing, 47
  tools, 45, 65
  transit mix, 48
  troweling, 66
  types, 45
  using power mixer, 47
Contractors, 21-29, 104-105
  concrete, 28-29
  electrical, 24-28
  framing, 29
  heating/cooling, 22, 24
  plumbing, 24, 104-105

Contracts, 21-22
Control joints, 132
  caulking, 132
  Michigan joint, 132
  premolded, 132
  tongue and groove, 132
Converting garage space, 142-150
Corners, 60, 61, 72
  locating, 60
  square, 61

Detached garage, 16, 23
  heating, 23
Doors, 82-85, 128-129, 135-136
  automatic, 83-84
  installation, 83
  overhead, 82-85
Drainage, 49, 50-51, 52, 54, 105
  baffles, 50, 52
  berm, 50
  catch basins, 50, 51, 54
  correcting devices, 50
  dry wells, 51, 54
  existing, 50
  foundation, 51, 105
  swale, 50
  water, 50-51
Drive, 10
Driveways, 10, 18, 19, 20, 40, 48, 138, 151-153
  approach, 10
  asphalt, 40, 151-152
  concrete, 152-153
  enlarging, 19
  planning, 18
  steep, 10
  types, 18, 20
Ductwork, 22
  connectors, 22
  tape, 22

Electrical, 22, 39, 86-91, 111
  boxes, 90-91
  box in block, 86
  cable, 88-89
  demand, 39
  eave connection, 87
  fishing wire, 90
  heating/cooling, 22
  LB fitting, 86
  plan, 39
  running cable, 88
  schedule, 39
  trench, 87-88
  underground wiring, 86
Elevation (drawing), 14-15, 31-33, 35, 36, 37
Elevation (ground slope), 61
  differences, 61
Erosion, 52-54
  baffles, 52-53
  catch basins, 54
  control, 52-56
  dry wells, 54
  groundcovers, 52
  rubble, 53
  stones, 52
  swales, 53
  terracing, 53
Excavation work, 29, 63, 104, 106, 138
  footing, 63
  slab, 63
  turn-down, 63

Excavators, 22
Exterior finishing materials, 79-85

Fiberboard, 80
  sheathing, 80
Floor plans, 22
Footings, 105, 106, 107, 138-139
Forms, 64-65, 106
Foundations, 57-69, 106, 107-108, 109, 114, 126-127, 138-139
  backfilling, 107-108
  carport, 114
  concrete/block, 65-67
  gravel fill, 108
  layout/location, 57-64
  pouring, 109
  vapor barrier, 108
  wire mesh, 108
  wood, 67-69

Framing, 35-36, 70-85, 110-111, 114-115, 137, 139, 149-151
  beam, 140-141
  ceiling joists, 72-73, 141
  doors, 71
  extending, 137
  plan, 35-36
  plate, 70-71, 137
  rafters, 76-79, 141
  removing, 139
  ridge, 73-76
  sill, 70-71
  studs, 70, 71, 139
  stud wall, 36, 70, 71
  trusses, 77-79
  vents, 71
  windows, 71, 72
Frost heave, 49, 51, 54
Furnaces, 12
  forced-air, 12

Garage, 16, 17, 23, 39, 57
  conversions, 16, 23
  corners, 57
  door opener, 39
  expansion, 17
  kits, 154-155
  metal, 156
Garage kits, 154-155
Grading, 51-52
  moving soil, 52
  stake/string grid, 52
Gutters and Downspouts, 93
Gypsumboard (see wallboard)

Heating and Cooling, 143, 145-149
  air conditioner, 148-149
  ductwork, 145-148
Heating oil, 22
HUD, 10, 31, 33, 54

Insulation, 97-101, 107
  around light fixtures, 99
  around openings, 100
  attic, 99
  batts, 97
  crawl spaces, 99
  rolls, 97
  slab, 107
  vapor barrier, 98, 100, 101
  walls, 99, 100

CONTRIBUTORS
ADDRESSES
PICTURE CREDITS

We wish to extend our thanks to the individuals, associations, and manufacturers who graciously provided information and photographs for this book.

American Plywood Association Box 1119A, Tacoma, WA 98401 44 left, 76 right

Monte Burch Route 1, Humansville, MO 65674 9 upper, 16 upper, 29 upper, 46, 47, 65, 66, 67 lower left, 129, 131, 132 upper left

California Redwood Association One Lombard Street, San Francisco, CA 94111 38, 40 upper, 96

Ego Productions James M. Auer 1849 North 72nd Street, Wauwatosa, WI 53213 16 lower, 21, 79, 86

Goldblatt Tool Co. 511 Osage, Kansas City, KS 66110 28, 45

Harris Lumber 4350 North 35th Street, Milwaukee, WI 53216 154

National Concrete Masonry Association P. O. Box 781, Herndon, VA 22070 133

Richard V. Nunn Media Mark Productions, Falls Church Inn, 6633 Arlington Boulevard, Falls Church, VA 22045 43, 41, 80, 81, 90, 91, 95, 97, 100, 102

Tom Philbin 14 Lakeside Drive, Centerport, New York 11721 41, 42

Portland Cement Association 5420 Old Orchard Road, Skokie, IL 60077 63, 129, 130, 132 lower left, 152

Stanley Door Systems Div. 2400 East Lincoln Place, Birmingham, MI 48012 19 upper, 44 right

Wausau Tile P. O. Box 1520, Wausau, WI 54401 29

Western Wood Products Association Yeon Building, Portland, OR 97204

One-car garage plans
INCLUDING (7) DIFFERENT STYLES

This package by nationally-known architect William G. Chirgotis, includes blueprints, materials lists, diagrams, and simple do-it-yourself instructions for building <u>seven different styles of one-car garages</u> <u>or six different styles of two-car garages.</u>

Included are gable, shed and hip roofs. The exteriors are designed to match your home: clapboard, brick veneer, stucco and half timber, board and batten siding, and wood shingles.

Two-car garage plans
INCLUDING (6) DIFFERENT STYLES

The do-it-yourself explanations and full materials lists simplify picking the right design and purchasing the materials. Then they guide you through the construction and finishing off of your garage.

- Complete professional blueprints
- Materials list included
- Easy to follow construction details
- Frame, brick veneer or masonry construction
- Conversion details for adding storage areas or garden equipment

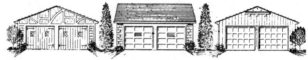

ORDER FORM

Please send garage plans:
Check box ☐ ONE CAR
☐ TWO CAR

1-Set Package	$30	$ _____
3-Set Package	$60	$ _____

Add the postage:

First Class	$3	$ _____
C.O.D.	$4	$ _____
TOTAL AMOUNT		$ _____

Make payment
In U.S. Currency to:
Creative Homeowner Press
Dept. GC
24 Park Way
Upper Saddle River, N.J. 07458

Prices subject to change without notice.

ORDER FORM

Please send garage plans:
Check box ☐ ONE CAR
☐ TWO CAR

1-Set Package	$30	$ _____
3-Set Package	$60	$ _____

Add the postage:

First Class	$3	$ _____
C.O.D.	$4	$ _____
TOTAL AMOUNT		$ _____

Make payment
In U.S. Currency to:
Creative Homeowner Press
Dept. GC
24 Park Way
Upper Saddle River, N.J. 07458

Prices subject to change without notice.

Metric Charts

LUMBER

Sizes: Metric cross-sections are so close to their nearest Imperial sizes, as noted below, that for most purposes they may be considered equivalents.

Lengths: Metric lengths are based on a 300mm module which is slightly shorter in length than an Imperial foot. It will therefore be important to check your requirements accurately to the nearest inch and consult the table below to find the metric length required.

Areas: The metric area is a square metre. Use the following conversion factors when converting from Imperial data: 100 sq. feet = 9.290 sq. metres.

METRIC SIZES SHOWN BESIDE NEAREST IMPERIAL EQUIVALENT

mm	Inches	mm	Inches
16 x 75	⅝ x 3	44 x 150	1¾ x 6
16 x 100	⅝ x 4	44 x 175	1¾ x 7
16 x 125	⅝ x 5	44 x 200	1¾ x 8
16 x 150	⅝ x 6	44 x 225	1¾ x 9
19 x 75	¾ x 3	44 x 250	1¾ x 10
19 x 100	¾ x 4	44 x 300	1¾ x 12
19 x 125	¾ x 5	50 x 75	2 x 3
19 x 150	¾ x 6	50 x 100	2 x 4
22 x 75	⅞ x 3	50 x 125	2 x 5
22 x 100	⅞ x 4	50 x 150	2 x 6
22 x 125	⅞ x 5	50 x 175	2 x 7
22 x 150	⅞ x 6	50 x 200	2 x 8
25 x 75	1 x 3	50 x 225	2 x 9
25 x 100	1 x 4	50 x 250	2 x 10
25 x 125	1 x 5	50 x 300	2 x 12
25 x 150	1 x 6	63 x 100	2½ x 4
25 x 175	1 x 7	63 x 125	2½ x 5
25 x 200	1 x 8	63 x 150	2½ x 6
25 x 225	1 x 9	63 x 175	2½ x 7
25 x 250	1 x 10	63 x 200	2½ x 8
25 x 300	1 x 12	63 x 225	2½ x 9
32 x 75	1¼ x 3	75 x 100	3 x 4
32 x 100	1¼ x 4	75 x 125	3 x 5
32 x 125	1¼ x 5	75 x 150	3 x 6
32 x 150	1¼ x 6	75 x 175	3 x 7
32 x 175	1¼ x 7	75 x 200	3 x 8
32 x 200	1¼ x 8	75 x 225	3 x 9
32 x 225	1¼ x 9	75 x 250	3 x 10
32 x 250	1¼ x 10	75 x 300	3 x 12
32 x 300	1¼ x 12	100 x 100	4 x 4
38 x 75	1½ x 3	100 x 150	4 x 6
38 x 100	1½ x 4	100 x 200	4 x 8
38 x 125	1½ x 5	100 x 250	4 x 10
38 x 150	1½ x 6	100 x 300	4 x 12
38 x 175	1½ x 7	150 x 150	6 x 6
38 x 200	1½ x 8	150 x 200	6 x 8
38 x 225	1½ x 9	150 x 300	6 x 12
44 x 75	1¾ x 3	200 x 200	8 x 8
44 x 100	1¾ x 4	250 x 250	10 x 10
44 x 125	1¾ x 5	300 x 300	12 x 12

METRIC LENGTHS

Lengths Metres	Equiv. Ft. & Inches
1.8m	5' 10⅞"
2.1m	6' 10⅝"
2.4m	7' 10½"
2.7m	8' 10¼"
3.0m	9' 10⅛"
3.3m	10' 9⅞"
3.6m	11' 9¾"
3.9m	12' 9½"
4.2m	13' 9⅜"
4.5m	14' 9⅓"
4.8m	15' 9"
5.1m	16' 8¾"
5.4m	17' 8⅝"
5.7m	18' 8⅜"
6.0m	19' 8¼"
6.3m	20' 8"
6.6m	21' 7⅞"
6.9m	22' 7⅝"
7.2m	23' 7½"
7.5m	24' 7¼"
7.8m	25' 7⅛"

All the dimensions are based on 1 inch = 25 mm.

NOMINAL SIZE (This is what you order.)	ACTUAL SIZE (This is what you get.)
Inches	Inches
1 x 1	¾ x ¾
1 x 2	¾ x 1½
1 x 3	¾ x 2½
1 x 4	¾ x 3½
1 x 6	¾ x 5½
1 x 8	¾ x 7¼
1 x 10	¾ x 9¼
1 x 12	¾ x 11¼
2 x 2	1¾ x 1¾
2 x 3	1½ x 2½
2 x 4	1½ x 3½
2 x 6	1½ x 5½
2 x 8	1½ x 7¼
2 x 10	1½ x 9¼
2 x 12	1½ x 11¼